INDIAN REMOVAL

A NORTON CASEBOOK

NORTON CASEBOOKS IN HISTORY SERIES

Indian Removal by David Heidler and Jeanne Heidler

FORTHCOMING TITLES INCLUDE:

Two Communities in the Civil War by Andrew Torget and
    Edward Ayers
Jim Crow by Jane Dailey
Global Revolutions of 1968 by Jeremi Suri
Pirates in the Age of Sail by Robert Antony
Mongols in Global History by Morris Rossabi

INDIAN REMOVAL

A NORTON CASEBOOK

David S. Heidler

and

Jeanne T. Heidler

W. W. NORTON & COMPANY

New York / London

W. W. Norton & Company has been independent since its founding in 1923, when William Warder Norton and Mary D. Herter Norton first published lectures delivered at the People's Institute, the adult education division of New York City's Cooper Union. The Nortons soon expanded their program beyond the Institute, publishing books by celebrated academics from America and abroad. By mid-century, the two major pillars of Norton's publishing program—trade books and college texts—were firmly established. In the 1950s, the Norton family transferred control of the company to its employees, and today—with a staff of four hundred and a comparable number of trade, college, and professional titles published each year—W. W. Norton & Company stands as the largest and oldest publishing house owned wholly by its employees.

Printed in the United States of America.
The text of this book is composed in Baskerville MT with the display set in Cloister Openface.
Composition by ElectraGraphics, Inc.
Series design by Jo Anne Metsch.
Manufacturing by Courier, Westford.
Project editor: Lory Frenkel.
Production manager: Benjamin Reynolds.

Library of Congress Cataloging-in-Publication Data

ISBN 0-393-92725-3
ISBN-13: 978-0-393-92725-2

W. W. Norton & Company, Inc., 500 Fifth Avenue, New York, N.Y. 10110-0017
www.wwnorton.com
W. W. Norton & Company Ltd., Castle House, 75/76 Wells Street, London W1T 3QT

1 2 3 4 5 6 7 8 9 0

CONTENTS

vi CONTENTS

LIST OF ILLUSTRATIONS AND MAPS

ILLUSTRATIONS

MAPS

vii

OVERVIEW

Everyone now judges the westward removal of eastern Indians as one of the great injustices in United States history. Marked by a callous disregard for principles and fair play, Indian removal has been considered by some historians as an unavoidable result of expanding white settlement during the early nineteenth century. But the architects of the early Republic did not consider removal as inevitable, and in the 1830s, the policy met with widespread resistance from religious and reform groups as well as from native populations. The story of Indian removal's evolution from unthinkable scheme to accepted policy is a complicated one—and not merely a tale of heroes and villains. Rather it is a story of truthful men who unwittingly lied, of wary people who unwisely trusted, of good people who risked their lives and reputations for decency and justice, and of greedy men who lied so convincingly that they themselves came to believe their deceits.

Indians east of the Mississippi River had been in regular contact with European settlers for almost two hundred years when the United States adopted the Constitution in 1788. President George Washington's administration was eager to end periodic Indian wars that had been a commonplace of colonial life. For their part, Indians who had remained neutral or had allied with Britain during the American Revolution were uneasy at its conclusion. They rightly feared being at the mercy of angry white Americans after Britain's departure, and indeed many in the Confederation Congress believed that Indians had forfeited their lands by refusing to help the patriot cause or by siding with the British.

The Confederation was militarily weak, however, and could not act on these resentments. Meanwhile, the cross-purposes of Indians and whites bred trouble. Some Indians saw American frailty as an

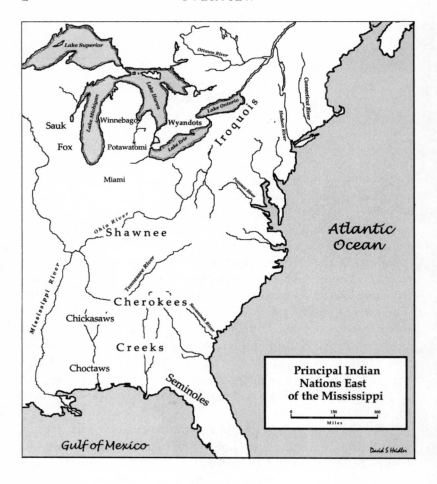

opportunity to regain territory lost to white settlement, while the virtually autonomous states of the Confederation tried to satisfy their impatient settlers by taking over even more Indian lands. State negotiators used a tactic that became a standard ploy: They bribed small Indian factions into relinquishing land on behalf of entire tribes. When that approach failed, the states simply opened Indian lands to white settlement. Friction understandably resulted, and fighting often broke out on the frontier. The weak Confederation government was unable to control this emerging situation, let alone suppress the violence it sparked.

Indian Policy in the Early Republic

The Constitution created a stronger central government that brought a measure of coherence to U.S. Indian policy. One improvement was that federal instead of state agents began conducting all negotiations with Indians. Nevertheless, as historian Harry Watson has noted, American Indian policy, before removal, was marked by "ignorance, benevolence, and greed."[1] Most white Americans were ignorant about Indian cultures and especially Native Americans' ties to their lands, but many people in government also sympathized with the Indians and wanted what was best for them. Impatient settlers, influential speculators, and the politicians who did their bidding, however, merely wanted the land and ultimately became heedless of the human toll in getting it.

Secretary of War Henry Knox, who was in charge of Indian affairs for the new government, worked to reconcile these conflicting interests. Knox knew that he could not eliminate whites' hunger for land and that George Washington's government would eventually be pressured to acquire more of it from Indians. Yet Knox's Enlightenment beliefs in orderly, rational progress, convinced him that such expansion could occur without completely displacing or destroying eastern Indians. Knox also believed that treating Indians dishonorably would violate the fundamental American doctrine of equal justice and would tarnish the United States' reputation, inviting comparisons with Spain's abuse of native populations in Mexico and Peru. He knew that white settlers were responsible for many recent Indian conflicts. If Indians could be persuaded to sell some of their lands, he hoped the frontier could be pacified, sparing both lives and the expense of keeping the peace.

Because the government's empty treasury and small army made any other solution unlikely, persuading rather than forcing Indians to sell land was key to the plan. The Enlightenment posited that human beings were not only perfectible but also naturally sought improvement. Knox and fellow devotees of the Age of Reason believed that American Indians were simply at a different level of civilization. Once acquainted with a more sophisticated way of life,

---

[1] Harry L. Watson, *Liberty and Power: The Politics of Jacksonian America* (New York: Hill and Wang, 1990), 105.

they would embrace it. The idea gave birth to a government civilization program for Indians. Domestic animals such as sheep, goats, poultry, and cattle were placed with some Indian groups who were also encouraged to adopt white agricultural methods. The government also encouraged white missionaries to live among Indians and provide models of white culture, all in the hope that if Indians accepted white husbandry and farming techniques, surplus would replace subsistence. If their need for land diminished, then they would be willing to part with more of it.

Despite Knox's condescending and patriarchal attitude, he did not believe that Indians were biologically inferior to whites. For instance, he did not object to white-Indian intermarriage—white

FIGURE 1

Henry Knox—This former Boston bookseller had distinguished himself in the American Revolution as one of George Washington's most trusted subordinates. As Washington's secretary of war, Knox was the guiding light for the civilization program, the government's plan to hasten Indian acculturation and reduce Indian dependence on large land holdings. *(Library of Congress)*

traders had been marrying Indian women for years—and saw the practice as aiding assimilation. Although assimilation was merely another way to erode Indian culture, Knox believed that this assimilation would preserve Indians as a people, and his sincere desire to accomplish that was at least a benign goal.

But many problems undermined the civilization program. Not the least of them was the persistence of centuries-old traditions among southeastern Native Americans. Southern tribes—Choctaws, Chickasaws, Cherokees, Creeks, and Seminoles who would later be the focus of most removal debates—had been practicing agriculture for centuries. In contrast to white farming, women did most of the work in Indian agriculture, with men limited mostly to heavy tasks such as clearing new fields. Men also defended against aggressors and hunted for food. They also collected animal hides that had become integral to trade with whites, an indispensable facet of Indian prosperity.

The deerskin trade had dramatically changed the lives of southeastern Indians by introducing them to textiles, metal pots, and firearms.[2] Guns made hunting more efficient, and household goods freed women from making clothes and cookery equipment, allowing them to concentrate on other pursuits. But conveniences came with a price. As they became increasingly dependent on these items, Indians relied more and more on deerskins to purchase these items. By the 1790s, overhunting had so thinned the deer population that there were hardly enough skins for barter. One historian asserts that white trade altered Indian cultures in subtler but no less tangible ways as well. As men became less dependent on women for items obtained through trade, they also traded skins for whiskey and consequently ceased to provide for their families.[3] Trade possibly intensified tensions between Indian men and women and perhaps made women more receptive to the civilization program.

Knox's desire to preserve Indians as a people was in sharp contrast to the dreams of frontier Americans. Frontiersmen were no

[2] For the most thorough examination of this impact on southeastern Indians, particularly the Creeks, see Kathryn Holland Braund, *Deerskins & Duffels: The Creek Indian Trade with Anglo-America, 1685–1815* (Lincoln: University of Nebraska Press, 1993).

[3] Claudio Saunt, *A New Order of Things: Property, Power, and the Transformation of the Creek Indians, 1733–1816* (New York: Cambridge University Press, 1999), 149–53.

friends of assimilation because it only promised to impede the acquisition of Indian lands, and though few put it so bluntly, the extinction of Native Americans would have suited them better. For the time being, they rationalized pushing Indians off their lands by asserting that Indians wasted God's bounty because of inefficient farming and wasteful hunting. In any case, aggressive frontiersmen threatened Knox's plans, and he urged Congress to prevent white trespassing on Indian lands. Congress responded in the 1790s by passing Trade and Intercourse Acts, which put restrictions on travel through Indian nations and allowed only licensed trade.

In addition to regulating contact between settlers and Indians, the government created agencies to operate among the Indians. Specially appointed agents often developed close relationships with Indians while they encouraged the adoption of white culture and facilitated land purchases. Yet the very presence of these agents could also alienate Indians who were resolved to resist assimilation.

While the emergence of U.S. political parties in the 1790s emphasized important differences over domestic and foreign affairs, both Federalists and Democratic-Republicans agreed that the civilization program was a good idea. In fact, the significant shift of power that followed the election of 1800—when Thomas Jefferson won the presidency and his fellow Republicans became the majority in Congress—did not alter the government's commitment to the program. America's foremost disciple of the Enlightenment, Jefferson proved to be an enthusiastic supporter of Knox's assimilation plan.[4]

In contemplating the future of the American Indian, Jefferson's commitment to their assimilation was unshakable, which was all the more peculiar because he remained unwavering in his belief that African slaves were incapable of assimilation into white culture.[5] Ironically, Jefferson's enthusiasm for the civilization program coincided with his belief that major land cessions would compel reluctant Indians to embrace white culture, a policy that caused more problems than it solved by increasing divisions within existing Indian nations.

[4] Henry Dearborn to Return J. Meigs, May 15, 1801, Willie Blount Papers, East Tennessee Historical Society, Knoxville, Tennessee.

[5] Thomas Jefferson, *Notes on the State of Virginia*, edited by William Peden (Chapel Hill: University of North Carolina Press, 1982), 138–40.

Nonetheless, the government pursued the policy with vigor. For example, the government had long tried to control trade with the Indians by reserving the exclusive right to operate stores in Indian nations. In addition to regulating trade, these establishments tended to foster Indian indebtedness. The Jefferson administration actually welcomed this result, because when Indians' debts fell in arrears, the government could acquire their land in the place of payment. Such land cessions stirred tremendous resentment among Indians who by 1810 were falling under the influence of nativist leaders urging a revival of Indian culture to eliminate dependence on white trade goods. Nativist movements assumed a religious character when prophets averred that wayward Indians were losing their land as punishment for abandoning the old ways of their fathers.

With their blatant rejection of acculturation, nativist movements threatened to subvert the entire civilization program. Nativists urged self-sufficiency by encouraging their people to return to the material and spiritual practices of their ancestors. If Indians in the eastern United States revived their traditional cultures, they would return to subsistence hunting that required large expanses of land. Indians would again produce the articles necessary for survival and cease relying on white trade goods and, in turn, on the U.S. government.

Nativism was not entirely original—it had occasionally appeared during the colonial and Revolutionary periods—but it became widespread in the early nineteenth century. In the years before the War of 1812, its influence was felt most in the Great Lakes region under the leadership of the Shawnee warrior Tecumseh and his brother Tenskwatawa, known as the Prophet. In addition to eliminating dependence on whites, Tecumseh wanted all Indians to unite across tribes and regions to resist additional white expansion.

Not all eastern Indians joined the nativists, but the movement's growing popularity caused concern for the government. Official responses to nativism—responses that ultimately resorted to war— labored under a confused misunderstanding of the movement's origins. Neither Jefferson nor his successor James Madison realized that the ethnocentrism and paternalism of their own civilization program encouraged nativism as much as white encroachments on Indian land did.

Even where the civilization program enjoyed limited success, it did not translate into large land cessions. Indians receptive to the civilization program justifiably believed that their efforts to live peacefully with whites would end the desire for additional land cessions. When the government broached the necessity for such cessions, Indians either refused or agreed to part with only small tracts. Because assimilation clearly opened only limited areas for white settlement and left Indian farmers in possession of the rest of their land, any miscarriage of the civilization program pleased states and territories with large Indian populations. To these expansionists the program's failure was proof that Indian and white cultures could not coexist, and they began to mutter that getting Indians out of the way was the only acceptable solution.

Ironically, it was Thomas Jefferson, the enthusiastic proponent of assimilation, who unwittingly provided critics of the civilization program with the answer of where to put evicted Indians. Jefferson suggested that the enormous expanse of land acquired from France in the Louisiana Purchase could provide a new home for Indians who rejected assimilation. Jefferson also hoped that assimilation would be given a chance to succeed, of course, but the reality of how power was wielded in the national government—basically through representation—made his expectations unrealistic.[6] In fact, frontier Americans had more at stake than merely opening new lands for covetous settlers. More land inhabited by voting citizens meant more influence in the government, especially in Congress where the House of Representatives was apportioned according to population. In light of this truth, even if assimilation opened land for settlement, any political benefits would be deferred while parts of the country without Indians reaped the advantages of growing settlement.[7] Consequently, land hungry settlers and their political representatives soon took up Jefferson's suggestion of

[6] Jefferson to Andrew Jackson, September 19, 1803, Andrew Jackson, *The Papers of Andrew Jackson*, 6 vols., edited by Sam B. Smith, Harriett C. Owsley, and Harold Moser (Knoxville: University of Tennessee Press, 1980–2003), 1: 365.

[7] Willie Blount to Tennessee Legislature, October 15, 1809, Willie Blount to R. J. Meigs, March 8, 1810, Willie Blount Papers, Perkins Library, Duke University; Anthony F. C. Wallace, *Jefferson and the Indians: The Tragic Fate of the First Americans* (Cambridge: The Belknap Press of Harvard University Press, 1999), 220–24.

providing a new home within the Louisiana Purchase and worked to make it policy.

Initially, Georgians pushed most aggressively for removal. They were encouraged by an 1802 pledge from the federal government that it would eliminate Indian land claims within Georgia in exchange for the state's relinquishing land west of the Chatta-hoochee River. Shortly after the Jefferson administration had brokered the Louisiana Purchase, Georgians wasted no time in de-manding that his administration fulfill its promise to take away Creek and Cherokee land and, by inference, move them out of the state. It did not happen that quickly, of course, but it would happen soon enough. After all, President Jefferson, an enlightened farmer, had inadvertently planted the seed for removal.

Others would see to its cultivation. Eventually, removal propo-nents modified their arguments for immediate removal into a blend of self-interest and political persuasion masked by insincere human-itarianism: They disingenuously claimed that moving Indians west of the Mississippi would protect them and their cultures from avari-cious settlers.[8] Pointing at the impractical idealism of the civiliza-tion program, they claimed that they were advocating a sensible as well as an altruistic solution to the "Indian problem."

The Creek War

In the Old Southwest, a faction within the Creek Nation known as Red Sticks (because of the red war-clubs they wielded in battle) began promoting nativism, partly in response to the aggressive ap-plication of the civilization program by federal Creek Indian agent Benjamin Hawkins. Having served as the Creek agent since 1796, Hawkins sincerely sympathized with the people he had come to regard almost as his own, but he also worked hard to fulfill his instructions from Washington to secure additional land cessions.

The Creek Nation sat in western Georgia and what is now modern-day Alabama. Geographically divided into Lower Towns that sat

---

[8] Reginald Horseman, "The Indian Policy of an 'Empire of Liberty,'" in Frederick E. Hoxie, Ronald Hoffman, and Peter J. Albert, eds., *Native Americans and the Early Republic* (Char-lottesville: University Press of Virginia), 54–56; Willie Blount to Return J. Meigs, March 8, 1810, Willie Blount Papers, Perkins Library, Duke University.

east of Upper Towns, the nation was illustrative of the political divisions caused by acculturation. Hawkins maintained his agency among the Lower Towns in western Georgia and eastern Alabama, the latter region forming part of the Mississippi Territory in the early nineteenth century.

Initially, nativist Creeks and those who favored acculturation merely differed over the best response to white expansion. For example, the construction of a federal road through the Creek Nation to white settlements north of Mobile offered an opportunity for some Creeks to profit from the collection of tolls and the operation of inns, but nativists condemned this enterprise as another form of white encroachment. It was during these tense times that Tecumseh visited in 1811 to recruit Creeks into his confederation. Because many Shawnee, including Tecumseh's parents, had previously lived among the Creeks before moving north, Tecumseh had close ties to the Creeks and was possibly related to some of them. Not only nativists listened enthusiastically to Tecumseh's talk; some acculturationists such as Big Warrior (Tustennuggee Thluco), headman of Tuckabatchee, also found Tecumseh's message persuasive. Yet Big Warrior was among those Creeks profiting from the civilization program. Creeks such as Big Warrior had even invested in the cotton culture's reliance on slavery to grow cotton for sale to whites. Furthermore, acculturationists knew the risks of offending the United States and refused to endorse Tecumseh's plan.

Nonetheless, Tecumseh did seem to present the only way to stop the slow expulsion of Creeks from their lands. An intrigued faction followed him to his Great Lakes home to hear more. When some returned south, they attacked and killed white settlers on the Duck River in Tennessee. Tennessee demanded that the perpetrators be punished. At Hawkins' urging the Creek National Council convened and sentenced the warriors responsible for the Duck River attack to death and then dispatched its enforcement squad—the lawmenders—to execute the sentence. The lawmenders soon had captured or killed several warriors, including one renowned Creek, Little Warrior.

The episode triggered a civil war, and angry Red Sticks promised to avenge their kinsmen. Red Sticks besieged towns like Tuckabatchee that inclined toward acculturation, while livestock and other emblems of the civilization program were destroyed. As pleas for help went out to other towns and to Hawkins' agency, white and mixed-heritage settlers congregated in settler-built forts from where they too sent out calls to the Mississippi Territorial government for protection.

While the siege of Tuckabatchee continued, prominent Red Stick warrior Peter McQueen led a party to Spanish Pensacola for gunpowder and shot. The Spanish government reluctantly supplied McQueen, but the enterprise had alarmed the Mississippi Territorial Militia. Colonel James Caller ambushed McQueen at Burnt Corn Creek on July 27, 1813, a muddled affair that finally saw McQueen and his warriors holding their own, but the engagement immediately clarified the opponents in this war, expanding it beyond an internal Indian conflict. It was a war between the Red Sticks and white settlers, which meant the United States government.

In the meantime, Red Sticks gained a new recruit in William Weatherford, another Creek of mixed heritage. In a violent reprisal for Burnt Corn Creek, Weatherford led an assault on one group of settlers at Fort Mims north of Mobile. After a desperate battle of several hours, Red Sticks killed most of Fort Mims' several hundred inhabitants.

The fight at Burnt Corn Creek had put surrounding states and territories on alert, but the attack on Fort Mims electrified the frontier. Militias from the Mississippi Territory, Georgia, and Tennessee converged on the Creek Nation to crush the Red Sticks.

To the Red Sticks the attack on Fort Mims was merely another blow at the civilization program and the ruinous assimilation it had produced. Fort Mims typified other settlements north of Mobile, where settlers of mixed Indian-white heritage lived and farmed. In the welter of competing concerns, these people found themselves truly caught in the middle, because just like frontier whites, Red Sticks saw assimilation as a threat to their way of life. Red Sticks feared for their culture and for the survival of the Creek Nation. Whites hungry for Creek lands saw even the smallest success of the civilization program as impeding white expansion and American prosperity.

The West Tennessee Militia—one of the groups mobilized because of Fort Mims—plainly viewed all eastern Indians as thwarting progress and economic opportunity. The militia's commander was Andrew Jackson, who was fated to become a central figure in this story. Jackson and militia commanders from the Mississippi Territory and Georgia entered the Creek Nation in the fall of 1813 to eliminate the Red Stick threat. The fact that achieving his goal would also open the area to white settlement was not lost on Jackson. The Creek War that followed saw Red Sticks fighting tenaciously in early campaigns but always on the run to escape white armies. It was a tactic as old as war itself, famously employed by the Roman Fabius Maximus against Hannibal in the Punic War two thousand years earlier. But Fabian tactics always carry a high price, and the Red Sticks paid it in this instance as advancing armies left many of their towns in smoldering ruins.

The Creek War occurred while the United States was also fighting Great Britain in the War of 1812, and that meant men and supplies for the southern campaigns were scarce. But by early 1814, Jackson's troops had been sufficiently reinforced to allow a major campaign against the Red Stick stronghold of Tohopeka (Horseshoe Bend on the Tallapoosa River). With an army of regulars, militiamen, and allied Creeks and Cherokees, Jackson attacked on March 27, 1814, killing about eight hundred Red Stick warriors and capturing about 350 women and children. Red Stick resistance collapsed after Horseshoe Bend. Many began moving to Florida, where they hoped the British would come to their aid. Others clustered in isolated camps where starvation became their most dreaded enemy, their stores of food from the previous year's harvest having been destroyed. The threat of Jackson's army was a pale specter in comparison, and Red Sticks searched out the man they had dubbed "Sharp Knife" to surrender to him. At Fort Jackson, a rough outpost at the confluence of the Coosa and Tallapoosa rivers, warriors began arriving, with their families, to submit. Even William Weatherford appeared at Fort Jackson to throw himself on Sharp Knife's mercy. He was released with the understanding that he would bring in more Red Sticks.

Weatherford's surrender and his fate afterward were both a cautionary example and ominous sign for defeated Creeks. Weatherford lived the remainder of his life as a prosperous Alabama planter. He died in 1824, before the imposition of Indian removal forced

Creeks like him to make hard choices. Weatherford was only one-eighth Indian and consequently was by all appearances a white man with a white name. Creeks more obviously Indian would face injustice first, but all of them, no matter how white, would ultimately face hard choices imposed by a policy contrived and politically realized by Sharp Knife only a few years later.

Treaty of Fort Jackson

With the Creek War at an apparent end, the War Department instructed Jackson to negotiate a treaty with the Creeks that would include a land cession sufficient to cover the cost of U.S. involvement in the war. Jackson instructed Agent Hawkins to summon Creek headmen to Fort Jackson for a meeting in August 1814, with the result that those who assembled at Fort Jackson were mainly those Creeks who had allied with the United States against the Red Sticks. These friends of the United States were shocked that the treaty was to be dic-tated, not negotiated, and that Jackson intended to extract a land cession from the entire Creek Nation. Signed on August 9, 1814, the Treaty of Fort Jackson ceded almost twenty-three million acres of Creek land to the United States. It was almost half of the Creek Nation, which Jackson referred to as "the cream of the creek country."[9]

National Expansion

Even before the Creek land cession had been surveyed and put up for sale, settlers were flooding into it. Meanwhile in the Northwest, Tecumseh's death during the War of 1812 ended his proposed confederation and opened more lands there to white settlement. By 1819, four new states (Indiana, Illinois, Alabama, and Mississippi) had been admitted to the Union, in part as a result of lands acquired from Indians during the War of 1812.[10] But instead of sating land hunger, these gains only whetted the appetite for more Indian lands. Westerners and southerners pushed their local governments and their representatives in Congress to accomplish

[9] Jackson to John Overton, August 10, 1814, Andrew Jackson Papers, Library of Congress.
[10] Daniel Feller, *The Public Lands in Jacksonian Politics* (Madison: University of Wisconsin Press, 1984), 15.

this goal with the ambitious demand that all Indian claims east of the Mississippi be abolished.

Such a demand plainly contradicted the goals of the civilization program, which appeared to be working too well with southeastern Indians, to some people's chagrin. Mixed-heritage Cherokees and Creeks were learning to read and write English, operate businesses, and work farms, occasionally using African American slaves. Not only were these clear signs of successful acculturation, but also the profitability of these enterprises discouraged Indians from selling land that was now valuable for cotton production. Critics of the civilization program chafed at the influence of these prosperous Indians in being able to thwart removal.[11] When Indians argued that they were doing exactly the government's bidding by participating in the American market economy, whites stubbornly countered that differences between the two races made coexistence impossible.[12]

Racist rationales were not new: they had always frustrated peaceful coexistence between Indians and European Americans. From the beginning of the colonial period in the seventeenth century, racism had justified the displacement and sometimes the extermination of thousands of Indians on the eastern seaboard. Racism had also gradually evolved to justify the enslavement of Africans. In the nineteenth century, especially in the South, the so-called Indian problem and racist attitudes became joined. Southerners wanted more land opened up for cotton growing. That land was in the hands of Indians who, like slaves, were people of another race toiling in the cotton fields. For whites to recognize the achievements of even the minority of Indians who tried to acculturate meant sequestering valuable land from white ownership.

These were the pecuniary motives for insisting on the innate inferiority of Indians, but there were other motives and reasons as well. The belief that "Anglo-Saxons" were superior to all other races was gaining credence in educated circles. White males' rights increased as a consequence of what was later called Jacksonian Democracy (a movement that clearly preceded Jackson's rise to

[11] Willie Blount to Return J. Meigs, May 20, 1811, Willie Blount Papers, East Tennessee Historical Society, Knoxville, Tennessee.

[12] Horseman, "Indian Policy," 59.

political power), but the rights of other races declined as race came to define citizenship. Most states that had recognized free blacks as citizens and had allowed adult males to vote drafted new state constitutions that took away those rights during the two decades following the War of 1812.[13]

Likewise, Indians who had embraced the civilization program found state or national citizenship increasingly unlikely. Ultimately, Indians who decided to remain on their lands rather than move west were told that even their limited rights would be further curtailed. As free persons of color, they could not defend their property against white intruders or testify in court against white thieves.[14]

Early Removal

In the years following the War of 1812, federal commissioners visited Indians throughout the country to persuade them to move west of the Mississippi River. Commissioners such as Andrew Jackson and his political friends from Tennessee arrived for talks with southern Indians. Jackson's behavior at Fort Jackson had roused both fear and resentment, and Creeks were understandably angry in the aftermath. So were Cherokees.

It is easy to see why. Large numbers of Creeks and Cherokees had allied with the United States during the War of 1812, but now they were being pressured to cede their lands and move west. The new demands from federal and state commissioners stiffened Cherokees against additional cessions and they lodged demands of their own. For one, they wanted monetary compensation for depredations against Cherokee towns by Tennessee militia during the Creek War. At the time of the attacks, Jackson had said Cherokee complaints were justifiable, but after the war, he changed his mind. He argued that compensating Cherokees would dishonor all Tennesseans who had fought in the war.[15]

[13] Watson, *Liberty and Power*, 53.

[14] Horseman, "Indian Policy," 59; Watson, *Liberty and Power*, 13, 53.

[15] Jackson to John Cocke, December 28, 1813, Jackson, *Papers*, 2: 511; Jackson to William Crawford, June 4, 1816, Andrew Jackson Letters, Perkins Library, Duke University; Return J. Meigs to William Crawford, August 19, 1816, Meigs to Jackson, August 8, 1816, *American State Papers, Indian Affairs*, 2 vols. (Washington, DC: Gales & Seaton, 1832), 2: 113.

Cherokees also claimed that the northern portion outlined in the Treaty of Fort Jackson cession belonged to them and should be excluded from sale and settlement. When James Madison's administration weighed the possibility of losing this large tract, it agreed to satisfy Cherokees' depredation claims, a decision that infuriated both Jackson and Tennessee. Nonetheless, most Cherokees did not want to give up the north Alabama tracts, and the government resorted to the old practice of pretending that a minority Cherokee faction represented the entire nation. Federal negotiators paid this splinter group for the depredations in return for the land in northern Alabama. The gesture was actually a savings in Madison's eyes, because moving large numbers of Indians to other regions was an expensive proposition, and the government did not have the money for such an undertaking. Later, when Jackson secured the passage of the Indian Removal Act and the funds it provided for removal, the practice of suborning minority factions would be used to commit entire nations to removal.

Not only did the Cherokee National Council strongly protest the land cession, many Cherokee women did so as well. In this matrilineal society where women controlled the farmland and passed that power to their daughters, alienating a large part of the nation threatened the very structure of Indian society.[16] But Andrew Jackson turned this objection to his advantage by arguing that if Cherokees faced the prospect of insufficient lands for their progeny, they were obligated to provide other land for their children and therefore needed to trade their remaining eastern lands for western tracts where white settlers could not pester them. The argument was effective, in part because divisions within the Cherokee Nation were ripe for offers by acquisitive whites. Although the Cherokee Council pledged to execute any of their people who encouraged emigration, about four thousand Cherokees agreed to pull up stakes and join the couple of thousand other Cherokees who had emigrated to northern Arkansas in 1808.[17]

[16] In matrilineal societies descent was only recognized through the mother. In other words, children were considered part of their mother's family or clan.

[17] Mary Elizabeth Young, "The Cherokee Nation: Mirror of the Republic," *American Quarterly* 33 (1981): 512; William G. McLoughlin, *Cherokee Renascence in the New Republic* (Princeton: Princeton University Press, 1986), 210–11, 231–33; Roger Spiller, "John C. Calhoun as Secretary of War, 1817–1825," Ph.D. dissertation, Louisiana State University, 1977, 200–01.

Even as these events unfolded, some government officials still believed that assimilation was the best way to reduce Indian holdings and preserve the peace. Secretary of War William Crawford, alarmed by increasing unrest among Creeks over the Fort Jackson cession, was reminiscent of those other men who had assessed the civilization program as progress, but Crawford also found himself confronting a younger generation of Americans who dismissed the program as misguided in conception and intolerable in application.

Crawford's concern over growing unrest on the southern border was warranted. Angry Creeks shadowed survey teams and threatened violence if their lands were sold to whites. Compounding the problem were the hundreds of white squatters pouring into the Fort Jackson cession, building crude cabins and appropriating Indian fields for their corn and cotton patches. Those Creeks who had essentially abandoned their ancestral lands by fleeing to Spanish Florida at the end of the Creek War were still angry over their forced removal, and they had the added insult of white squatters in southern Georgia and Alabama mounting raids across the border to steal livestock and reclaim runaway slaves. It was natural for Creeks who had fled to Florida to develop an informal alliance with Seminoles, since many of the latter, a collection of various ethnic and linguistic groups, were descended from Creeks who had moved to Florida in the eighteenth century. Raids by American frontiersmen targeted Creek and Seminole property indiscriminately, particularly cattle and slaves, which further cemented the bond between the two Indian tribes.

Spanish Florida was a tempting refuge for slaves hoping to escape the grueling labor of southern farms and plantations. The Spanish presence in the colony was meager, and settlements of fugitive slaves offered a haven for American runaways. Seminoles loosely owned these settlements, but actually slavery as practiced by the Seminoles resembled more a feudal alliance than chattel bondage. Seminoles' slaves, often called maroons, lived in separate towns and worked their own fields, a payment of tribute in kind being their only obligation to their ostensible owners. Seminoles and maroons intermarried, and some slave men rose to positions of importance in the Seminole community to serve as advisors and interpreters to headmen and fight alongside Seminole warriors. Tales of this

benign form of slavery worked their way onto the cotton plantations of Georgia and Alabama and beckoned American slaves southward. Understandably, alarmed white southerners saw the large
communities of free blacks on their borders as a threat to their way
of life. The situation on the Florida border promised to erupt into
an expensive war, and clashes between whites and Indians made
the Fort Jackson cession less attractive to settlers and consequently
less lucrative for the government. Compounding rather than resolv-
ing this problem were American soldiers sent to quell the violence
on the frontier. In some cases, they made the situation worse.

In July 1816, the U.S. Army was sent into Florida to rendezvous
with the navy coming up the Apalachicola River. Their goal was
the destruction of an abandoned British outpost dubbed "Negro
Fort" because it had become a refuge for runaway slaves. A heated
artillery shell from a naval gun exploded the fort's powder magazine, killing almost everyone in it and enraging Florida's Seminoles
and Creeks. Hostilities on the border immediately increased.

In the fall of 1817, Brigadier General Edmund Pendleton Gaines,
the American commander policing from Fort Scott on the Georgia–
Florida border, ordered the destruction of the Creek Fowltown
because Neamathla, its headman, insisted that Fort Scott's garrison
cease cutting down trees on Fowltown's land. When Indians swiftly
retaliated by attacking soldiers and their families while they made
their way up the Apalachicola River, the War Department dispatched the commanding general of the southern department,
Andrew Jackson, to chastise the Florida Indians. In March 1818,
Jackson began his invasion, with clear instructions not to assail
Florida's Spanish owners, but he had other plans.

Jackson destroyed a few abandoned Indian villages en route, but
his real purpose was to take the Spanish fort at St. Marks. Overwhelmingly outnumbered by Jackson's army, the Spanish commander at St. Marks had little choice but to surrender, and Jackson
personally raised the U.S. flag over the fort. At St. Marks, the
Americans found Alexander Arbuthnot, an elderly Scottish trader,
who had written letters for the Florida Indians to the U.S. government asking for redress of their grievances. Jackson regarded these
acts of kindness as encouraging Indians to violence and had
Arbuthnot arrested.

Standing off St. Marks in the Gulf of Mexico, an American naval vessel had earlier lured two Red Stick leaders by flying the British flag. Jackson brought them ashore and summarily hanged them. He then marched his army east to skirmish with Seminoles and Creeks, burned Seminole towns along the Suwanee River, and accidentally captured Robert Ambrister, a former British marine in Florida recruiting Indians and maroons for a filibustering expedition to Latin America. Back in St. Marks, a military court tried both Arbuthnot and Ambrister for inciting Indians to make war on the United States. Although both were found guilty and sentenced to death, the court recommended leniency for Ambrister. Jackson refused the recommendation and had both men executed. He then moved west on Pensacola, the capital of West Florida.[18] Pensacola's Spanish garrison retreated to the town's fortifications but surrendered after enduring a brief bombardment. In his dispatches to Washington, Jackson justified the taking of both St. Marks and Pensacola on the grounds that Spaniards in Florida were harboring Indians, but Jackson's transparent intent in Florida had been to wrest the territory from Spain. Although his foray raised a diplomatic and political storm, he ultimately succeeded. After protesting Jackson's actions, Spanish minister Don Luis de Onís grimly negotiated with Secretary of State John Quincy Adams to cede Florida to the United States. After the United States took possession of Florida in 1821, Andrew Jackson became its first territorial governor, and Florida Indians ominously found themselves under American jurisdiction.

They had cause for apprehension. Jackson spent his brief tenure as territorial governor trying to secure land cessions from Seminoles. His ultimate goal was to sequester them to a small area surrounded by white settlements until they could be completely removed from Florida. Negotiations with the Seminoles continued after his departure and culminated in the Treaty of Moultrie Creek in 1823, which forced most Seminoles off rich agricultural and

---

[18] The British owned Florida from 1763 to 1783 and divided it into eastern and western provinces. East Florida comprised the peninsula and had its capital at St. Augustine. West Florida was the panhandle with its capital at Pensacola. When Spain again took possession of the Floridas at the end of the American Revolution, it kept the administrative arrangement in place. The United States eliminated that arrangement when it took possession of Florida in 1821.

cattle grazing lands in northern Florida and relocated them to tracts in south-central Florida, a swampy region far from any lands then coveted by whites.[19]

Andrew Jackson was among those proponents of Indian removal publicly couching their plans in humanitarian terms—men who claimed that rescuing Indians from extinction was their only objective. But Jackson's private correspondence revealed a starkly different sentiment. He warned to beware of "the treachery of the Indian character."[20] And while serving as territorial governor in Florida, he told Secretary of War John C. Calhoun that to make treaties with Indians was "not only useless but absurd."[21]

Jacksons' belief that if Indians were not using the land properly the government should take it typified Western sentiment. By the 1820s, such attitudes were driving federal Indian policy. Congressmen from the South and West maneuvered to dominate congressional committees that dealt with Indian affairs and kept steady pressure on the president for aggressive removal treaties. As noted, Thomas Jefferson saw removal as a possible option, and subsequent presidents James Monroe and John Quincy Adams did so as well, but the government had persisted in its cautious approach of making treaties with small groups of Indians exchanging small holdings for equivalent acreage in Arkansas and that part of the Louisiana Purchase later designated as the Indian Territory.

As before, Georgia took the lead in insisting that all Indian claims within its borders be extinguished. Contemplating the remaining lands of the Creeks, Georgia governor George M. Troup prodded the Adams administration to finish what Andrew Jackson had started with the Treaty of Fort Jackson. Federal negotiators met with Creek leader William McIntosh in 1825. McIntosh, the son of a Scottish trader and a prominent Creek woman, had fought alongside Andrew Jackson against Red Sticks during the Creek War and was related to several prominent Georgians, includ-

[19] John K. Mahon, "The Treaty of Moultrie Creek, 1823," *Florida Historical Quarterly* 40 (1962): 353–66.

[20] Jackson to Henry Atkinson, May 15, 1819, John C. Calhoun, *The Papers of John C. Calhoun*, edited by Robert Meriwether, William Edwin Hemphill, and Clyde Norman Wilson, 20 vols. (Columbia: University of South Carolina Press, 1959–1988), 4: 63.

[21] Jackson to Calhoun, September 17, 1821, in ibid., 6: 373.

ing Governor Troup. A prosperous businessman, McIntosh thus had interests in both the Creek and white worlds. Moreover, he had come to believe that Indian resistance to white expansion was futile, and he saw money to be made—not necessarily honestly—by facilitating removal. After receiving a hefty bribe, McIntosh led a few other compliant headmen in signing the Second Treaty of Indian Springs, which incredibly ceded all Creek lands within Georgia to the United States.[22]

It was soon clear, however, that McIntosh had no authority to negotiate for the Creek Nation. Only the Creek National Council had the power to approve land cessions, and to emphasize that sole authority, the council had passed a law mandating death for any Creek who alienated additional Creek lands. Accordingly, the council responded to the Second Treaty of Indian Springs by handing down a death sentence for McIntosh. Lawmenders—years before, McIntosh had been one—cornered him in one of his homes and set it ablaze. When McIntosh finally emerged, the lawmenders shot him, dragged him from his porch, and stabbed him to death.

The Creek author of the Second Indian Springs Treaty was dead, and the obvious fraud surrounding the treaty even caused the federal government to repudiate it. But white persistence disheartened Georgia Creeks. New negotiators were dispatched, and in 1826 another treaty provided sufficient payment to the Creek Nation to persuade it to cede its remaining lands to Georgia.

The Cherokees and the Civilization Program

Georgia's title to Creek lands emboldened the state, and it immediately turned its attention to the Cherokees. For years the Cherokees had escaped close scrutiny because their hilly and occasionally mountainous lands were judged worthless and ill-suited for growing cotton. But more than their land, it was the Cherokees themselves who attracted notice. Most Cherokees lived according to traditional ways, with women tilling the fields, making clothes, and taking care

[22] In 1821, McIntosh had negotiated the first Treaty of Indian Springs, which ceded to Georgia Creek land between the Ocmulgee and Flint rivers. Upper Creeks were outraged by this agreement and were responsible for securing a death penalty for anyone who ceded additional Creek territory.

of children while men traded and tended livestock. But a significant number of Cherokees had also embraced the government's civilization program. Gravely injured by the American Revolution and economically debilitated by the declining deerskin trade, Cherokees saw acculturation as the road to recovery.[23] Cherokee elites, many of mixed Indian-white heritage, worked farms, ran stores, and owned black slaves. Cherokees welcomed Protestant missionaries into their communities and embraced schools and churches as symbols of progress. Cherokee children learned to read and write English, and the great Cherokee sage Sequoyah invented a Cherokee alphabet featured in their bilingual newspaper, the *Cherokee Phoenix.*

These social and intellectual accomplishments were matched by political ones. By 1809, Cherokees had created a centralized government headed by the National Council that met once a year to confer about important decisions. Elites dominated the council and called a convention in the 1820s to draft a constitution and enact laws for the entire nation. Similar to Creeks, Cherokees protected their land with an automatic death sentence for anyone who sold or ceded it.

Rather than applauding this success of the civilization program, Georgia was troubled by it. Yet not until gold was discovered on Cherokee land did the state move in such way as to make the civilization program irrelevant.

Gold was discovered in 1828, the same year that Andrew Jackson was elected president. It was a portentous coincidence for Cherokees. Now having a reason to do so and with a president friendly to their goals, Georgia commenced a program of astonishing harassment and intimidation against the Cherokees. The Georgia legislature extended its laws over the Cherokee Nation, a move that legally defined Cherokees as free persons of color but with one important stipulation: Unlike other free persons of color in the state, Cherokees could not hold legitimate titles to any property. Georgia also prohibited Cherokees from mining gold within their nation and audaciously organized a land lottery to distribute Cherokee lands to white Georgians. Because religious and philan-

---

[23] Theda Perdue, *Cherokee Women: Gender and Culture Change, 1700–1835* (Lincoln: University of Nebraska Press, 1998), 111.

thropic groups such as the American Board of Commissioners for Foreign Missions supported Indians, Georgia targeted the missionaries living among the Cherokees by requiring that all whites within the Cherokee Nation swear allegiance to the state and obtain a license to reside with Indians.

This ambitious and extensive program inspired emulation in other states with Indian populations. Knowing that President Jackson was in sympathy with their efforts, Georgians adopted unprecedented policies designed to torment Indians, confident that such treatment would ease the negotiation of removal treaties.[24] As it turned out, they had read both their man and the situation correctly.

Jacksonian Indian Policy

Andrew Jackson was always an advocate for Indian removal. Prior to defeating John Quincy Adams for the presidency in 1828, he had urged Adams to achieve complete removal. After assuming office, Jackson appointed staunch supporters of removal to key positions within his government, particularly Attorney General John Berrien of Georgia and Secretary of War John Eaton of Tennessee. In addition, he sent emissaries to the Creeks and Cherokees urging them to exchange all lands in the East for equivalent lands west of the Mississippi. The government, said Jackson, would pay Indians for their livestock and for improvements on their property.

In addition, Jackson offered those Indians who wanted to remain in the East individual land allotments that would allow them to operate family farms. That option, however, made them subject to state laws that designated them only as free persons of color. It would be worse, Jackson warned, to refuse either option, because in that case the government would do nothing to prevent states from simply confiscating Indian lands.[25]

Jackson made certain that Indians knew he meant business, but he also wanted to avoid violent unrest. He had political worries as well. Realizing that many throughout the country would not

---

[24] David S. Heidler and Jeanne T. Heidler, *Manifest Destiny* (Westport, CT: Greenwood Press, 2003), 78.

[25] John Eaton to Governor of Alabama, May 21, 1829, Andrew Jackson Letters, Perkins Library, Duke University.

support unvarnished removal, he undertook to convince the public about the policy's wisdom. He recruited religious leaders and well-known proponents of Indian rights, such as Superintendent of Indian Trade Thomas L. McKenney, to explain that removal was actually in the best interests of the Indians.[26] In his first Annual Message he informed Congress of the pressing need for Indian removal and asked for money to accomplish it. As he habitually did in his public statements, Jackson framed his sentiments in humanitarian terms about the good effects removal would have on Indians. He was exceedingly disingenuous in insisting that eastern Indians were nomadic hunters whose cultures could only be saved by removing them from white influence.[27] Jackson knew the truth as something else altogether, since he had seen Indian towns surrounded by cornfields and herded cattle.

Nonetheless, his political popularity was so unassailable that pensive nonsense about noble savages guided much of the subsequent debate when Congress took up the issue in 1830. Although opponents of removal were frequently Jackson's political opponents and consequently were open to charges of partisanship, they obviously had a better claim to the moral high ground than pro-removal forces. Pointing to the humane Indian policies of people like William Penn as an example to which the country should aspire, these antiremoval proponents declared the civilization program a success and insisted that it would be unconscionable to take away everything that the Indians had worked to build. It was an argument as effective as it was simple because it appealed to Americans' natural sense of fair play. Advocates of removal also took up the benevolent banner, insisting that they too only had the best interests of Indians at heart. They decried the cruelty of leaving Indians at the mercy of white settlers and state governments; the only way for Indians really to achieve the goals of the civilization program, they argued, was through removal from the very white civilization they were supposed to be imitating.

---

[26] Ronald N. Satz, *American Indian Policy in the Jacksonian Era* (Lincoln: University of Nebraska Press, 1974), 14–17.

[27] James D. Richardson, comp., *A Compilation of the Messages and Papers of the Presidents, 1789–1908*, vol. 2 (Washington, DC: Bureau of National Literature and Art, 1908), 456–59.

But their posture had a hollow ring, and the pro-removal advocates sought to bolster their claims to compassion with additional racial, legal, and political arguments. They pointed to the number of brutal Indian wars as proof that the savage race of Indians could not live in peace with whites. They referred to the federal government's 1802 agreement with Georgia (to extinguish all Indian land titles) as a solemn obligation. They appealed to states' rights sentiments by insisting that the federal government could not rightfully interfere to protect Indians within states.

When all was said, Indian removal proved too attractive to too many congressmen and senators. Jackson's popularity would have likely been sufficient to ram through the legislation. He had cleverly proposed it early in his administration while supporters were still energized by his victory and before opponents had organized a coherent challenge. The Removal Act passed in a close vote (28 to 19 in the Senate and 102 to 97 in the House), but it passed. Most important, it funded removal more aggressively than any previous policy with Indians, allocating $500,000 to negotiate removal treaties and pay for the transportation of entire tribes of Indians out of the East.[28] The civilization program and all it had promised was a dead letter.

The Cherokee Legal Fight

Andrew Jackson quickly signed the Removal Bill into law, but opposition by Indians and their supporters continued. While Jackson dispatched commissioners to Indian nations to negotiate removal treaties, the Cherokees mounted legal challenges to stop Georgia from taking their lands through a state lottery. Georgia had accelerated the lottery to persuade Cherokees to accept the federal government's removal plans. The Cherokees instead appealed to the courts.[29]

In the case of *Cherokee Nation* v. *Georgia*, Chief Justice John Marshall appeared sympathetic to the Cherokees when he described

---

[28] Satz, *Indian Policy*, 25–30; Henry E. Fritz, "Humanitarian Rhetoric and Andrew Jackson's Removal Policy," *Chronicles of Oklahoma* 79 (2001): 70, 79–80; Jason Meyers, "No Idle Past: Uses of History in the 1830 Indian Removal Debates," *The Historian* 63 (Fall 2000): 54–65.

[29] Satz, *Indian Policy*, 39–42; Watson, *Liberty and Power*, 107–09.

Indians as "domestic dependent Nations." Yet Marshall also noted
a legal impediment in the framing of the Cherokee case: The Indians had approached the Supreme Court as a foreign nation to give
the court original jurisdiction. Marshall consequently claimed that
the Court could not make a ruling because, per his description,
Indian nations were not foreign entities. The message was clear,
and the unspoken message was equally so: Cherokees could not sue.
American citizens could.[30]

Almost immediately, Americans did. Elizur Butler and Samuel
Worcester, missionaries who had been arrested for disobeying the
Georgia law that required whites to obtain licenses to live among
the Cherokees, hired William Wirt, formerly James Monroe's attorney general, to represent them. Both Butler and Worcester had
intentionally violated the license law in order to force the federal
courts into ruling on Georgia's authority over the Cherokee Nation.
In a majority decision rendered in 1832, Marshall said that because
the Cherokee Nation was a "domestic dependent nation" guaranteed by U.S. treaties, Georgia law had no power over it.[31]

Cherokees interpreted the decision as a great victory, but the
decision ultimately proved nugatory. Georgia refused to obey the
Supreme Court's ruling, and Andrew Jackson declined to insist that
the state do so. The famous story of Jackson responding to Marshall's ruling by muttering, "Well: John Marshall has made his
decision: *now let him enforce it*," is probably false.[32] The sentiment,
however, was authentic. In a letter to friend John Coffee, Jackson
crowed that "the decision of the supreme court has fell still born."[33]

In short, Jackson's refusal to enforce Marshall's ruling rendered
it a nullity. His reasons for refusal have invited speculation. Some

[30] Satz, *Indian Policy*, 42–47; Mark R. Scherer, "'Now Let Him Enforce It': Exploring the
Myth of Andrew Jackson's Reponse to Worcester v. Georgia (1832)," *Chronicles of Oklahoma*
74 (Spring 1996): 20–27.

[31] Satz, *Indian Policy*, 47–49; *Worcester v. Georgia*, in Richard Peters, ed., *Report of Cases Argued
and Adjudged in the Supreme Court of the United States* (Philadelphia: Thomas, Cowperthwait,
1845), 6: 515–97.

[32] Horace Greeley, *American Conflict: A History of the Great Rebellion in the United States of America,
1860–65*, 2 vols. (Hartford, CT: Case, 1865), 1: 106.

[33] Jackson to Coffee, April 7, 1832, in Andrew Jackson, *The Correspondence of Andrew Jackson*,
7 vols., edited by John Spencer Bassett (Washington, DC: The Carnegie Institution of Washington, 1927–1928), 4: 430.

have seen the Nullification crisis over the protective tariff that pitted the federal government against South Carolina as a clue to explaining Jackson's actions. He needed support in the South to prevent South Carolina from recruiting other states to defy federal tariff laws. His helping Georgia and other southern states with Indian populations was possibly intended to court their support in the fight against Nullification. Perhaps this was so, but Jackson's support for Indian removal long predated the Nullification crisis. In any case, Jackson was not likely to have enforced Marshall's decision, since he really saw no inconsistency in supporting states' rights with regard to Indian removal and in condemning states' rights in the form of Nullification. He needed no other reason than his own predilections to increase pressure on eastern Indians to sign removal treaties. That states were willing to strip Indians of their lands was not a problem for the government; it was a way to coerce a solution.

During the 1830s there were more than seventy treaties with eastern Indians. These agreements surrendered some one hundred million acres in exchange for lands in the West and annuity payments in cash or goods. The western land that the Indians obtained

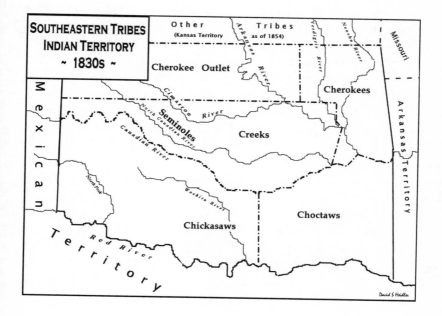

in the swap was not undesirable in itself, but unlike the land they were leaving, it was unimproved. Worse, it often bordered or overlapped land claimed by other Indians who were hostile towards interlopers. Because removal destinations were always undeveloped and frequently unfriendly, the fairness of these presumably equivalent exchanges was questionable at best.

Opposition to Indian Removal

Many Americans considered what was happening to eastern Indians a rank injustice and therefore opposed the government's removal plans. Such attitudes were part of a general reform movement sweeping the country, spawned by the fear that Americans were slipping into irredeemable sin. Reformers who condemned removal as un-Christian also condemned slavery as a sin against God, and accordingly abolitionists led protests against the treatment of Native Americans. Correspondingly, other Americans who first agitated against removal became abolitionists as well.

Their stance was understandable. Antislavery stemmed from the same point of view that had first envisioned the civilization program for southern Indians. After the American Revolution, many Americans uncomfortably recognized the contradictions between the high-minded rhetoric of liberty and the sordid existence of slavery. Northern states gradually abolished slavery, and a few slave owners freed their slaves, especially in the upper South. To allay fears that emancipation would cause social chaos, abolitionists opened schools for freed slaves to prove that they could be fashioned into productive members of society. Just as Enlightenment beliefs had led to the civilization program, these early attempts to educate freed blacks derived from the abolitionist zeal for progress and moral improvement. Who, they innocently asked, could object to that?[34]

Regrettably quite a few people did object, and many of the forces that had doomed the civilization program undermined embryonic abolitionism. Slavery, an expensive, inefficient relic of colonial labor shortages, had seemed in decline at the close of the Revolution. But beginning in the 1790s, it commenced an unremit-

[34] Merton L. Dillon, *The Abolitionists: The Growth of a Dissenting Minority* (New York: W. W. Norton, 1979), 10, 21.

ting expansion when the invention of the cotton gin made planta-
tion agriculture profitable. Not only was slavery revived, it became
indispensable in the interior, black-soiled regions of the Deep
South, where cotton flourished and the demand for cheap labor
intensified. At the same time and because of this economic necessity, racial views hardened. The argument that whites and Indians
could not live together peacefully easily translated into claims
that freed slaves could never be included in American society. From
that self-interested fatalism, it was only a short step to claiming that
America and its blessings of liberty and opportunity should be
reserved for whites only.

The connection between Indian removal and the expansion of
slavery was not lost on the abolitionists. The relatively conciliatory
antislavery movement became more aggressive in the 1820s. Earlier
abolitionists had been willing to wait for gradual emancipation and
had accepted the argument of groups such as the American Colonization Society, which held that after emancipation, freed slaves
should be colonized in Africa or the Caribbean. In the 1820s, when
abolitionists began vehemently arguing that Indian removal was
unnecessary, they also demanded immediate emancipation with no colonization. Logic demanded the consistency, since the proposed colonization of freed slaves was just as immoral as removing Indians.[35]

Thus leading abolitionists such as William Lloyd Garrison,
Theodore Dwight Weld, and Sarah and Angelina Grimké used
meetings, newspapers, and pamphlets to oppose Indian removal
just as they did slavery. For the first time in the American experience, women organized themselves nationally to promote a cause
other than their own and gained important skills of persuasion they
would later use in fighting other civil rights issues.[36]

One of the strongest condemnations of both slavery and Indian
removal appeared in the "William Penn Essays" written by Jeremiah Evarts, secretary of the American Board of Commissioners
for Foreign Missions. Number 22 of the series posed the question:
"Is it more clearly wrong to take Africans from their native land,
than it is to make slaves of the Cherokees upon *their* native land? or,

[35] Mary Hershberger, "Mobilizing Women, Anticipating Abolition: The Struggle against
Indian Removal," *Journal of American History* 86 (June 1999): 17, 35; Dillon, *Abolitionists*, 11–12, 19.
[36] Hershberger, "Mobilizing Women," 25, 33.

on penalty of their being thus enslaved, driving them into exile?"[37] Evarts did not appeal to Americans' consciences alone; he expertly analyzed the legal questions involved and argued that American treaty law prevented both the United States and state governments from interfering with the status of any Indians.

Petitions were drafted and mass meetings were convened to protest both slavery and Indian removal, and eventually reformers derided as crackpots in their own time would be later lauded as prophets. Yet, strong emotional appeals, valid legal arguments, petition drives, and mass meetings could not sway those committed to evicting Indians any more effectively than they could win over those committed to maintaining slavery. Ironically, the egalitarianism later referred to as Jacksonian Democracy hurt both the antislavery and antiremoval movements. Most new voters in the South and the West wanted Indian removal. Most new voters in the South wanted slavery. The ugly legacies of these twin evils were assured.

Northern Indian Removal

Much attention at the time was on the removal of southeastern Indians, primarily because of the value of southern cotton lands. But Indian removal was not limited to the South. The government also forced smaller groups of northern and midwestern tribes to move west of the Mississippi River. As it had with southern Indians, the War of 1812 weakened these people, especially because their association with Tecumseh had corrupted them in the eyes of whites. Parts of the Winnebago, Potawatomi, and Sauk nations had either aided or openly joined Tecumseh's confederation, and his death and the British departure from the Northwest in 1813 put these groups at the mercy of the United States.

Unlike the South, where cotton fever gripped settlers, the North did not experience as much pressure for land cessions. Even in wilderness regions of the Old Northwest, the fur trade's lucrative days were numbered because overhunting had depleted most game, forcing hunters and trappers west to the upper Missouri River and Rocky Mountains. Meanwhile, the government appointed agents

[37] Jeremiah Evarts, *Cherokee Removal: The "William Penn" Essays and Other Writings*, ed. Francis Paul Prucha (Knoxville: University of Tennessee Press, 1981), 173.

and established trading posts (known as factories) to smooth the progress of peaceful relations with northern Indians.

Treaties with northern Indians nonetheless secured enough land cessions to satisfy settlers eager for agricultural expansion. For example, Michigan territorial governor Lewis Cass negotiated the Treaty of Fort Meigs in 1817, which ceded Indian lands in Michigan to the United States. During Cass' tenure in Michigan he developed a strong interest in Indian languages and cultures, and though he came to the apparently sincere belief that Indian culture could only survive through removal, he did not believe that this good end justified any means. Cass thought that given time to understand their plight, Indians would voluntarily distance themselves from abuse by white settlers and from the injurious influence of alcohol.

Yet Indians in the Old Northwest were as reluctant to leave their homes as were their southern counterparts. Some, however, sensed that a change in their status was inevitable, and even before the passage of the Indian Removal Act of 1830, they were voluntarily giving up their lands. For example, a number of Seneca and Shawnee moved from Ohio to Kansas during the 1820s. In August 1825, a major conference of numerous tribes and U.S. government agents at Prairie du Chien drew boundaries between all major tribes, which later made land cessions easier to negotiate.

This gradual approach to land cessions and removal seemed to work better in the Northwest until Wisconsin's lead deposits attracted a rapid influx of settlers that exasperated the region's Winnebago Indians. Violence broke out in 1827 and soon intensified into the Winnebago War. A large show of military force by General Henry Atkinson brought the conflict to an end, with the Indians ceding large portions of their land.

With the passage of the Removal Act, the government increased its pressure on the Indians of the Northwest to follow the example of earlier emigrants. Commissioners traveled the Northwest to negotiate removal treaties with remaining Seneca, Shawnee, and Ottawa. In 1832, the Kaskaskia, Peoria, and other small Illinois tribes ceded their lands in Illinois and moved to eastern Kansas. While most agreed to make their way over difficult trails to Kansas, the fate of the Wyandot of Ohio and Michigan was telling. Although they consistently rejected the offer of land west of the

Missouri River, they did consent during the 1830s to enough land sales to the government to deplete seriously their Ohio holdings. Finally succumbing to pressure, Wyandots agreed to purchase part of the Shawnees' holdings in Kansas, but that arrangement fell through. When increasing harassment by whites went unpunished, the Wyandot consented to removal to Kansas in 1843. Their numbers by now were negligible—only about six hundred made the journey—and as latecomers they had to purchase Delaware Indian land for a place to live.

And so it was with most of the Indians who agreed to remove from the Old Northwest. They exchanged their lands for tracts in Kansas and occasionally for expanses to the north, but all such land trades were predicated on the idea that removing Indians to these regions would not only place them away from whites but also would situate them on land that whites did not want. But because of the fertility of eastern Kansas's soil and its closeness to white-settled areas such as Missouri, relocated Indians were only temporarily left in peace. When plans for a transcontinental railroad proposed laying track through the region, pressures again mounted on the relocated Indians to move even farther west. White pledges of good faith and titles to property were as empty as the phrase that had typically graced trade agreements, words promising that Indians would have their new lands as long as rivers flowed and grass grew.

The Black Hawk War

The government's removal policy sparked armed conflict with another Indian tribe in the Old Northwest. Settlement pouring into Illinois and Wisconsin after the War of 1812 spurred demands for the ouster of Indians in that region, and by 1831, the situation had become grave.

Caught in this vise of white encroachment were the Sauk and Fox Indians, Algonquian people whose relationship dated from the early eighteenth century when they both had fought the French. Led by the respected warrior Black Hawk, portions of the Sauk-Fox vehemently protested a fifty-million-acre land cession to the United States, consented to by some questionable tribal representatives in 1804. The cession gave away an area comprising almost half of northwestern Illinois, the eastern part of Missouri, and most of southwestern Wisconsin. Black Hawk's anger led him to side with the British during the War of 1812, and after the war, the Sauk-Fox rejected a peace agreement with the United States in September 1815. For the time being, however, the remote nature of their settlements prevented friction with Americans.

But relying on distance to preserve the peace proved a false hope as soon as white settlers began surging into western Illinois. In 1831, confronting white interlopers in his own village of Saukenuk near Rock Island, Illinois, Black Hawk contemplated war, but Illinois militia and U.S. regular forces quickly intimidated the aging leader. Instead of resisting what was seemingly irresistible, Black Hawk submitted to removal and led his followers across the Mississippi River into Iowa. The move was disastrous. Uprooted from their homes and forced to wander into unfamiliar lands, the Sauk-Fox were unwelcome by Indians in the region, especially their hereditary enemy, the Sioux. Such open hostility and the prospect of starvation compelled Black Hawk to lead his band of about four hundred men and their families back into Illinois in early 1832. Although these famished Indians planned to settle with the hospitable Winnebago and put in a stand of corn, Illinois went into near panic over Black Hawk's "invasion." General Henry Atkinson demanded that Black Hawk return to Iowa, but the Sauk-Fox refused. U.S. Army units then took the field and the Illinois militia was mustered (including a young Abraham Lincoln) to wage what became known as the Black Hawk War.

In many respects, the affair was a tragic misunderstanding with violent consequences. Black Hawk's consternation—that his attempt to return to his homelands had evoked such a large military response—prompted him to surrender, but his peace emissary was murdered. Encountering the Illinois militia, he again tried to surrender but was attacked nonetheless. His warriors returned fire, scattering the militia. This initial victory, however, sealed the Indians' fate. Pursued by forces increasing in both number and determination, Black Hawk moved his people as quickly as he could up the Rock River toward Wisconsin as rearguard skirmishes pestered their progress. On July 21, 1832, militia under Henry Dodge attacked Black Hawk's forces at Wisconsin Heights, sending them scurrying westward. By August 2, the Indians had reached the Mississippi and were trying to cross when regulars under Atkinson and Dodge's militia fell upon them at the mouth of the Bad Axe River, and with such fury that only a small number escaped. Black Hawk was among the survivors, fleeing to a Winnebago village in Wisconsin, but he soon surrendered to the government. He remained a prisoner in the East—though with considerable liberty at times. He was in fact taken on a tour of the East where he met with Andrew Jackson in June 1833 in Baltimore.[38] Except for Jackson's indulging a habit of lecturing Indians on civic responsibilities and their need to be submissive, the meeting was brief and uneventful. Black Hawk returned to his devastated people in Iowa and died there in 1838 at about the age of seventy.

The Black Hawk War was the last Indian conflict in the Old Northwest. Its aftermath saw a wholesale punishment of the principal remaining tribes in the region. In September 1832, General Winfield Scott gathered Winnebago, Sauk, and Fox leaders and forced them to give up the remainder of their lands in Wisconsin and eastern Iowa. Thereafter they formed small enclaves in Iowa, Kansas, and Oklahoma.

Choctaw Removal

Southern Indians were ironically known as the Five Civilized Tribes because they had most eagerly cooperated with the federal government's civilization program. Of these, the Choctaw Indians constituted one of the most populous tribes in the country, numbering about twenty thousand in the 1820s. Living in the southern part of modern-day Mississippi, Choctaws had been urged to relinquish ever-larger tracts of land to the federal government since the early nineteenth century. When Mississippi became a state in 1817, the government finally proposed that the Choctaws make the customary exchange of land for territory west of the Mississippi River. In response, elderly headman Pushmataha took a delegation to Washington to argue against the exchange, but the journey was too much for him, and he died in the capital. Choctaw resolve remained firm,

---

[38] *Niles Weekly Register,* June 15, 1833.

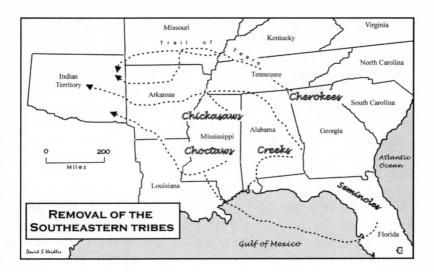

however, and younger leaders, most of them of mixed heritage like Greenwood LeFlore and David Folsom, continued to resist removal.[39]

Nonetheless, the same chain of events that had played out in Georgia occurred in Mississippi. Andrew Jackson's election and Mississippi's extending its laws over the Choctaw Nation in January 1830 persuaded Choctaws to sign the Treaty of Dancing Rabbit Creek, which bore the distinction of being the first removal treaty signed under the 1830 legislation. Dancing Rabbit Creek thus became the model for events throughout the South.

Jackson promised that Choctaw families who wanted to remain in Mississippi would each receive a land allotment. Others would move west of the Mississippi and receive an annuity from the federal government to compensate for improvements and for any livestock left behind. Jackson intended to sell ceded Choctaw land to fund the annuity.[40] It seemed like an orderly solution that would benefit everyone. The result, however, was anything but tidy.

Many Choctaws remained in Mississippi, hoping that the U.S. Senate would not ratify the treaty. Even before the Senate took the

---

[39] Arthur H. De Rosier, Jr., *The Removal of the Choctaw Indians* (Knoxville: University of Tennessee Press, 1970), 92.

[40] Jackson to Coffee, October 23, 1831, Jackson, *Correspondence*, 4: 363.

matter under consideration, squatters were pouring into the Choctaw Nation, some using erroneous claims of Choctaw debts to take
allotments away from families. Meanwhile, the Choctaws who were
already leaving Mississippi fared no better. During the winter of
1830–31, the first migration began, often over trackless land
toward the Red River and without any of the supplies that the
government had promised. As one historian of Indian removal
asserted, Jackson intended for removal to occur "quickly, cheaply,
and humanely," although the last of these three conditions was
often deemed unessential.[41]

Indeed, rather than seeking to correct mistakes evident in these
Choctaw journeys, the government repeated them while threatening any Indians who protested. The following autumn, when the
next wave of Choctaw migration began, criminals stalked the journey to steal the few possessions the Indians carried. Disease was
another predator with outbreaks of cholera amplifying the Indians'
misery as the illness thinned their ranks. Two years of such treks
had not only removed about half of the Choctaws from Mississippi,
it had killed a sizeable number along the way. Those who remained
in Mississippi descended into abject poverty while unscrupulous
whites systematically cheated them out of their lands. In a few
years, the remaining Choctaws too were willing to leave, leaving
only a small number of elite Choctaws who had managed to keep
relatively large allotments. These remnants of the once populous
Choctaws eventually became citizens and melded into American
society, but they did so because they were, in both appearance and
name, essentially white.

Creek Removal

Other states watched the rapid removal of the large number of
Choctaws with great interest. Soon these states were also pestering
their own Indian populations to conclude removal treaties, actions
that emboldened squatters to move on to Indian lands, stealing livestock and farm implements as they went. The states threatened
retaliation if Indians resisted.

---

[41] Satz, *Indian Policy*, 64–71.

Creeks in Alabama, suffering at the hands of such land-hungry whites, decided like the Choctaws to send a delegation to speak directly with President Jackson in Washington. Many Creek men had fought alongside Jackson against Red Sticks in the Creek War, and despite his behavior at Fort Jackson they hoped that their old comrade would be sympathetic to their plight. Any illusions about the matter were quickly dispelled. Jackson refused even to see the delegation. Instead, Secretary of War John Eaton scolded the Creeks for resisting removal and warned that removal was their best hope for survival. Deflated Creek leaders finally agreed to an arrangement like that offered to the Choctaws. Creeks who migrated west would be given land and an annuity, and those families who remained in Alabama would each receive a land allotment.[42]

The government intended to conduct a census of the Creeks, a deliberate plan that was to take five years. Ordinarily this would have provided plenty of time to designate allotments for Creeks who wanted to stay, to arrange transportation and supplies for those moving west, and to survey ceded lands for sale to settlers. The systematic process was planned for 1833, but it quickly unraveled when rapacious whites descended on the Creeks who intended to leave as well as those who intended to stay, intimidating the former into selling their possessions and swindling the latter out of their allotments.[43] White behavior was so wanton that even government officials were shocked by the fraud and violence. Alabama officials spoke as if they wanted to curb the abuse, but realizing that today's criminals were tomorrow's voters, the state ultimately did little to protect the Creeks. In fact, many officials realized that threats of uncontrolled violence might best persuade Creeks to move west. Earlier Creek migrants were brought back as propagandists for removal, with effective results, and Creek removal increased over the next two years.

As the Choctaw had, Creeks traveling west endured terrible hardships, especially because many waited until after the fall harvest to commence the journey. This meant traveling in winter with

[42] Michael D. Green, *The Politics of Indian Removal: Creek Government and Society in Crisis* (Lincoln: University of Nebraska Press, 1982), 159–63.

[43] John Milton to John Fontaine, July 4, 1834, John Fontaine Papers, University of Georgia Libraries, Hargrett Rare Book and Manuscript Library, Athens, Georgia.

provisions that would have been inadequate even in a good season. Possibly a third of the Creeks who made the journey between 1833 and 1835 died.

Many Creeks had accepted allotments and remained in Alabama, but they became increasingly angry over their treatment and resentful of the government's failure to protect them. Finally, law-abiding Alabamians, appalled by white behavior, asked the federal government to intervene. Proving that voters had considerably more influence with Washington than Indians did, the federal government stopped sales of Creek land until it could investigate the situation. By then, many homeless Creeks were starving, and their warriors were threatening to attack whites living on former Creek farms.

Such talk alarmed cautious Creek leaders who knew that war could destroy a people who had neither the men nor the arms to fight the United States. Others, however, believed that only violence would compel the government to live up to the promises of the 1832 treaty. Despite numerous signs that the crisis was about to erupt, the government did little more than conduct a cursory investigation of the frauds. Moreover, agents persisted in delivering the warning that the federal government could not protect the Creeks, at the same time advising them to move as far from whites as possible. While warriors' anger boiled, these same agents handed out money to Creeks to purchase supplies for westward journeys they never intended to make.

More cash into the nation meant more attempts by whites to swindle the Creeks out of the money. Some Creeks submissively gathered in camps to await transportation west, but others fled to the countryside or took refuge with Cherokees in north Georgia, a development that disgruntled authorities there. Georgians were too busy harassing Cherokees into accepting removal, and the last thing they wanted were more Indians. Their militia was dispatched to chase Creeks back into Alabama and thus began the so-called Creek War of 1836. The war featured little fighting but much hiding by Creeks who were watching their children starve. Removal came to a standstill when only a few hundred Indians traveled west.

Hunger finally compelled Creeks to raid farms for food even as leaders urged restraint to prevent retaliation. Brigadier General Thomas S. Jesup used federal troops to capture Creeks and move them west, using the pretense of the Creek War to justify what amounted to compulsory removal. After it was all over, few Creeks remained. Like the Choctaw, a few mixed-heritage Creeks retained title to their farms and eventually melded into the white Alabama population. Others were treated even more shabbily. When the United States recruited Creek warriors to pursue Seminoles in Florida, their families were herded into embarkation points at Mobile. Their husbands and fathers found them there upon returning from Florida. Everyone was unceremoniously loaded on boats and shipped west.[44]

Chickasaw Removal

The Chickasaws were a smaller nation in northwestern Alabama and northeastern Mississippi who nonetheless had a strong warrior tradition resistant to the government's civilization program. Jackson met with Chickasaw leaders in 1830 and bluntly told them that there was nothing he could do to protect them from Alabama and Mississippi whites, and true enough, by 1832 settlers were pouring onto Chickasaw lands. A group of mixed-heritage Chickasaws forlornly agreed to the Treaty of Pontotoc Creek, which contained presumably generous terms. Before migrating, Chickasaw leaders could visit Indian Territory to choose their lands. Furthermore, Chickasaws were to keep the proceeds from the eventual sale of their lands in the East. Despite these concessions, full-blooded Chickasaws condemned the treaty as a betrayal of their birthright and vowed to resist removal. Their numbers were no match for the tide of surveyors and settlers flooding their lands, though, and during the summer of 1837 most Chickasaws began the difficult journey west. The remainder followed over the next few years.

Cherokee Removal

As Choctaws, Creeks, and Chickasaws were herded out of the region, many Cherokees were confident that their successful acculturation would exempt them from removal. Some Cherokees,

[44] Green, *Indian Removal*, 185.

however, warily gauged what was happening to other Indians and
counseled caution. These differing perceptions created two factions
within the nation, the Treaty Party that wanted to negotiate for voluntary removal under the best possible terms and the opponents
who unwaveringly opposed removal under any circumstances. The
latter faction was quite influential because it included the Cherokee
National Council under the principal chief of the nation, John
Ross, who was prepared to block acceptance of any removal treaty.
Meanwhile, a few Cherokees surveyed the rift among their own
people and the onerous treks of other Indian tribes westward and
succumbed to hopelessness. They simply began packing their
belongings and moving toward the Indian Territory.

Hoping to persuade more Cherokees to flee the state, Georgia
finalized its lottery system and began distributing Cherokee lands to
white settlers. The Treaty Party sprung into action, making trips to
Washington in 1834 and 1835 in the hopes of negotiating a favorable removal treaty. John Ross traveled to Washington as well, not
to secure a benign removal agreement but to demand that the government rein in Georgia.[45] The government would not listen, and
Georgia retaliated by confiscating Ross's considerable estates for
the land lottery.

Washington was indifferent to the Cherokee, but federal officials
were also exasperated with Georgia for its refusal to allow individual land allotments to Cherokee families wanting to remain in
the state. Such a concession, empty though it might be, had eased
the acceptance of removal treaties with other tribes, but Georgia
would not even consider it: All Indians had to go. Many Cherokees—
especially mixed-heritage elites—owned large farms that were
bustling with livestock and worked by slaves; these Cherokees were
understandably unwilling to leave everything behind. Many less
prosperous Cherokees, especially in traditional households, did not
want to leave Georgia either.

Any Indian rationale for opposing removal was immaterial to
Andrew Jackson and his agents. Georgia governor Wilson Lumpkin
had made clear to Jackson that the state would not accept any treaty

---

[45] Ross and Cherokee delegation to Jackson, January 23, 1835, Jackson, *Correspondence*, 5:
319–20.

granting allotments to or conferring citizenship on Indians.[46] Impatient for an end to the Indian presence in the East, Jackson sent commissioners under the leadership of John F. Schermerhorn to the Cherokee Nation to secure a treaty. Schermerhorn took heed of his instructions to deliver a treaty by any means and thus opened talks with a small minority of Cherokees at New Echota in 1835. The treaty that resulted agreed to the removal of all Cherokees. Although the Cherokee National Council denounced it, the treaty was rushed through the U.S. Senate and ratified after heated debate.

Stunned Cherokees protested that the treaty was simply illegitimate. Only a few Cherokees had consented to it, and the council had never ratified it. Procedural arguments were irrelevant to the national and state governments, however. New Echota was deemed a valid agreement, and troops began rounding up Cherokees for the move west. The army found the task distasteful, though, and Brigadier General John Wool granted Cherokee leaders time to appeal the government's actions. For this modest show of compassion, the government replaced Wool with Winfield Scott.

It all took time to play out, and by this point Jackson had left office. His handpicked successor was Martin Van Buren, who was as uncompromising in his instructions to Scott as Jackson would have been. Removal began in the spring of 1838. Camps were established and soldiers continued funneling Cherokees into them. A few Cherokees hid in the mountains and eked out a meager existence in the rough terrain, but most were caught.

Partly by land, partly by river, large groups trod what infamously became known as the Trail of Tears. A poor supply system and wretched weather made it a death march for about a quarter of the Cherokee Nation, most of the victims the elderly and the very young. Those who survived suffered ongoing ill-treatment. Two years later they still had not received a single payment for the numerous improvements they had made on their Georgia farms.[47] It was just one more promise broken in a long line that began years before with the plan for acculturation, a government program that in the case of the Cherokee had been discarded because it was successful.

[46] Lumpkin to Jackson, February 9, 1835, Jackson, *Correspondence*, 5: 327.

[47] Nicholas S. Peck to William H. Thomas, June 18, 1840, William H. Thomas Papers, University of Georgia Libraries, Hargrett Rare Book and Manuscript Library, Athens, Georgia.

The Seminoles and Their War

While Cherokees resisted removal through the courts, many Florida Seminoles resisted through war. They had lived apart from white civilization longer than any southern nation and had a tradition of antagonism toward the American government. Creek Red Sticks who had fought the United States in the first Creek War were part of their number, and Seminoles themselves greeted the civilization program and white settlement on their lands with uniform hostility. For a time, whites indulged this brooding aloofness because Seminole land was regarded as marginal. They had been pushed from the valuable agricultural region of northern Florida to steamy, swampy land in south central Florida, and few whites wanted it. Seminoles ran afoul of whites for other reasons. Settlers in the panhandle, along the northern coast, and in southern Georgia and Alabama feared the Seminoles as a security threat and resented them for the haven they provided to runaway slaves. Soon enough, they called on the federal government to get rid of these Indians.

Commissioners went to Florida in 1832 and negotiated the Treaty of Payne's Landing. The treaty contained the same attractive plum proffered to the Chickasaws. Seminoles were to send a delegation to Indian Territory to inspect their prospective new home before committing to removal. The delegation was supposed to return to Florida with a report for the entire Seminole leadership that would then decide about removal. But the delegation's journey to Indian Territory was the only part of this promise that the government kept. While in the West, the Seminole delegation was induced to sign another agreement that prematurely finalized Payne's Landing. The Treaty of Fort Gibson required all Seminoles to begin removal by the end of 1835, their destination the portion of the Indian Territory already designated for the Creek Nation. They were to receive scant compensation for their Florida lands.

Most Seminoles rejected these appalling terms. Led by the charismatic Osceola, they began preparing for war and soon had one. At the end of December 1835, Osceola coordinated simultaneous attacks on the Seminole agency, killing agent Wiley Thompson, and a column of soldiers under Major Francis Dade marching from Fort Brooke at Tampa Bay to Fort King in the interior, slaughtering all but three of 110 men. The assault on the agency and the Dade Massacre began the Second Seminole War.

It would be the longest continuous Indian war in United States history, but at first the government thought it was only a small uprising and planned to quash it with militia and a handful of regulars. But Florida comprised both the Eastern and Western Departments of the U.S. Army, and the administrative confusion that resulted was a portent of more serious problems to come. Western Department commander Brigadier General Edmund Pendleton Gaines assumed that he would direct the campaign against the Seminoles. He left his headquarters in New Orleans with a contingent of regulars and militia, landed on the coast of Florida, and marched into the interior where Seminoles promptly besieged his encampment along the Withlacoochee River. To extricate himself from this predicament, Gaines signed a treaty with the Seminoles that promised them a permanent home in southern Florida. He then headed back to New Orleans claiming he had ended the war.

The War Department did not know Gaines was even in Florida, let alone that he ended the war by essentially losing it. The department in fact had given command of the Florida campaign to Brigadier General Winfield Scott, commander of the Eastern Department. After being apprised of Gaines's extraordinary agreement, the government bluntly renounced it and ordered Scott to bring the Seminoles to heel and ready them for removal. Scott, however, was only more successful than Gaines in that he was not compelled to surrender. Seminole warriors moved their women and children into remote south Florida and then conducted hit and run attacks against American forces. One of the most respected regular officers in the army, Scott could not adjust to such irregular tactics and persisted in arraying his men in orderly columns that proved tempting and effective targets for Seminoles. President Jackson had a long history of arguing with Scott and needed little excuse to replace him with Brigadier General Thomas S. Jesup.

Maroons, the runaway slaves who allied with the Seminoles, also complicated the army's job in Florida. Many maroons were related to Seminoles through marriage, and even those Seminoles not reflexively opposed to removal insisted that these people be allowed to come with them to the West. That slave hunters were intent on returning maroons to American plantations not only stiffened the determination of both Indians and blacks to resist removal to the last man but also animated abolitionists in Congress. The Second Seminole War thus melded antislavery and Indian removal into a large, unsettling controversy.

Abolitionists who were disposed to take up the maroon cause now combined their antislavery principles with their opposition to removal. Congressman Joshua Giddings of Ohio (who would write *Exiles of Florida,* a detailed history of the Second Seminole War), condemned the capture of freedom-loving maroons as barbarous, and General Jesup came to believe that the conflict was "a Negro, not an Indian war" that would lead to serious uprisings among southern slaves.[48]

The old Indian fighter Andrew Jackson urged the army to concentrate on Seminoles, advising Jesup to hold Seminole women and children as hostages until their husbands and fathers surrendered. Jackson left office in March 1837, with the situation in Florida still unresolved, but he continued to offer sharp counsel to the War Department. Smarting under such criticism, Jesup called for another meeting with Osceola, this one a trap under a flag of truce. Jesup's officers were dismayed by the bad faith, but when Osceola arrived in October 1837, Jesup had him arrested. Jailed at Fort Moultrie in Charleston Harbor, Osceola lasted only a year.[49]

Seminoles sorely felt the loss of Osceola, but they and their African American allies tenaciously fought on. Jesup used bloodhounds imported from Cuba to track down Indians and slaves, achieving some measure of success, but such measures were regarded as infamous. His men grew tired of Florida's stifling climate and the diseases it caused. Regular officers not only found service in Florida distasteful but also increasingly dishonorable. They began to criticize the war, echoing voices in Congress and the

---

[48] Jesup to Benjamin F. Butler, December 9, 1936, *American State Papers, Military Affairs,* 7 vols. (Washington, DC: Gales & Seaton, 1832–1961), 7: 821.

[49] Jackson to Jesup, August 2, 1836, August 3, 1836, November 5, 1836, October 7, 1837, Andrew Jackson Letters, Perkins Library, Duke University; Memorandum on the Florida Campaign, April 1837; Jackson to Joel R. Poinsett, August 27, 1837, October 1, 1837, Jackson, *Correspondence,* 5: 512; John K. Mahon, *History of the Second Seminole War, 1835–1842* (Gainesville: University of Florida, 1967), 214–18.

newspapers, and more and more people began expressing consternation over resources being expended to expel some five thousand Indians from a place that no one wanted. Disgusted by the war and frustrated by its inconclusiveness, Jesup endorsed a letter written by his officers recommending that the Seminoles be left alone in southern Florida. General of the Army Alexander Macomb promptly replaced him.

Macomb fruitlessly tried to negotiate with Seminole leaders, and Colonel Zachary Taylor soon replaced him. Taylor designed a grid system for central and southern Florida with the plan of establishing a garrison in every square. Soldiers could then patrol the region more systematically. While the plan enjoyed some success, Taylor never received enough men to implement it fully. Ultimately as disgusted as Jesup had been, Taylor left Florida in 1841.

By the time Colonel William Jenkins Worth assumed command in Florida, the war had been going on for almost five years and had stirred heated controversies over slavery, removal, and expansion. The government wanted the matter concluded, and Worth accordingly conducted a relentless campaign of summer raids on Seminole food sources that saw hundreds of Indians surrendering to escape starvation. After shipping his captives off to the West, Worth declared the war over in 1842. It ended as had all other chapters in the removal story. Several hundred unrepentant Seminoles remained in Florida, concealing themselves in the impenetrable Everglades and refusing to make agreements with whites except on their terms. Their descendants live in Florida today, having earned a place in the state's culture and society, on their own terms.

Conclusion

Indian removal did not expel all Indians from the East. Mixed-heritage Indians remained on their modest allotments in Alabama and Mississippi, able to do so because these Indians were often by appearance and behavior indistinguishable from whites. In fact, they melded with white society and lost virtually all vestiges of their Indian identity. Other Indians remained by inhabiting lands no one else wanted. Cherokees, for example, lived in isolation in the remote mountains of North Carolina; Seminoles became denizens of the swamps of south Florida; Iroquois remained on tiny hold-ings in upstate New York; and small groups of Creeks wandered wilderness regions of Alabama.

By the late 1840s, though, most eastern Indians were west of the Mississippi River, living in enclaves that dotted the frontier from Iowa to eastern Texas. The heaviest concentration was in the Indian Territory, first called Indian Country when Secretary of War John C. Calhoun had marked it off on a map of the Louisiana Purchase in 1825. Jackson used it as the destination for most removals, and it was soon dubbed the Indian Territory. Congress formally reserved this nebulous expanse for Indians in 1834 with the Trade and Intercourse Act. Until 1854, when the Kansas-Nebraska Act set new limits on the Indian Territory's boundaries, the territory was quite large, spanning present-day Oklahoma north of the Red River across Kansas and Nebraska, east to the Missouri and Arkansas borders, and west to the 100th meridian.

Tribes other than those of the Southeast were also placed in the Indian Territory, a policy that caused discord and spurred occasional violence. Government commissions tried to keep the peace, but the jumble of different tribal cultures from so many different parts of the country meant that American military interventions were occasionally necessary. Original Indian inhabitants—roaming Great Plains hunters such as the Pawnee, Omaha, Cheyenne, Arapaho, Comanche, Kiowa, and Apache, who were unfamiliar with the concept of borders in the first place—suddenly found in their midst Indians from the Old Northwest and Southeast, and they sporadically made clear their hostility toward the newcomers. The United States expected these transplants to live within artificially assigned areas under their respective tribal governments, but adjustments were difficult at best and became even more challenging when white caravans began snaking through the region. Merchants on the way to Santa Fe, settlers to Oregon, or Mormons to Utah were only the beginning; the California Gold Rush in 1849 and subsequent plans for the Transcontinental Railroad were increasingly ominous signs that the Indian Territory would not remain inviolate.

The Kansas-Nebraska Act in 1854 lopped off the territory's northern expanse, and the Homestead Act of 1862 opened those regions to white settlement. Additional changes following the Civil

War finally culminated in the Dawes Severalty Act in 1887. By dismantling tribal land-holdings and allotting them to households, the law removed traditional Indian curbs on alienating property. In the next ten years, enormous amounts of Indian acreage found its way into white hands, some by legitimate transactions but most by deceit and fraud. In 1889, the Indian Territory was opened to white settlement, and on an appointed day the Boomer movement sent thousands of whites speeding across the plains in Conestoga wagons to stake out homesteads. The Oklahoma Territory was created the following year. Most of the land promised in perpetuity by countless removal treaties was no longer the Indian Territory, and additional legislation in 1898 dissolved tribal governments to place the Five Civilized Tribes under the allotment system. The measure was born of yet another strange mixture of white greed for Indian land and altruistic impulses to improve Indians by making them white. It was moreover a sardonic closing of the circle of anguish and tragedy for these buffeted people.

In the end, they were buffeted but not undone. In 1907, when Oklahoma became a state, it absorbed the small Indian lands that remained and formally extinguished the Indian Territory. But Oklahoma would also forever feature Indian place names that strangely echoed those of towns and rivers and people back east. Eufaula, Coweta, Okmulgee, Olustee, Tecumseh, and Wetumka are only a few of the places that serve as a testament to the determined optimism of those Indians whose grueling journeys years before had spilled them out in a strange land. There they had gathered themselves and had labored to make new homes by laying out and improving farms and raising their children. There they had resolved to preserve their cultures, in part by tangibly memorializing the homes of their mothers and fathers. There they had given names to these new places in bittersweet tribute to the homes they had lost, in all but their memories and dreams. They, like those dreams, had been buffeted but not undone.

DOCUMENTS

I
Treaties

*T*reaties almost always left Indians the losers. During the colonial period, Europeans used treaties to ally with influential tribes, especially to strengthen local armies when wars broke out with rival colonial powers. After American independence, treaties with Indians increasingly became a way for the new U.S. government to acquire land. The arrangements, always cloaked in high ceremonial language, were a blend of white avarice and ethics. Government negotiators were not always unscrupulous, but they were always servants to the ruthless master of expanding settlement. Although the Northwest Ordinance of 1787 had pledged that Indians would only be expected to surrender lands voluntarily and, by implication, with appropriate compensation, the opening decades of the nineteenth century saw a different attitude emerge and a different reality unfold. Ultimately, treaties marked empty rituals whose purpose was to take Indian lands. Removal treaties did this and more by evicting Indians from the regions they called home. The following five treaties reveal both ongoing similarities in such arrangements and their evolving purpose.

The first selection is the Treaty of Greenville, which concluded an Indian war in the Old Northwest. After the American Revolution, U.S. behavior toward Indians west of the Appalachian Mountains roused first brooding resentment and then overt hostility. After Indians soundly defeated an American army in 1791, General Anthony Wayne won the Battle of Fallen Timbers (near modern Toledo, Ohio) in the summer of 1794. The vanquished tribes were compelled to sign a treaty the following year, giving up significant expanses of the Ohio Valley in return for pledges of immediate payment and a perpetual peace that was to be undisturbed either by Indian depredations or by white encroachments on Indian lands. Yet the opening of these regions to white settlement made perpetual peace unlikely.

Treaty of Greenville
August 3, 1795

A treaty of peace between the United States of America and the Tribes of Indians, called the Wyandots, Delawares, Shawanoes, Ottawas, Chipewas, Putawatimes, Miamis, Eel-river, Weeás, Kickapoos, Piankashaws, and Kaskaskias.

To put an end to a destructive war, to settle all controversies, and to restore harmony and a friendly intercourse between the said United States, and Indian tribes; Anthony Wayne, major-general, commanding the army of the United States, and sole commissioner for the good purposes above-mentioned, and the said tribes of Indians, by their Sachems, chiefs, and warriors, met together at Greeneville, the head quarters of the said army, have agreed on the following articles, which, when ratified by the President, with the advice and consent of the Senate of the United States, shall be binding on them and the said Indian tribes.

ARTICLE I.

Henceforth all hostilities shall cease; peace is hereby established, and shall be perpetual; and a friendly intercourse shall take place, between the said United States and Indian tribes.

ARTICLE II.

All prisoners shall on both sides be restored. The Indians, prisoners to the United States, shall be immediately set at liberty. The people of the United States, still remaining prisoners among the Indians, shall be delivered up in ninety days from the date hereof, to the general or commanding officer at Greeneville, Fort Wayne or Fort Defiance; and ten chiefs of the said tribes shall remain at Greeneville as hostages, until the delivery of the prisoners shall be effected.

ARTICLE III.

The general boundary line between the lands of the United States, and the lands of the said Indian tribes, shall begin at the mouth of Cayahoga river, and run thence up the same to the portage between that and the Tuscarawas branch of the Muskingum; thence down that branch to the crossing place above Fort Lawrence; thence westerly to a fork of that branch of the great Miami river running into the Ohio, at or near which fork stood Loromie's store, and where commences the portage between the Miami of the Ohio, and St. Mary's river, which is a branch of the Miami, which runs into Lake Erie; thence a westerly course to Fort Recovery, which stands on a branch of the Wabash; then southwesterly in a direct line to the Ohio, so as to intersect that river opposite the mouth of Kentucke or Cuttawa river. And in consideration of the peace now established; of the goods formerly received from the United States; of those now to be delivered, and of the yearly delivery of goods now stipulated to be made hereafter, and to indemnify the United States for the injuries and expenses they have sustained during the war; the said Indian tribes do hereby cede and relinquish forever, all their claims to the lands lying eastwardly and southwardly of the general boundary line now described; and these lands, or any part of them, shall never hereafter be made a cause or pretence, on the part of the said tribes or any of them, of war or injury to the United States, or any of the people thereof.

* * *

ARTICLE IV.

* * * the United States relinquish their claims to all other Indian lands northward of the river Ohio, eastward of the Mississippi, and westward and southward of the Great Lakes and the waters uniting them, according to the boundary line agreed on by the United States and the king of Great-Britain, in the treaty of peace made between them in the year 1783. * * *

And for the same considerations and with the same views as above mentioned, the United States now deliver to the said Indian tribes a quantity of goods to the value of twenty thousand dollars, the receipt whereof they do hereby acknowledge; and henceforward every year forever the United States will deliver at some convenient place northward of the river Ohio, like useful goods, suited to the circumstances of the Indians, of the value of nine thousand five hundred dollars; reckoning that value at the first cost of the goods in the city or place in the United States, where they shall be procured.

* * *

ARTICLE V.

To prevent any misunderstanding about the Indian lands relinquished by the United States in the fourth article, it is now explicitly declared, that the meaning of that relinquishment is this: The Indian tribes who have a right to those lands, are quietly to enjoy them, hunting, planting, and dwelling thereon so long as they please, without any molestation from the United States; but when those tribes, or any of them, shall be disposed to sell their lands, or any part of them, they are to be sold only to the United States; and until such sale, the United States will protect all the said Indian tribes in the quiet enjoyment of their lands against all citizens of the United States, and against all other white persons who intrude upon the same. And the said Indian tribes again acknowledge themselves to be under the protection of the said United States and no other power whatever.

ARTICLE VI.

If any citizen of the United States, or any other white person or persons, shall presume to settle upon the lands now relinquished by the United States, such citizen or other person shall be out of the protection of the United States; and the Indian tribe, on whose land the settlement shall be made, may drive off the settler, or punish him in such manner as they shall think fit; and because such settlements made without the consent of the United States, will be injurious to them as well as to the Indians, the United States shall be at liberty to break them up, and remove and punish the settlers as they shall think proper, and so effect that protection of the Indian lands herein before stipulated.

ARTICLE VII.

The said tribes of Indians, parties to this treaty, shall be at liberty to hunt within the territory and lands which they have now ceded to the United States, without hindrance or molestation, so long as they demean themselves peaceably, and offer no injury to the people of the United States.

ARTICLE VIII.

Trade shall be opened with the said Indian tribes; and they do hereby respectively engage to afford protection to such persons, with their property, as shall be duly licensed to reside among them for the purpose of trade, and to their agents and servants; but no person shall be permitted to reside at any of their towns or hunting camps as a trader, who is not furnished with a license for that purpose, under the hand and seal of the superintendent of the department north-west of the Ohio, or such other person as the President of the United States shall authorize to grant such licenses; to the end, that the said Indians may not be imposed on in their trade. And if any licensed trader shall abuse his privilege by unfair dealing, upon complaint and proof thereof, his license shall be taken from him, and he shall be further punished according to the laws of the United States. And if any person shall intrude himself as a trader, without such license, the said Indians shall take and bring him before the superintendent or his deputy, to be dealt with according to law. And to prevent impositions by forged licenses, the said Indians shall at least once a year give information to the superintendent or his deputies, of the names of the traders residing among them.

ARTICLE IX.

Lest the firm peace and friendship now established should be interrupted by the misconduct of individuals, the United States, and the said Indian tribes agree, that for injuries done by individuals on either side, no private revenge or retaliation shall take place; but instead thereof, complaint shall be made by the party injured, to the other: By the said Indian tribes, or any of them, to the President of the United States, or the superintendent by him appointed;

and by the superintendent or other person appointed by the President, to the principal chiefs of the said Indian tribes, or of the tribe to which the offender belongs; and such prudent measures shall then be pursued as shall be necessary to preserve the said peace and friendship unbroken, until the Legislature (or Great Council) of the United States, shall make other equitable provision in the case, to the satisfaction of both parties. Should any Indian tribes meditate a war against the United States or either of them, and the same shall come to the knowledge of the before-mentioned tribes, or either of them, they do hereby engage to give immediate notice thereof to the general or officer commanding the troops of the United States, at the nearest post. And should any tribe, with hostile intentions against the United States, or either of them, attempt to pass through their country, they will endeavor to prevent the same, and in like manner give information of such attempt, to the general or officer commanding, as soon as possible, that all causes of mistrust and suspicion may be avoided between them and the United States. In like manner the United States shall give notice to the said Indian tribes of any harm that may be meditated against them, or either of them, that shall come to their knowledge; and do all in their power to hinder and prevent the same, that the friendship between them may be uninterrupted.

Charles J. Kappler, *Indian Affairs: Laws and Treaties, Vol. II (Treaties)* (Washington, DC: GPO, 1904), 39–40, 41–43.

Treaty of Fort Jackson
August 9, 1814

Less than twenty years after the Treaty of Greenville, another treaty ended another Indian war, this one in the American South. After defeating Red Stick Creeks at Horseshoe Bend in March 1814, Andrew Jackson exacted a harsh penalty on all Creeks, including those who had fought on the side of the United States. The Treaty of Fort Jackson's first article, the lengthiest in the treaty, delineated twenty-three million acres of land to be ceded to the United States as

FIGURE 2

Selocta—An American ally during the Creek War, Selocta served as Andrew
Jackson's translator at Fort Jackson when the treaty was signed there in 1814.
He was, like other Allied Creeks, horrified by the enormous loss of land.
Moreover, he was extremely disheartened by Jackson's indifference to his
entreaties that the cession was unfair, because he had considered Jackson a
friend. He later opposed removal, but his former ties to Jackson served him
no better in that instance than they had years before. *(Library of Congress)*

*compensation for the expense of prosecuting the Creek War. The cession amounted
to about half of all Creek lands in the Mississippi Territory, soon to become the
state of Alabama. The change in tone from the Treaty of Greenville was ominous in itself, but that it was aimed at U.S. allies as well as those Indians who
had fought against the United States marked the treaty as uniquely and unfairly
punitive. Even worse for the stunned Indians who were compelled to sign the
treaty was that the lands they surrendered were prime for growing cotton and
would be soon open to white settlement, circumstances that would increase rather
than diminish pressures for future cessions.*

*Articles of agreement and capitulation, made and concluded this ninth day of
August, one thousand eight hundred and fourteen, between major general Andrew
Jackson, on behalf of the President of the United States of America, and the
chiefs, deputies, and warriors of the Creek Nation.*

WHEREAS an unprovoked, inhuman, and sanguinary war, waged by the hostile Creeks against the United States, hath been repelled, prosecuted and determined, successfully, on the part of the said States, in conformity with principles of national justice and honorable warfare— * * *

1st—The United States demand an equivalent for all expenses incurred in prosecuting the war to its termination, by a cession of all the territory belonging to the Creek nation within the territories of the United States, lying west, south, and south-eastwardly, of a line to be run and described by persons duly authorized and appointed by the President of the United States—Beginning at a point on the eastern bank of the Coosa river, where the south boundary line of the Cherokee nation crosses the same; running from thence down the said Coosa river with its eastern bank according to its various meanders to a point one mile above the mouth of Cedar creek, at Fort Williams, thence east two miles, thence south two miles, thence west to the eastern bank of the said Coosa river, thence down the eastern bank thereof according to its various meanders to a point opposite the upper end of the great falls, (called by the natives Woetumka,) thence east from a true meridian line to a point due north of the mouth of Ofucshee, thence south by a like meridian line to the mouth of Ofucshee on the south side of the Tallapoosa river, thence up the same, according to its various meanders, to a point where a direct course will cross the same at the distance of ten miles from the mouth thereof, thence a direct line to the mouth of Summochico creek, which empties into the Chatahouchie river on the east side thereof below the Eufaulau town, thence east from a true meridian line to a point which shall intersect the line now dividing the lands claimed by the said Creek nation from those claimed and owned by the state of Georgia: Provided, nevertheless, that where any possession of any chief or warrior of the Creek nation, who shall have been friendly to the United States during the war, and taken an active part therein, shall be within the territory ceded by these articles to the United States, every such person shall be entitled to a reservation of land within the said territory of one mile square, to include his improvements as near the centre thereof as may be, which shall inure to the said chief or warrior, and his descendants, so long as he or they shall continue to occupy the same, who shall be protected by and subject to the laws of the United States; but upon the voluntary abandonment thereof, by such possessor or his descendants, the right of occupancy or possession of said lands shall devolve to the United States, and be identified with the right of property ceded hereby.

2nd—The United States will guarantee to the Creek nation, the integrity of all their territory eastwardly and northwardly of the said line to be run and described as mentioned in the first article.

3d—The United States demand, that the Creek nation abandon all communication, and cease to hold any intercourse with any British or Spanish post, garrison, or town; and that they shall not admit among them, any agent or trader, who shall not derive authority to hold commercial, or other intercourse with them, by licence from the President or authorized agent of the United States.

4th—The United States demand an acknowledgment of the right to establish military posts and trading houses, and to open roads within the territory, guaranteed to the Creek nation by the second article, and a right to the free navigation of all its waters.

* * *

8th—A permanent peace shall ensue from the date of these presents forever, between the Creek nation and the United States, and between the Creek nation and the Cherokee, Chickasaw, and Choctaw nations.

Charles J. Kappler, *Indian Affairs: Laws and Treaties, Vol. II (Treaties)* (Washington, DC: GPO, 1904), 107, 108–09.

Second Treaty of Indian Springs
February 12, 1825

For years Georgia had wanted its Indian populations to consent not only to massive land cessions but also to leave the state altogether, and Georgia officials repeatedly criticized the federal government for not helping to achieve that goal, something the government had pledged to do in 1802. In 1821, a treaty signed at Indian Springs by the prominent Creek William McIntosh ceded a significant

FIGURE 3
Menewa—Leader of Red Stick nativists during the Creek War of 1813–
1814, Menewa was seriously wounded at Horseshoe Bend but escaped. He
steadfastly opposed Creek removal and was one of the lawmenders who
carried out the execution of William McIntosh for having negotiated the
Second Treaty of Indian Springs in 1825. Finally resigned to the inevitability of removal, he accompanied his people to the Indian Territory where he
disappeared from prominence. *(Library of Congress)*

*amount of Creek land and caused outrage in a substantial part of the Creek
Nation. Only ten years after the immense Fort Jackson cession had radically
diminished Creek holdings in Alabama, U.S. commissioners managed to bribe
McIntosh into agreeing to a second Treaty of Indian Springs that extinguished
the title to all Creek lands in Georgia and arranged for removal west of the Mississippi River. The treaty marked an important policy shift: Not only did it
depart from the traditional, piecemeal approach to land acquisitions, it also openly
embraced removal. The treaty, however, provoked so much fury among Creeks that
they killed McIntosh, and the corruption that tainted its negotiation kept President John Quincy Adams from submitting it to the Senate.*

    *Nonetheless, the treaty featured some elements that became standard in sub-
sequent agreements. For example, Indians were to receive what appeared to be
munificent payments, they were to have the right to inspect their prospective new*

lands before agreeing to settle on them, and they were to be protected from white predators as they prepared to leave the state. Later removal treaties would include similar provisions, but despite the good intentions of even fair-minded commissioners, such terms usually turned out to be enticements rather than guarantees.

Articles of a convention, entered into and concluded at the Indian Springs, between Duncan G. Campbell, and James Meriwether, Commissioners on the part of the United States of America, duly authorised, and the Chiefs of the Creek Nation, in Council assembled.

WHEREAS the said Commissioners, on the part of the United States, have represented to the said Creek Nation that it is the policy and earnest wish of the General Government, that the several Indian tribes within the limits of any of the states of the Union should remove to territory to be designated on the west side of the Mississippi river, as well for the better protection and security of said tribes, and their improvement in civilization, as for the purpose of enabling the United States, in this instance, to comply with the compact entered into with the State of Georgia, on the twenty-fourth day of April, in the year one thousand eight hundred and two: And the said Commissioners having laid the late Message of the President of the United States, upon this subject, before a General Council of said Creek Nation, to the end that their removal might be effected upon terms advantageous to both parties:

And whereas the Chiefs of the Creek Towns have assented to the reasonableness of said proposition, and expressed a willingness to emigrate beyond the Mississippi, *those of Tokaubatchee excepted:*

These presents therefore witness, that the contracting parties have this day entered into the following Convention:

ART. 1. The Creek nation cede to the United States all the lands lying within the boundaries of the State of Georgia, as defined by the compact herein before cited, now occupied by said Nation, or to which said Nation have title or claim; and also, all other lands which they now occupy, or to which they have title or claim, lying north and west of a line to be run from the first principal falls upon the Chatauhoochie river, above Cowetau town, to Ocfuskee Old Town, upon the Tallapoosa, thence to the falls of the Coosaw river, at or near a place called the Hickory Ground.

ART. 2. It is further agreed between the contracting parties, that the United States will give, in exchange for the lands hereby acquired, the like quantity, acre for acre, westward of the Mississippi, on the Arkansas river, commencing at the mouth of the Canadian Fork thereof, and running westward between said rivers Arkansas and Canadian Fork, for quantity. But whereas said Creek Nation have considerable improvements within the limits of the territory hereby ceded, and will moreover have to incur expenses in their removal, it is further stipulated, that, for the purpose of rendering a fair equivalent for the losses and inconveniences which said Nation will sustain by removal, and to enable them to obtain supplies in their new settlement, the United States agree to pay to the Nation emigrating from the lands herein ceded, the sum of four hundred thousand dollars, of which amount there shall be paid to said party of the second part, as soon as practicable after the ratification of this treaty, the sum of two hundred thousand dollars. And as soon as the said party of the second part shall notify the Government of the United States of their readiness to commence their removal, there shall be paid the further sum of one hundred thousand dollars. And the first year after said emigrating party shall have settled in their new country, they shall receive of the amount first above named, the further sum of twenty-five thousand dollars. And the second year, the sum of twenty-five thousand dollars. And annually, thereafter, the sum of five thousand dollars, until the whole is paid.

ART. 3. And whereas the Creek Nation are now entitled to annuities of thirty thousand dollars each, in consideration of cessions of territory heretofore made, it is further stipulated that said last mentioned annuities are to be hereafter divided in a just proportion between the party emigrating and those that may remain.

ART. 4. It is further stipulated that a deputation from the said parties of the second part, may be sent out to explore the territory herein offered them in exchange; and if the same be not acceptable to them, then they may select any other territory, west of the Mississippi, on Red, Canadian, Arkansas, or Missouri Rivers—the territory occupied by the Cherokees and Choctaws excepted; and if the territory so to be selected shall be in the occupancy of other Indian tribes, then the United States will extinguish the title of such occupants for the benefit of said emigrants.

ART. 5. It is further stipulated, at the particular request of the said parties of the second part, that the payment and disbursement of the first sum herein provided for, shall be made by the present Commissioners negotiating this treaty.

ART. 6. It is further stipulated, that the payments appointed to be made, the first and second years, after settlement in the West, shall be either in money, merchandise, or provisions, at the option of the emigrating party.

ART. 7. The United States agree to provide and support a blacksmith and wheelwright for the said party of the second part, and give them instruction in agriculture, as long, and in such manner, as the President may think proper.

ART. 8. Whereas the said emigrating party cannot prepare for immediate removal, the United States stipulate, for their protection against the incroachments, hostilities, and impositions of the whites, and of all others; but the period of removal shall not extend beyond the first day of September, in the year eighteen hundred and twenty-six.

ART. 9. This treaty shall be obligatory on the contracting parties, so soon as the same shall be ratified by the President of the United States, by and with the consent of the Senate thereof.

Charles J. Kappler, *Indian Affairs: Laws and Treaties, Vol. II (Treaties)* (Washington, DC: GPO, 1904), 214–15.

Treaty of Dancing Rabbit Creek
September 27, 1830

Andrew Jackson's election as president of the United States fundamentally altered all aspects of Indian ownership of lands east of the Mississippi River, rich tracts that planters and settlers in Georgia, Alabama, and Mississippi had yearned to acquire for years. On December 8, 1829, Jackson used part of his Annual Message to assess the potential fate of eastern Indian tribes and resolved that a novel policy was necessary to rescue them from extinction. The sincerity or dishonesty of his motive notwithstanding, his recommendation set in motion the congressional machinery that resulted in the Indian Removal Act of 1830. The law provided for a fair exchange of eastern for western lands with the Indians, a bargain described as inviolable and permanent, and supplied funds to facilitate the transport of Indians to the West.

The first treaty arranged under the Removal Act was with the Choctaws of Mississippi. At Dancing Rabbit Creek, the Choctaw Nation ceded more than ten million acres of land to the United States in exchange for land in the West. The treaty was long and comprehensive, addressing issues such as government funded education for relocated Indians, compensation for improvements and livestock, and detailed inventories of goods and implements that the government would provide Choctaws in their new homes.

Originally opposed to removal, Choctaw headmen were evidently induced to sign the treaty by Article XIV, which allowed any Choctaw the right to remain in Mississippi and receive a fixed land allotment for himself and members of his family. Many Choctaws greeted news of Dancing Rabbit Creek with dismay, however, and the Choctaw Nation was soon rent with dissent and factions. Nevertheless, removal was under way even before the Senate had ratified the treaty and continued on a grueling timetable afterward.

As with subsequent removal treaties, many of the grand provisions were only grand in the reading. Land allotments were successful for barely a few mixed-heritage members of the tribe, and squatters began staking out most Choctaw lands as soon the treaty was announced. The abundant supplies promised for the journeys west were instead meager and substandard, and the whites who supervised the trek were indifferent or cruel or, when benevolent, hamstrung by daunting logistics.

A treaty of perpetual, friendship, cession and limits, entered into by John H. Eaton and John Coffee, for and in behalf of the Government of the United States, and the Mingoes, Chiefs, Captains and Warriors of the Choctaw Nation, begun and held at Dancing Rabbit Creek, on the fifteenth of September, in the year eighteen hundred and thirty.

WHEREAS the General Assembly of the State of Mississippi has extended the laws of said State to persons and property within the chartered limits of the same, and the President of the United States has said that he cannot protect the Choctaw people from the operation of these laws; Now therefore that the Choctaw may live under their own laws in peace with the United States and the State of Mississippi they have determined to sell their lands east of the Mississippi and have accordingly agreed to the following articles of treaty: *["This paragraph was not ratified"—Kappler]*

* * *

ARTICLE II. The United States under a grant specially to be made by the President of the U.S. shall cause to be conveyed to the Choctaw Nation a tract of country west of the Mississippi River, in fee simple to them and their descendants, to inure to them while they shall exist as a nation and live on it, beginning near Fort Smith where the Arkansas boundary crosses the Arkansas River, running thence to the source of the Canadian fork; if in the limits of the United States, or to those limits; thence due south to Red River, and down Red River to the west boundary of the Territory of Arkansas; thence north along that line to the beginning. The boundary of the same to be agreeably to the Treaty made and concluded at Washington City in the year 1825. The grant to be executed so soon as the present Treaty shall be ratified.

ARTICLE III. In consideration of the provisions contained in the several articles of this Treaty, the Choctaw nation of Indians consent and hereby cede to the United States, the entire country they own and possess, east of the Mississippi River; and they agree to move beyond the Mississippi River, early as practicable, and will so arrange their removal, that as many as possible of their people not exceeding one half of the whole number, shall depart during the falls of 1831 and 1832; the residue to follow during the succeeding fall of 1833, a better opportunity in this manner will be afforded the Government, to extend to them the facilities and comforts which it is desirable should be extended in conveying them to their new homes.

ARTICLE IV. The Government and people of the United States are hereby obliged to secure to the said Choctaw Nation of Red People the jurisdiction and government of all the persons and property that may be within their limits west, so that no Territory or state shall ever have a right to pass laws for the government of the Choctaw Nation of Red People and their descendants; and that no part of the land granted them shall ever be embraced in any Territory or State. * * *

ARTICLE V. The United States are obliged to protect the Choctaws from domestic strife and from foreign enemies on the same principles that the citizens of the United States are protected, so that whatever would be a legal demand upon the U.S. for defense or for wrongs committed by an enemy, on a citizen of the U.S. shall be equally binding in favor of the Choctaws.

* * *

ARTICLE XII. All intruders shall be removed from the Choctaw Nation and kept without it. Private property to be always respected and on no occasion taken for public purposes without just compensation being made therefor to the rightful owner. If an Indian unlawfully take or steal any property from a white man a citizen of the U.S. the offender shall be punished. And if a white man unlawfully take or steal any thing from an Indian, the property shall be restored and the offender punished. It is further agreed that when a Choctaw shall be given up to be tried for any offense against the laws of the U.S. if unable to employ counsel to defend him, the U.S. will do it, that his trial may be fair and impartial.

* * *

ARTICLE XIV. Each Choctaw head of a family being desirous to remain and become a citizen of the States, shall be permitted to do so, by signifying his intention to the Agent within six months from the ratification of this Treaty, and he or she shall thereupon be entitled to a reservation of one section of six hundred and forty acres of land, to be bounded by sectional lines of survey; in like manner shall be entitled to one half that quantity for each unmarried child which is living with him over ten years of age; and a quarter section to such child as may be under 10 years of age, to adjoin the location of the parent. If they reside upon said lands intending to become citizens of the States for five years after the ratification of this Treaty, in that case a grant in fee simple shall issue; said reservation shall include the present improvement of the head of the family, or a portion of it. Persons who claim under this article shall not lose the privilege of a Choctaw citizen, but if they ever remove are not to be entitled to any portion of the Choctaw annuity.

ARTICLE XV. To each of the Chiefs in the Choctaw Nation (to wit) Greenwood Laflore, Nutackachie, and Mushulatubbe there is granted a reservation of four sections of land, two of which shall include and adjoin their present improvement, and the other two located where they please but on unoccupied unimproved lands, such sections shall be bounded by sectional lines, and with the consent of the President they may sell the same.

* * *

ARTICLE XVI. In wagons; and with steam boats as may be found necessary—the U.S. agree to remove the Indians to their new homes at their expense and under the care of discreet and careful persons, who will be kind and brotherly to them. They agree to furnish them with ample corn and beef, or pork for themselves and families for twelve months after reaching their new homes. It is agreed further that the U.S. will take all their cattle, at the valuation of some discreet person to be appointed by the President, and the same shall be paid for in money after their arrival at their new homes; or other cattle such as may be desired shall be furnished them, notice being given through their Agent of their wishes upon this subject before their removal that time to supply the demand may be afforded.

ARTICLE XVII. The several annuities and sums secured under former Treaties to the Choctaw nation and people shall continue as though this Treaty had never been made.

And it is further agreed that the U.S. in addition will pay the sum of twenty thousand dollars for twenty years, commencing after their removal to the west, of which, in the first year after their removal, ten thousand dollars shall be divided and arranged to such as may not receive reservations under this Treaty.

ARTICLE XVIII. The U.S. shall cause the lands hereby ceded to be surveyed; and surveyors may enter the Choctaw Country for that purpose, conducting themselves properly and disturbing or interrupting none of the Choctaw people. But no person is to be permitted to settle within the nation, or the lands to be sold before the Choctaws shall remove. And for the payment of the several amounts secured in this Treaty, the lands hereby ceded are to remain a fund pledged to that purpose, until the debt shall be provided for and arranged. And further it is agreed, that in the construction of this Treaty wherever well founded doubt shall arise, it shall be construed most favorably towards the Choctaws.

Charles J. Kappler, *Indian Affairs: Laws and Treaties, Vol. II (Treaties)* (Washington, DC: GPO, 1904), 310–11, 312, 313–14.

Treaty of New Echota
December 29, 1835

The fate of the Cherokee Nation is unique among removal stories, because no other tribe had so thoroughly embraced the civilization program. Moreover, the Cherokee removal treaty revealed that the government's relocation policy, always advertised as voluntary, was actually compulsory. The Treaty of New Echota matched the second Treaty of Indian Springs for deceit and fraud, in part because federal commissioners negotiated it with a small group of accommodating Cherokees portrayed as representing the entire Cherokee Nation. The treaty's lengthy preamble strained to explain the reasons for these negotiations, but in protesting too much, it revealed a disquieting uneasiness about the process. Otherwise, the treaty was modeled on other removal agreements and included the usual special enticements and promises of fair treatment. It even featured (in its original form) the promise of land allotments for Cherokees who wished to remain in Georgia. Unlike other southern states, however, Georgia refused to allow land allotments for Indians rejecting removal. The clear aim was the thorough expulsion of all Indians and the simultaneous acquisition of all their lands; the result was the crowning duplicity of including allotment articles that were later canceled. The Treaty of New Echota was an abomination to most Cherokees anyway, but its unambiguous intent of compelling removal made it insufferable. Neither petitions to the Senate nor entreaties to public opinion made any difference. Under the revised terms of New Echota, the Cherokees were forced from their homes and driven to the Indian Territory in 1838.

Articles of a treaty, concluded at New Echota in the State of Georgia on the 29th day of Decr. 1835 by General William Carroll and John F. Schermerhorn commissioners on the part of the United States and the Chiefs Head Men and People of the Cherokee tribe of Indians.

WHEREAS the Cherokees are anxious to make some arrangements with the Government of the United States whereby the difficulties they have experienced by a residence within the settled parts of the United States under the jurisdiction and laws of the State Governments may be terminated and adjusted; and with a view to reuniting their people in one body and securing a permanent home for themselves and their posterity in the country selected by their forefathers without the territorial limits of the State sovereignties, and where they can establish and enjoy a government of their choice and perpetuate such a state of society as may be most consonant with their views, habits and condition; and as may tend to their individual comfort and their advancement in civilization.

And whereas a delegation of the Cherokee nation composed of Messrs. John Ross[,] Richard Taylor[,] Danl. McCoy[,] Samuel Gunter[,] and William Rogers with full power and authority to conclude a treaty with the United States did on the 28th day of February 1835 stipulate and agree with the Government of the United States to submit to the Senate to fix the amount which should be allowed the Cherokees for their claims and for a cession of their lands east of the Mississippi river, and did agree to abide by the award of the Senate of the United States themselves and to recommend the same to their people for their final determination.

And whereas on such submission the Senate advised "that a sum not exceeding five millions of dollars be paid to the Cherokee Indians for all their lands and possessions east of the Mississippi river."

And whereas this delegation after said award of the Senate had been made, were called upon to submit propositions as to its disposition to be arranged in a treaty which they refused to do, but insisted that the same "should be referred to their nation and there in general council to deliberate and determine on the subject in order to ensure harmony and good feeling among themselves."

And whereas a certain other delegation composed of John Ridge[,] Elias Boudinot[,] Archilla Smith[,] S. W. Bell[,] John West[,] Wm. A. Davis[,] and Ezekiel West, who represented that portion of the nation in favor of emigration to the Cherokee country west of the Mississippi entered into propositions for a treaty with John F. Schermerhorn commissioner on the part of the United States which were to be submitted to their nation for their final action and determination:

And whereas the Cherokee people at their last October council at Red Clay, fully authorized and empowered a delegation or committee of twenty persons of their nation to enter into and conclude a treaty with the United States commissioner then present, at that place or elsewhere and as the people had good reason to believe that a treaty would then and there be made or at a subsequent council at New Echota which the commissioners it was well known and understood, were authorized and instructed to convene for said purpose; and since the said delegation have gone on to Washington city, with a view to close negotiations there, as stated by them notwithstanding they were officially informed by the United States commissioner that they would not be received by the President of the United States; and that the Government would transact no business of this nature with them, and that if a treaty was made it must be done here in the nation, where the delegation at Washington last winter urged that it should be done for the purpose of promoting peace and harmony among the people; and since these facts have also been corroborated to us by a communication recently received by the commissioner from the Government of the United States and read and explained to the people in open council and therefore believing said delegation can effect nothing and since our difficulties are daily increasing and our situation is rendered more and more precarious uncertain and insecure in consequence of the legislation of the States; and seeing no effectual way of relief, but in accepting the liberal overtures of the United States.

And whereas Genl William Carroll and John F. Schermerhorn were appointed commissioners on the part of the United States, with full power and authority to conclude a treaty with the Cherokees east and were directed by the President to convene the people of the nation in general council at New Echota and to submit said propositions to them with power and authority to vary the same so as to meet the views of the Cherokees in reference to its details.

And whereas the said commissioners did appoint and notify a general council of the nation to convene at New Echota on the 21st day of December 1835; and informed them that the commissioners would be prepared to make a treaty with the Cherokee people who should assemble there and those who did not come they should conclude gave their assent and sanction to whatever should be transacted at this council and the people having met in council according to said notice.

Therefore the following articles of a treaty are agreed upon and concluded between William Carroll and John F. Schermerhorn commissioners on the part of the United States and the chiefs and head men and people of the Cherokee nation in general council assembled this 29th day of Decr 1835.

ARTICLE 1. The Cherokee nation hereby cede relinquish and convey to the United States all the lands owned claimed or possessed by them east of the Mississippi river, and hereby release all their claims upon the United States for spoliations of every kind for and in consideration of the sum of five millions of dollars to be expended paid and invested in the manner stipulated and agreed upon in the following articles But as a question has arisen between the commissioners and the Cherokees whether the Senate in their resolution by which they advised "that a sum not exceeding five millions of dollars be paid to the Cherokee Indians for all their lands and possessions east of the Mississippi river" have included and made any allowance or consideration for claims for spoliations it is therefore agreed on the part of the United States that this question shall be again submitted to the Senate for their consideration and decision and if no allowance was made for spoliations that then an additional sum of three hundred thousand dollars be allowed for the same.

* * *

ARTICLE 5. The United States hereby covenant and agree that the lands ceded to the Cherokee nation * * * shall, in no future time without their consent, be included within the territorial limits or jurisdiction of any State or Territory. But they shall secure to the Cherokee nation the right by their national councils to make and carry into effect all such laws as they may deem necessary for the government and protection of the persons and property within their own country belonging to their people or such persons as have connected themselves with them: provided always that they shall not be inconsistent with the constitution of the United States and such acts of Congress as have been or may be passed regulating trade and intercourse with the Indians; and also, that they shall not be considered as extending to such citizens and army of the United States as may travel or reside in the Indian country by permission according to the laws and regulations established by the Government of the same.

* * *

ARTICLE 8. The United States also agree and stipulate to remove the Cherokees to their new homes and to subsist them one year after their arrival there and that a sufficient number of steamboats and baggage-wagons shall be furnished to remove them comfortably, and so as not to endanger their health, and that a physician well supplied with medicines shall accompany each detachment of emigrants removed by the Government. Such persons and families as in the opinion of the emigrating agent are capable of subsisting and removing themselves shall be permitted to do so; and they shall be allowed in full for all claims for the same twenty dollars for each member of their family; and in lieu of their one year's rations they shall be paid the sum of thirty-three dollars and thirty-three cents if they prefer it.

Such Cherokees also as reside at present out of the nation and shall remove with them in two years west of the Mississippi shall be entitled to allowance for removal and subsistence as above provided.

ARTICLE 9. The United States agree to appoint suitable agents who shall make a just and fair valuation of all such improvements now in the possession of the Cherokees as add any value to the lands; and also of the ferries owned by them, according to their net income; and such improvements and ferries from which they have been dispossessed in a lawless manner or under any existing laws of the State where the same may be situated.

The just debts of the Indians shall be paid out of any monies due them for their improvements and claims; and they shall also be furnished at the discretion of the President of the United States with a sufficient sum to enable them to obtain the necessary means to remove themselves to their new homes, and the balance of their dues shall be paid them at the Cherokee agency west of the Mississippi. The missionary establishments shall also be valued and appraised in a like manner and the amount of them paid over by the United States to the treasurers of the respective missionary societies by whom they have been established and improved in order to enable them to erect such buildings and make such improvements among the Cherokees west of the Mississippi as they may deem necessary for their benefit. Such teachers at present among the Cherokees as this council shall select and designate shall be removed west of the Mississippi with the Cherokee nation and on the same terms allowed to them.

* * *

ARTICLE 12. Those individuals and families of the Cherokee nation that are averse to a removal to the Cherokee country west of the Mississippi and are desirous to become citizens of the States where they reside and such as are qualified to take care of themselves and their property shall be entitled to receive their due portion of all the personal benefits accruing under this treaty for their claims, improvements and per capita; as soon as an appropriation is made for this treaty.

Such heads of Cherokee families as are desirous to reside within the States of No. Carolina, Tennessee, and Alabama subject to the laws of the same; and who are qualified or calculated to become useful citizens shall be entitled, on the certificate of the commissioners to a preemption right to one hundred and sixty acres of land or one quarter section at the minimum Congress price; so as to include the present buildings or improvements of those who now reside there and such as do not live there at present shall be permitted to locate within two years any lands not already occupied by persons entitled to pre-emption privilege under this treaty and if two or more families live on the same quarter section and they desire to continue their residence in these States and are qualified as above specified they shall, on receiving their pre-emption certificate be entitled to the right of pre-emption to such lands as they may select not already taken by any person entitled to them under this treaty.

* * *

ARTICLE 13. In order to make a final settlement of all the claims of the Cherokees for reservations granted under former treaties to any individuals belonging to the nation by the United States it is therefore hereby stipulated and agreed and expressly understood by the parties to this treaty—that all the Cherokees and their heirs and descendants to whom any reservations have been made under any former treaties with the United States, and who have not sold or conveyed the same by deed or otherwise and who in the opinion of the commissioners have complied with the terms on which the reservations were granted as far as practicable in the several cases; and which reservations have since been sold by the United States shall constitute a just claim against the United States and the original reservee or their heirs or descendants shall be entitled to receive the present value thereof from the United States as unimproved lands. And all such reservations as have not been sold by the United States and where the terms on which the reservations were made in the opinion of the commissioners have been complied with as far as practicable, they or their heirs or descendants shall be entitled to the same. They are hereby granted and confirmed to them—and also all persons who were entitled to reservations under the treaty of 1817 and who as far as practicable in the opinion of the commissioners, have complied with the stipulations of said treaty, although by the treaty of 1819 such reservations were included in the unceded lands belonging to the Cherokee nation are hereby confirmed to them and they shall be entitled to receive a grant for the same. And all such reservees as were obliged by the laws of the States in which their reservations were situated, to abandon the same or purchase them from the States shall be deemed to have a just claim against the United States for the amount by them paid to the States with interest thereon for such reservations and if obliged to abandon the same, to the present value of such reservations as unimproved lands but in all cases where the reservees have sold their reservations or any part thereof and conveyed the same by deed or otherwise and have been paid for the same, they their heirs or descendants or their assigns shall not be considered as having any claims upon the United States under this article of the treaty nor be entitled to receive any compensation for the lands thus disposed of. It is expressly understood by the parties to this treaty that the amount to be allowed for reservations under this article shall not be deducted out of the consideration money allowed to the Cherokees for their claims for spoilations and the cession of their lands; but the same is to be paid for independently by the United States as it is only a just fulfillment of former treaty stipulations.[1]

* * *

ARTICLE 16. It is hereby stipulated and agreed by the Cherokees that they shall remove to their new homes within two years from the ratification of this treaty and that during such time the United States shall protect and defend them in their possessions and property and free use and occupation of the same and such persons as have been dispossessed of their improvements and houses; and for which no grant has actually issued previously to the enactment of the law of the State of Georgia, of December 1835 to regulate Indian occupancy shall be again put in possession and placed in the same situation and condition, in reference to the laws of the State of Georgia, as the Indians that have not been dispossessed; and if this is not done, and the people are left unprotected, then the United States shall pay the several Cherokees for their losses and damages sustained by them in consequence thereof. And it is also stipulated and agreed that the public buildings and improvements on which they are situated at New Echota for which no grant has been actually made previous to the passage of the above recited act if not occupied by the Cherokee people shall be reserved for the public and free use of the United States and the Cherokee Indians for the purpose of settling and closing all the Indian business arising under this treaty between the commissioners of claims and the Indians.

[1] Articles 12 and 13 were nullified by a supplemental article added in March 1836. The explanatory preamble stated: "WHEREAS the undersigned were authorized at the general meeting of the Cherokee people held at New Echota as above stated, to make and assent to such alterations in the preceding treaty as might be thought necessary, and whereas the President of the United States has expressed his determination not to allow any pre-emptions or reservations his desire being that the whole Cherokee people should remove together and establish themselves in the country provided for them west of the Mississippi river."
"Article 1. It is therefore agreed that all the pre-emption rights and reservations provided for in articles 12 and 13 shall be and are hereby relinquished and declared void." See Kappler, 2: 448.

The United States, and the several States interested in the Chero-kee lands, shall immediately proceed to survey the lands ceded by this treaty; but it is expressly agreed and understood between the parties that the agency buildings and that tract of land surveyed and laid off for the use of Colonel R. J. Meigs Indian agent or heretofore enjoyed and occupied by his successors in office shall continue sub-ject to the use and occupancy of the United States, or such agent as may be engaged specially superintending the removal of the tribe.

Charles J. Kappler, *Indian Affairs: Laws and Treaties, Vol. II (Treaties)* (Washington, DC: GPO, 1904), 439–40, 442, 443, 444, 445, 446.

II
Contemporary Views of Indians

*W*hite perceptions of Indians spanned a broad spectrum that characterized them as savages (sometimes as noble, sometimes as simply savage), children of nature, or just as human beings, although never equals of whites. In the selections that follow, we see these differing sorts of thoughts. All, however, contain the constant of regarding Indians as alien. Some saw them as curiously exotic innocents, while others judged their different ways as marking treachery and brutality. Whether that alien nature was perceived as sinister or benign often tells us more about the times and the historical context of the writer than about the Indians being described.

    This first selection, by John Lawson, was published in 1709; the excerpts are taken from a 1714 edition. Lawson left his native London to become surveyor-general of North Carolina in 1700 and spent some of his time with companions and Indian guides exploring the mid-Atlantic interior. His observations were the basis for his book A New Voyage to Carolina *that in part described in sharp detail the region's Indians. While he considered Indians as natural denizens of the wilderness, he neither romanticized nor vilified them. Instead, he tried to describe his subjects from a social and scientific objectivity that provides a fascinating portrait of American Indians in an early stage of European contact. Ironically, Lawson would be a primary reason for the dissolution of the Tuscarora people in the Carolinas, because on his last journey into the interior in 1711 he was captured and killed by them. The English colony's reaction was rapid, fierce, and thorough. Many Tuscaroras were killed in the ensuing reprisals and even more were captured and sold into slavery. Remnants of the once powerful Tuscarora Nation fled the region in the early 1720s to live among the Iroquois farther north.*

Customs and Character
of Carolina Indians, 1709

The Succession falls not to the King's Son, but to his Sister's Son, which is a sure way to prevent Impostors in the Succession. Sometimes they poison the Heir to make way for another, which is not seldom done, when they do not approve of the Youth that is to succeed them. * * *

They are so well versed in Poison, that they are often found to poison whole Families; nay, most of a Town; and which is most to be admired, they will poison a running Spring, or Fountain of Water, so that whosoever drinks thereof, shall infallible die. When the Offender is discovered, his very Relations urge for Death, whom nothing will appease, but the most cruel Torment imaginable, which is executed in the most publick Manner that it's possible to act such a Tragedy in. For all the whole Nation, and all the Indians within a hundred Miles, (if it is possible to send for them), are summoned to come and appear at such a Place and Time, to see and rejoice at the Torments and Death of such a Person, who is the common and professed Enemy to all the friendly Indians thereabouts, who now lies under the Condemnation of the whole Nation, and accordingly is to be put to Death. Then all appear (young and old) from all the adjacent Parts, and meet, with all the Expressions of Joy, to consummate this horrid and barbarous Feast, which is carried on after this dismal Manner. First, they bring the Prisoner to the Place appointed for the Execution, where he is set down on his Breech on the Ground. Then they all get about him, and you shall not see one sorrowful or dejected Countenance amongst them, but all very merrily disposed, as if some Comedy was to be acted, instead of a Tragedy. He that is appointed to be the chief Executioner, takes a Knife, and bids him hold out his

Hands, which he does, and then cuts round the Wrist through the Skin, which is drawn off like a Glove, and flead quite off at the Fingers' Ends, then they break his Joints and Bones, and buffet and torment him after a very inhumane Manner, till some violent Blow perhaps ends his Days; then they burn him to Ashes, and throw them down the River. Afterwards they eat, drink and are merry, repeating all the Actions of the Tormentors and the Prisoner, with a great deal of Mirth and Satisfaction. This Accusation is laid against an Indian Heroe sometimes wrongfully, or when they have a mind to get rid of a Man that has more Courage and Conduct than his neighboring Kings or great Men; then they alledge the Practice of poisoning Indians against him, and make a Rehearsal of every Indian that died for a year or two, and say, that they were poisoned by such an Indian; which Reports stir up all the Relations of the deceased against the said Person, and by such means make him away presently. In some Affairs, these Savages are very reserved and politick, and will attend a long time with a great deal of Patience, to bring about their Designs; they being never impatient or hasty in executing any of their Designs of Revenge.

Now I am gone so far in giving an Account of the Indian's Temper, I will proceed, and can give you no other Character of them, but that they are a very wary People, and are never hasty or impatient. They will endure a great many Misfortunes, Losses, and Disappointments without showing themselves, in the least, vexed or uneasy. When they go by Water, if there proves a Head-Wind, they never vex and fret as the Europeans do, and let what Misfortune come to them, as will or can happen, they never relent. Besides, there is one Vice very common every where, which I never found amongst them, which is Envying other Men's Happiness, because their Station is not equal to, or above, their Neighbors. Of this Sin I cannot say I ever saw an Example, though they are a People that set as great a Value upon themselves, as any sort of Men in the World; upon which Account they find something Valuable in themselves above Riches. Thus, he that is a good Warriour is the proudest Creature living; and he that is an expert Hunter, is esteemed by the People and himself; yet all these are natural Vertues and Gifts, and not Riches, which are as often in the Possession of a Fool as a

Wise-Man. Several of the Indians are possessed of a great many Skins, Wampum, Ammunition, and what other things are esteemed Riches amongst them; yet such an Indian is no more esteemed amongst them, than any other ordinary Fellow, provided he has no personal Endowments, which are the Ornaments that must gain him an Esteem among them; for a great Dealer, amongst the Indians, is no otherwise respected and esteemed, than as a Man that strains his Wits, and fatigues himself, to furnish others with Necessaries of Life, that live much easier and enjoy more of the World, than he himself does with all his Self. If they are taken Captives, and expect a miserable Exit, they sing; if Death approach them in Sickness, they are not afraid of it; nor are ever heard to say, Grant me some time. They know by Instinct, and daily Example, that they must die; wherefore, they have that great and noble Gift to submit to every thing that happens, and value nothing that attacks them.

Their Cruelty to their Prisoners of War is what they are seemingly guilty of an Error in, (I mean as to a natural Failing) because they strive to invent the most inhumane Butcheries for them, that the Devils themselves could invent, or hammer out of Hell; they esteeming Death no Punishment, but rather an Advantage to him, that is exported out of this into another World.

* * *

One of their Expeditions afforded an Instance, worthy mention, which was thus; Two Nations of Indians here in Carolina were at War together, and a Party of each were in the Forest ranging to see what Enemies they could take. The lesser Number found they were discovered, and could not well get over a River (that lay betwixt them and their home) without engaging the other Party, whose Numbers were much the greater; so they called a Council, which met, and having weighed their present Circumstances with a great deal of Argument and Debate, for a considerable time, and found their Enemies Advantage, and that they could expect no Success in Engaging such an unequal Number; they, at last, concluded on this Stratagem, which, in my Opinion, carried a great deal of Policy along with it. It was, That the same Night, they should make a great Fire, which they were certain would be discovered by the adverse

Party, and there dress up Logs of Wood in their Cloaths, and make them exactly seem like Indians, that were asleep by the Fireside; (which is their Way, when in the Woods) so, said they, our Enemies will sire upon these Images, supposing them to be us, who will lie in Ambuscade, and, after their Guns are unloaded, shall deal well enough with them. This Result was immediately put in Execution, and the Fire was made by the side of a Valley, where they lay perdu very advantageously. Thus, a little before Break of Day, (which commonly is the Hour they surprise their Enemies in) the Indians came down to their Fire, and at once fired in upon those Logs in the Indians Cloaths, and run up to them, expecting they had killed every Man dead; but they found themselves mistaken, for then the other Indians, who had lain all the Night stark-naked in the Bottom, attacked them with their loaded Pieces, which so surprised them, that every Man was taken Prisoner, and brought in bound to their Town.

* * *

The Indians are very revengeful, and never forget an Injury done, till they have receiv'd Satisfaction. Yet they are the freest People from Heats and Passions (which possess the Europeans) of any I ever heard of. They never call any Man to account for what he did, when he was drunk; but say, it was the Drink that caused his Misbehaviour, therefore he ought to be forgiven: They never frequent a Christian's House that is given to Passion, nor will they ever buy or sell with him, if they can get the same Commodities of any other Person; for they say, such Men are mad Wolves, and no more Men.

They know not what Jealousy is, because they never think their Wives are unconstant, unless they are Eye-witnesses thereof. They are generally very bashful, especially the young Maids, who when they come into a strange Cabin, where they are not acquainted, never ask for any thing, though never so hungry or thirsty, but sit down, without speaking a Word (be it never so long) till some of the House asks them a Question, or falls into Discourse, with the Stranger. I never saw a Scold amongst them, and to their Children they are extraordinary tender and indulgent; neither did I ever see a Parent correct a Child, excepting one Woman, that was the King's

Wife, and she (indeed) did possess a Temper that is not commonly found amongst them. They are free from all manner of Compliments, except Shaking of Hands, and Scratching on the Shoulder, which two are the greatest Marks of Sincerity and Friendship, that can be shewed one to another. They cannot express *fare-you-well*, but when they leave the House, will say, *I go straightway*, which is to intimate their Departure; and if the Man of the House has any Message to send by the going Man, he may acquaint him therewith. Their Tongue allows not to say, *Sir, I am your Servants;* because they have no different Titles for Man, only King, War-Captain, Old Man, or Young Man, which respect the Stations and Circumstances Men are employed in, and arrived to, and not Ceremony. As for Servant, they have no such thing, except Slave, and their Dogs, Cats, tame or domestic Beasts, and Birds, are called by the same Name: For the Indian Word for Slave includes them all. So when an Indian tells you he has got a Slave for you, it may (in general Terms, as they use) be a young Eagle, a Dog, Otter, or any other thing of that Nature, which is obsequiously to depend on the Master for its Sustenance.

John Lawson, *Lawson's History of North Carolina* (London: W. Taylor, 1714; reprint, Richmond, Garrett and Massie, 1952), 207–09, 211, 212–13.

Andrew Jackson Describes Indians, 1793

At the end of the eighteenth century, attitudes about Indians on the expanding American frontier had undergone a significant transformation. Rather than regarding Indians as mysteriously different, American pioneers had come to loathe them as false and dangerous rivals for limited resources. In this letter to John McKee, who the following year would become temporary agent to the Cherokees, twenty-five-year-old Andrew Jackson expressed outrage over the behavior of Indians and the white response to it, especially in regard to treaty making. Jackson regarded such exercises as futile appeasement. The treaty he refers to was the Holston Treaty of 1791 that tried to designate certain lands for white settlement in Tennessee, a measure that Jackson predicted the Indians would ignore.

Cumberland January 30th 1793

[Dear Sir,]

* * * The Late Express that [proclaimed peace] to our Western Country [attended with] the Late Depredations and [Murders] Committed by the Indians [on our] frontier has occassioned a Great [Clamour] amonghts the people of this [District] and it is Two Much to be [dreaded] that the Indians has made [use of] this Finesse to Lull the peo[ple to] sleep that they might save [their Towns] and open amore Easy Road to [Commit] Murder with impunity; this [is proved] by their late Conduct, for since [that] Express not Less than Twelve [have] been Killed and wounded in this [District:] one Question I Would beg leave to [ask] why do we now attempt to hold a [Treaty with them;] have they attended to the [Last] Treaty; I answer in the Negative [then] why do we attem[pt] to Treat with [a Savage] Tribe tha[t] will neither ad[here to] Treaties, nor the law of Nations, [upon these] particu[la]rs I would thank [you for] your Sent[i]ments in your [next.] I have the honour to be [wi]th the highes Estem your Mo. ob. Serv.

Andrew Jackson

Sam B. Smith and Harriet Chappell Owsley, eds., *The Papers of Andrew Jackson, Volume 1, 1770–1803* (Knoxville: The University of Tennessee Press, 1980), 40.

James Fenimore Cooper Describes Indians

James Fenimore Cooper was not only one of America's first great novelists, he was also a keen observer of the social changes sweeping across the country because of Jacksonian Democracy. Moreover, he established an indelible description of Indians for Americans of his time, one that has invited criticism from knowledgeable critics who charge that Cooper's Indians were unrealistically adept at woods lore, usually one-dimensional, and often based on romantic notions that revealed Cooper's ignorance about real native peoples. While Cooper himself once confessed that most of his knowledge about Indians came from books, he also defended his characterization of Indians in his preface to The Last of the

Mohicans. *And a few years later, his travel narrative* Notions of the Americans *took up the subject of Indians in a more discursive and coldly objective fashion. Like Lawson a century before, Cooper harbored no hostility toward Indians and regarded them with an almost scientific curiosity. Yet he was also convinced that Indians were doomed because they were incompatible with a white culture he judged as infinitely superior and ultimately irresistible. In that regard, he was completely in step with most Americans at the time of removal.*

Preface to *The Last of the Mohicans* (1826)

Few men exhibit greater diversity, or, if we may so express it, greater antithesis of character, than the native warrior of North America. In war, he is daring, boastful, cunning, ruthless, self-denying, and self-devoted; in peace, just, generous, hospitable, revengeful, superstitious, modest, and commonly chaste. These are qualities, it is true, which do not distinguish all alike; but they are so far the predominating traits of these remarkable people as to be characteristic.

It is generally believed that the Aborigines of the American continent have an Asiatic origin. There are many physical as well as moral facts which corroborate this opinion, and some few that would seem to weigh against it.

The color of the Indian, the writer believes, is peculiar to himself, and while his cheek-bones have a very striking indication of a Tartar origin, his eyes have not. Climate may have had great influence on the former, but it is difficult to see how it can have produced the substantial difference which exists in the latter. The imagery of the Indian, both in his poetry and in his oratory, is oriental; chastened, and perhaps improved, by the limited range of his practical knowledge. He draws his metaphors from the clouds, the seasons, the birds, the beasts, and the vegetable world. In this, perhaps, he does no more than any other energetic and imaginative race would do, being compelled to set bounds to fancy by experience; but the North American Indian clothes his ideas in a dress which is different from that of the African, and is oriental in itself. His language has the richness and sententious fullness of the Chinese. He will express a phrase in a word, and he will qualify the meaning of an entire sentence by a syllable; he will even convey different significations by the simplest inflections of the voice.

* * *

Like nations of higher pretensions, the American Indian gives a very different account of his own tribe or race from that which is given by other people. He is much addicted to overestimating his own perfections, and to undervaluing those of his rival or his enemy; a trait which may possibly be thought corroborative of the Mosaic account of the creation.[2]

* * *

The Mohicans were the possessors of the country first occupied by the Europeans in this portion of the continent. They were, consequently, the first dispossessed; and the seemingly inevitable fate of all these people, who disappear before the advances, or it might be termed the inroads, of civilization, as the verdure of their native forests falls before the nipping frosts, is represented as having already befallen them. There is sufficient historical truth in the picture to justify the use that has been made of it.

James Fenimore Cooper, *The Last of the Mohicans, A Narrative of 1757* (New York: Stringer & Townsend, 1856), iv–v, vii, viii.

From *Notions on Americans* (1830)

By far the most numerous, and the most important of the native tribes, which still continue in the immediate vicinity of the whites, are those which occupy reservations in Georgia, the Floridas, Alabama, Mississippi, and Tennessee. The lingering fragments of a hundred tribes are certainly seen scattered over the immense surface of this country, living on greater or less tracts that had been secured to them, or dwelling by sufferance in the woods; but the only people now residing east of the Mississippi who can aspire to the names of nations, are the Creeks, the Choctaws, the Chickasaws, the Cherokees, and the Seminoles, all of whom dwell in the portion of country I have named.

As a rule, the red man disappears before the superior moral and physical influence of the white, just as I believe the black man will

[2] The description of the creation in the book of Genesis.

eventually do the same thing, unless he shall seek shelter in some other region. In nine cases in ten, the tribes have gradually removed west; and there is now a confused assemblage of nations and languages collected on the immense hunting grounds of the Prairies.

* * *

The ordinary manner of the disappearance of the Indian, is by a removal deeper into the forest. Still, many linger near the graves of their fathers, to which their superstitions, no less than a fine natural feeling, lend a deeper interest. The fate of the latter is inevitable; they become victims to the abuses of civilization, without ever attaining to any of its moral elevation.

* * *

In point of civilization, comforts, and character, the Indians, who remain near the coasts, are about on a level with the lowest classes of European peasantry. Perhaps they are somewhat below the English, but I think not below the Irish peasants. They are much below the condition of the mass of the slaves. It is but another proof of the wayward vanity of man, that the latter always hold the Indians in contempt, though it is some proof that they feel their own condition to be physically better: morally, in one sense, it certainly is not.

* * *

In the more interior parts of the Country, I frequently met families of the Indians, either travelling or proceeding to some village, with their wares. They were all alike, a stunted, dirty, and degraded race. Sometimes they encamped in the forests, lighted their fires, and remained for weeks in a place; and at others, they kept roaming daily, until the time arrived when they should return to their reservations.

The reservations in the old States, and with tribes that cannot aspire to the dignity of nations, are managed on a sufficiently humane principle. The laws of the State, or of the United States, have jurisdiction there, in all matters between white men, or between a white man and an Indian; but the Indians themselves are commonly permitted to control the whole of their own internal policy. Bargains, exceeding certain amounts, are not valid between them and the whites, who cannot, for instance, purchase their lands. Schools are usually provided, in the more important tribes, by the general government, and in the less, by charity. Religious instruction is also furnished by the latter means.

I saw reservations in which no mean advances had been made in civilization. Farms were imperfectly tilled, and cattle were seen grazing in the fields. Still, civilization advances slowly among a people who consider labour a degradation, in addition to the bodily dislike that all men have to its occupations.

James Fenimore Cooper, *Notions on Americans Picked up by a Travelling Bachelor*, 2 vols. (New York: Frederick Under Publishing, Co., 1963), 277–78, 279, 281–82.

III

The Indian Perspective

*I*ndians reacted to whites with the normal range of human emotions. Indians were suspicious, curious, hostile, or benevolent depending on the circumstances and the melding or clashing of personalities. Too often, however, Indians found themselves put upon, and time and again victimized in their contact with whites.

As this first selection shows, white-Indian relations always had the potential for the tragic event. Tachnechdorus, known to whites as Logan, was a Mingo chief who settled in the Ohio Valley in the 1770s. Although a warrior, he consistently urged peace toward white settlers moving into the Ohio region, yet in 1774 Virginia militia raided his village and murdered many of his people, including his mother and sister. Logan swore revenge and mounted raids that sparked Lord Dunmore's War, a conflict named after the royal governor of colonial Virginia whose soldiers defeated the Indians after a few months of bitter fighting. Utterly aggrieved, Logan refused to attend peace negotiations. Instead, he sent the following speech to be read at the meeting; despite his claim that his vengeance was satisfied, he continued to prey on whites until his death some fifteen years later.

"Logan's Lament"

I appeal to any white man to say, if ever he entered Logan's cabin hungry, and he gave him not meat; if ever he came cold and naked, and he clothed him not. During the course of the last long and bloody war, Logan remained idle in his cabin, an advocate for peace. Such was my love for the whites, that my countrymen pointed as they passed, and said, Logan is the friend of the white men. I have even thought to live with you but for the injuries of one man. Col. Cresap, the last spring, in cold blood, and unprovoked, murdered all the relations of Logan, not sparing even my women and children. There runs not a drop of my blood in the veins of any living creature. This has called on me for revenge. I have sought it: I have killed many: I have fully glutted my vengeance. For my country, I rejoice at the beams of peace. But do not harbour a thought that mine is the joy of fear. Logan never felt fear. He will not turn on his heel to save his life. Who is there to mourn for Logan? Not one.

Samuel G. Drake, *The Aboriginal Races of North America,* 15th ed. (New York: Hurst & Company, 1880), 163–64.

Cornplanter, Big Tree, and Half-Town to George Washington, 1790

Cornplanter was an influential Seneca chief, a member of the Six Nations of the Iroquois Confederacy. He unwisely allied with the British during the American Revolution, and after its conclusion, he tried to placate angry Americans by consenting to a series of Seneca land cessions that made him unpopular with his

*own people. By 1790 Cornplanter was disillusioned by his attempts to concil-
iate whites, and along with Seneca chiefs objected to President George Washington about whites' seemingly insatiable demand for more Indian land. Despite his
doubts, Cornplanter remained loyal to the United States, helping to resolve
white-Indian disputes and possibly contributing to the government's resolve to
attempt the fair treatment of Indians that resulted in the civilization program.
He died in 1836.*

Father: The voice of the Seneca nations speaks to you; the great
counsellor, in whose heart the wise men of all the *thirteen fires* [13
U.S.][3] have placed their wisdom. It may be very small in our ears,
and we, therefore, entreat you to hearken with attention; for we are
able to speak of things which are to us very great.

When your army entered the country of the Six Nations, we
called you the *town destroyer;* to this day, when your name is heard,
our women look behind them and turn pale, and our children cling
close to the necks of their mothers.

When our chiefs returned from Fort Stanwix, and laid before our
council what had been done there, our nation was surprised to hear
how great a country you had compelled them to give up to you,
without your paying to us any thing for it. Every one said, that your
hearts were yet swelled with resentment against us for what had
happened during the war, but that one day you would consider it
with more kindness. We asked each other, *What have we done to deserve
such severe chastisement?*

Father: when you kindled your 13 fires separately, the wise men
assembled at them told us that you were all brothers; the children
of one great father, who regarded the red people as his children.
They called us brothers, and invited us to his protection. They told
us that he resided beyond the great water where the sun first rises;
and that he was a king whose power no people could resist, and that
his goodness was as bright as the sun. What they said went to our
hearts. We accepted the invitation, and promised to obey him.
What the Seneca nation promises, they faithfully perform. When

---

[3] A reference to the thirteen states that then constituted the Union.

you refused obedience to that king, he commanded us to assist his beloved men in making you sober. In obeying him, we did no more than yourselves had led us to promise. We were deceived; but your people teaching us to confide in that king, had helped to deceive us; and we now appeal to your breast. *Is all the blame ours?*

Father: when we saw that we had been deceived, and heard the invitation which you gave us to draw near to the fire you had kindled, and talk with you concerning peace, we made haste towards it. You told us you could crush us to nothing; and you demanded from us a great country, as the price of that peace which you had offered to us: *as if our want of strength had destroyed our rights.* Our chiefs had felt your power, and were unable to contend against you, and they therefore gave up that country. What they agreed to has bound our nation, but your anger against us must by this time be cooled, and although our strength is not increased, nor your power become less, we ask you to consider calmly—*Were the terms dictated to us by your commissioners reasonable and just?*

* * *

Father: you have said that we were in your hand, and that by closing it you could crush us to nothing. Are you determined to crush us? If you are, tell us so; that those of our nation who have become your children, and have determined to die so, may know what to do. In this case, one chief has said, he would ask you to put him out of his pain. Another, who will not think of dying by the hand of his father, or his brother, has said he will retire to the Chataughque, eat of the fatal root, and sleep with his fathers in peace.

All the land we have been speaking of belonged to the Six Nations. No part of it ever belonged to the king of England, and he could not give it to you.

Hear us once more. At Fort Stanwix we agreed to deliver up those of our people who should do you any wrong, and that you might try them and punish them according to your law. We delivered up two men accordingly. But instead of trying them according to your law, the lowest of your people took them from your magistrate, and put them immediately to death. It is just to punish the murder with death; but the Senecas will not deliver up their people to men who disregard the treaties of their own nation.

Samuel G. Drake, *The Aboriginal Races of North America*, 15th ed. (New York: Hurst & Company, 1880), 609–11.

Corn Tassel Protests White Plans, 1785

Years before the government's civilization program was envisioned, the Cherokees warned about its pitfalls. It was later a high irony that the Cherokees were among those Indians who resolutely did so, because they would eventually accept acculturation more avidly than any other Indian nation. But in the 1780s they were wary. They had sided with the British during the Revolution, and the close of that conflict left them anxious about maintaining their autonomy, let alone their dominion. One of the most respected Cherokees of his time, Corn Tassel reacted to a proposed peace treaty with the following objections and advice.

It is a little surprising that when we entered into treaties with our brothers, the whites, their whole cry is more land! Indeed, formerly it seemed to be a matter of formality with them to demand what they knew we durst not refuse. But on the principles of fairness, of which we have received assurances during the conducting of the present treaty, and in the name of free will and equality, I must reject your demand.

Suppose, in considering the nature of your claim (and in justice to my nation I shall and will do it freely), I were to ask one of you, my brother warriors, under what kind of authority, by what law, or on what pretense he makes this exorbitant demand of nearly all the lands we hold between your settlements and our towns, as the cement and consideration of our peace.

Would he tell me that it is by right of conquest? No! If he did, I should retort on him that we had last marched over his territory; even up to this very place which he has fortified so far within his former limits; nay, that some of our young warriors (whom we have not yet had an opportunity to recall or give notice to, of the general treaty) are still in the woods, and continue to keep his people in fear, and that it was but till lately that these identical walls were your strongholds, out of which you durst scarcely advance.

If, therefore, a bare march, or reconnoitering a country is sufficient reason to ground a claim to it, we shall insist upon transposing the demand, and your relinquishing your settlements on the western waters and removing one hundred miles back towards the east, whither some of our warriors advanced against you in the course of last year's campaign.

Let us examine the facts of your present eruption into our country, and we shall discover your pretentions [sic] on that ground. What did you do? You marched into our territories with a superior force; our vigilance gave us no timely notice of your maneuvers; your numbers far exceeded us, and we fled to the stronghold of our extensive woods, there to secure our women and children.

Thus, you marched into our towns; they were left to your mercy; you killed a few scattered and defenseless individuals, spread fire and desolation wherever you pleased, and returned again to your own habitations. If you meant this, indeed, as a conquest you omitted the most essential point; you should have fortified the junction of the Holstein and Tennessee rivers, and have thereby conquered all the waters above you. But, as all are fair advantages during the existence of a state of war, it is now too late for us to suffer for your mishap of generalship!

Again, were we to inquire by what law or authority you set up a claim,

I answer, none! Your laws extend not into our country, nor ever did. You talk of the law of nature and the law of nations, and they are both against you.

Indeed, much has been advanced on the want of what you term civilization among the Indians; and many proposals have been made to us to adopt your laws, your religion, your manners and your customs. But, we confess that we do not yet see the propriety, or practicability of such a reformation, and should be better pleased with beholding the good effect of these doctrines in your own practices than with hearing you talk about them, or reading your papers to us upon such subjects.

You say: Why do not the Indians till the ground and live as we do? May we not, with equal propriety, ask, Why the white people do not hunt and live as we do? You profess to think it no injustice to warn us not to kill our deer and other game from the mere love of waste; but it is very criminal in our young men if they chance to kill a cow or a hog for their sustenance when they happen to be in your lands. We wish, however, to be at peace with you, and to do as we would be done by. We do not quarrel with you for killing an occasional buffalo, bear or deer on our lands when you need one to eat; but you go much farther; your people hunt to gain a livelihood by it; they kill all our game; our young men resent the injury, and it is followed by bloodshed and war.

This is not a mere affected injury; it is a grievance which we equitably complain of and it demands a permanent redress.

The great God of Nature has placed us in different situations. It is true that he has endowed you with many superior advantages; but he has not created us to be your slaves. We are a separate people! He has given each their lands, under distinct considerations and circumstances; he has stocked yours with cows, ours with buffalo; yours with hog, ours with bear; yours with sheep, ours with deer. He has, indeed, given you an advantage in this, that your cattle are tame and domestic while ours are wild and demand not only a larger space for range, but art to hunt and kill them; they are, nevertheless, as much our property as other animals are yours, and ought not to be taken away without our consent, or for something equivalent.

CORN TASSEL, *Cherokee*

Peter Nabokov, ed. *Native American Testimony: A Chronicle of Indian-White Relations from Prophecy to the Present, 1492–1992* (New York: Viking, 1991), 121–23.

Red Jacket on Land Cessions and Removal, 1811

As pressure for more land cessions from the Seneca continued, Red Jacket, chief of their nation, spoke, with succinct decisiveness, to the issue of cessions. He also provided a perceptive rationale for not eliminating remaining Seneca land holdings and moving west, because he realized the danger of leaving his home to establish new quarters among other, likely hostile, Indians.

FIGURE 4

Red Jacket—This Seneca chief met with George Washington and received from him a large silver medallion, which he is wearing in this portrait. Of noble bearing and measured words, Red Jacket would later protest mounting white pressure for Indian lands with an eloquent explanation of why the Seneca could not leave their homes. *(Library of Congress)*

Brother!—We opened our ears to the talk you *lately* delivered to us, at our council-fire. In doing important business it is best not to tell long stories, but to come to it in a few words. We therefore shall not repeat your talk, which is fresh in our minds. We have well considered it, and the advantages and disadvantages of your offers. We request your attention to our answer, which is not from the speaker alone, but from all the Sachems and Chiefs now around our council-fire.

Brother!—We know that great men, as well as great nations, have different interests and different minds, and do not see the same light—but we hope our answer will be agreeable to you and your employers.

Brother!—Your application for the purchase of our lands is to our minds very extraordinary. It has been made in a crooked manner. You have not walked in the straight path pointed out by the great Council of your nation. You have no writings from your great Father, the President. In making up our minds we have looked back, and remembered how the Yorkers purchased our lands in former times. They bought them, piece after piece—for a little money paid to a few men in our nation, and not to all our brethren—until our planting and hunting-grounds have become very small, and if we sell *them*, we know not where to spread our blankets.

Brother!—You tell us your employers have purchased of the Council of Yorkers,[4] a right to buy our lands. We do not understand how this can be. The lands do not belong to the Yorkers; they are ours, and were given to us by the Great Spirit.

Brother!—We think it strange that you should jump over the lands of our brethren in the East, to come to our council-fire so far off, to get our lands. When we sold our lands in the East to the white people, we determined never to sell those we kept, which are as small as we can comfortably live on.

Brother!—You want us to travel with you and look for new lands. If we should sell our lands and move off into a distant country towards the setting sun, we should be looked upon in the country to which we go, as foreigners and strangers. We should be despised by the red, as well as the white men, and we should soon be surrounded by the white people, who will there also kill our game, and come upon our lands and try to get them from us.

[4] The New York state legislature.

Brother!—We are determined not to sell our lands, but to continue on them. We like them. They are fruitful, and produce us corn in abundance for the support of our women and children, and grass and herbs for our cattle.

Brother!—At the treaties held for the purchase of our lands, the white men, with sweet voices and smiling faces, told us they loved us, and that they would not cheat us, but that the king's children on the other side of the lake would cheat us. When we go on the other side of the lake, the king's children tell us your people will cheat us. These things puzzle our heads, and we believe that the Indians must take care of themselves, and not trust either in your people, or in the king's children.

Brother!—At a late council we requested our agents to tell you that we would not sell our lands, and we think you have not spoken to our agents, or they would have told you so, and we should not have met you at our council-fire at this time.

Brother!—The white people buy and sell false rights to our lands, and your employers have, you say, paid a great price for their rights. They must have a plenty of money, to spend it in buying false rights to lands belonging to Indians. The loss of it will not hurt them, but our lands are of great value to us, and we wish you to go back with our talk to your employers, and tell them and the Yorkers that they have no right to buy and sell false rights to our lands.

Brother!—We hope you clearly understand the ideas we have offered. This is all we have to say.

———————

B. B. Thatcher, *Indian Biography*, 2 vols. (New York, Harper & Brothers, 1843), 2: 282–84.

Tecumseh to William Henry Harrison, 1810

Even before Red Jacket objected to pressure for additional land cessions, farther to the west the popular Shawnee Tecumseh and his brother Tenskwatawa (the Prophet) were organizing a confederation of northwestern tribes to resist white settlement. Tecumseh's efforts would eventually extend throughout the region and beyond to the southeastern Indians. In 1810, his oration to Governor William

Henry Harrison of the Indiana Territory illuminated the guiding purpose behind forming the confederation, the belief that all Indian lands were a common birthright that could not be forsaken in part without violating the whole.

It is true I am a Shawanee. My forefathers were warriors. Their son is a warrior. From them I only take my existence; from my tribe I take nothing. I am the maker of my own fortune; and oh! that I could make that of my red people, and of my country, as great as the conceptions of my mind, when I think of the Spirit that rules the universe. I would not then come to Governor *Harrison*, to ask him to tear the treaty, and to obliterate the landmark; but I would say to him, Sir, you have liberty to return to your own country. The being within, communing with past ages, tells me, that once, nor until lately, there was no white man on this continent. That it then all belonged to red men, children of the same parents, placed on it by the Great Spirit that made them, to keep it, to traverse it, to enjoy its productions, and to fill it with the same race. Once a happy race. Since made miserable by the white people, who are never contented, but always encroaching. The way, and the only way to check and stop this evil, is, for all the red men to unite in claiming a common and equal right in the land, as it was at first, and should be yet; for it never was divided, but belongs to all, for the use of each. That no part has a right to sell, even to each other, much less to strangers; those who want all, and will not do with less. The white people have no right to take the land from the Indians, because they had it first; it is theirs. They may sell, but all must join. Any sale not made by all is not valid. The late sale is bad. It was made by a part only. Part do not know how to sell. It requires all to make a bargain for all. All red men have equal rights to the unoccupied land. The right of occupancy is as good in one place as in another. There cannot be two occupations in the same place. The first excludes all others. It is not so in hunting or travelling; for there the same ground will serve many, as they may follow each other all day; but the camp is stationary, and that is occupancy. It belongs to the first who sits down on his blanket or skins, which he has thrown upon the ground, and till he leaves it no other has a right.

Samuel G. Drake, *The Aboriginal Races of North America*, 15th ed. (New York: Hurst & Company, 1880), 617–18.

Indians Do Not Break Treaties, 1815

At the end of the War of 1812, Tecumseh was dead and disastrous defeats had set back Indians' cause in both the Northwest and the South. Indians were mindful of the new conditions under which they now lived, but they were equally perplexed that their best efforts to accommodate white wishes were sometimes dismissed or misrepresented. In the following selection, Black Thunder, a chief of the Fox Indians of the Great Lakes region, disputed to American commissioners claims that his people had been untrustworthy and deceitful in their treaty arrangements, but he also made clear that there were limits to how far Indians could go in obliging white demands for additional territory.

My father, restrain your feelings, and hear calmly what I shall say. I shall say it plainly. I shall not speak with fear and trembling. I have never injured you, and innocence can feel no fear. I turn to you all, red-skins and white-skins—where is the man who will appear as my accuser? Father, I understand not clearly how things are working. I have just been set at liberty. Am I again to be plunged into bondage? Frowns are all around me; but I am incapable of change. You, perhaps, may be ignorant of what I tell you; but it is a truth, which I call heaven and earth to witness. It is a fact which can easily be proved, that I have been assailed in almost every possible way that pride, fear, feeling, or interest, could touch me—that I have been pushed to the last to raise the tomahawk against you; but all in vain. I never could be made to feel that you were my enemy. *If this be the conduct of an enemy, I shall never be your friend.* You are acquainted with my removal above Prairie des Chiens. I went, and formed a settlement, and called my warriors around me.

We took counsel, and from that counsel we never have departed. We smoked, and resolved to make common cause with the U. States. I sent you the pipe—it resembled this—and I sent it by the Missouri, that the Indians of the Mississippi might not know what we were doing. You received it. I then told you that your friends should be my friends—that your enemies should be my enemies—and that I only awaited your signal to make war. *If this be the conduct of an enemy, I shall never be your friend.*—Why do I tell you this? Because it is a truth, and a melancholy truth, that the good things which men do are often buried in the ground, while their evil deeds are stripped naked, and exposed to the world. When I came here, I came to you in friendship. I little thought I should have had to defend myself. I have no defence to make. If I were guilty, I should have come prepared; but I have ever held you by the hand, and I am come without excuses. If I had fought against you, I would have told you so: but I have nothing now to say here in your councils, except to repeat what I said before to my great father, the president of your nation. You heard it, and no doubt remember it. It was simply this. My lands can never be surrendered; I was cheated, and basely cheated, in the contract; I will not surrender my country but with my life. Again I call heaven and earth to witness, and I smoke this pipe in evidence of my sincerity. If you are sincere, you will receive it from me. My only desire is, that we should smoke it together—that I should grasp your sacred hand, and I claim for myself and my tribe the protection of your country. When this pipe touches your lip, may it operate as a blessing upon all my tribe.—*May the smoke rise like a cloud, and carry away with it all the animosities which have arisen between us.*

Samuel G. Drake, *The Aboriginal Races of North America*, 15th ed. (New York: Hurst & Company, 1880), 632.

Constitution of the Cherokee Nation, 1827

The Cherokee Nation became the most successful acculturation story in the government's civilization program. By 1820, the Cherokees had formed a republican government specifically emulating that of the United States. They had an elected chief that resembled the U.S. president and a legislature consisting of a senate and house of representatives. This government was institutionalized in 1827, when the Cherokees drafted a constitution that formally established the Cherokee Nation.

Formed by a Convention of Delegates from the several Districts, at New Echota, July 1827.

WE THE REPRESENTATIVES of the people of the CHEROKEE NATION in Convention assembled, in order to establish justice, ensure tranquility, promote our common welfare, and secure to ourselves and our posterity the blessings of liberty, acknowledging with humility and gratitude the goodness of the sovereign Ruler of the Universe, in offering as an opportunity so favorable to the design, and imploring his aid and direction in its accomplishment, do ordain and establish this Constitution for the Government of the Cherokee Nation.

ARTICLE I

Sec. 1. THE BOUNDARIES of this nation, embracing the lands solemnly guarantied and reserved forever to the Cherokee Nation by the Treaties concluded with the United States, are as follows; and shall forever hereafter remain unalterably the same-to wit-Beginning on the North Bank of Tennessee River at the upper part of the Chickasaw old fields; thence along the main channel of said river, including all the islands therein, to the mouth of the Hiwassee River, thence up the main channel of said river, including islands, to the first hill which closes in on said river, about two miles above Hiwassee Old Town; thence along the ridge which divides the waters of the Hiwassee and Little Tellico, to the Tennessee River at Tallasasei, thence along the main channel, including islands, to the junction of the Cowee and Nanteyalee; thence along the ridge in the fork of said river, to the top of the Blue Ridge; thence along the Blue Ridge to the Unicoy Turnpike road; thence by a straight line to the main source of the Chestatee; thence along its main channel, including islands, to the Chattahoochy; and thence down the same to the Creek boundary at Buzzard Roost; thence along the boundary line which separates this and the Creek Nation, to a point on the Coosa River opposite the mouth of Will's Creek; thence down along the south bank of the same to a point opposite to Fort Strother; thence up the river to the mouth of Will's Creek; thence up along the east bank of said creek to the west branch thereof, and up the same to its source; and thence along the ridge which separates the Tombechee and Tennessee waters, to a point on the top of said ridge; thence due north to Camp Coffee on the Tennessee River, which is opposite the Chickasaw Island; thence to the place of beginning.

Sec. 2. The Sovereignty and Jurisdiction of this Government shall extend over the country within the boundaries above described, and the lands therein are, and shall remain the common property of the Nation; but the improvements made thereon, and in the possession of the citizens of the Nation, are the exclusive and indefeasible property of the citizens respectively who made, or may rightfully be in possession of them; Provided, That the citizens of the Nation, possessing exclusive and indefeasible right to their respective improvements, as expressed in this article, shall possess no right nor power to dispose of their improvements in any manner whatever to the United States, individual states, nor to individual citizens hereof; and that, whenever any such citizen or citizens shall remove with their effects out of the limits of this Nation, and become citizens of any other government, all their rights and privileges as citizens of this nation shall cease; Provided nevertheless, That the Legislature shall have power to re-admit by law to all the rights of citizenship any such person or persons, who may at any time desire to return to the Nation on their memorializing the General Council for such readmission. Moreover, the Legislature shall have power to adopt such laws and regulations, as its wisdom may deem expedient and proper, to prevent the citizens from monopolizing improvements with the view of speculation.

ARTICLE II

Sec. 1. The Power of this Government, shall be divided into three distinct departments; the Legislative, the Executive, and the Judicial.

Sec. 2. No person or persons, belonging to one of these Departments, shall exercise any of the powers properly belonging to either of the others, except in the cases hereinafter expressly directed or permitted.

ARTICLE III

Sec. 1. THE LEGISLATIVE POWER shall be vested in two distinct branches; a Committee, and a Council; each to have a negative on the other, and both to be styled, the General Council of the Cherokee Nation; and the style of their acts and laws shall be,

"RESOLVED by the Committee and Council in General Council convened."

Sec. 2. The Cherokee Nation, as laid off into eight Districts, shall so remain.

Sec. 3. The Committee shall consist of two members from each district, and the Council shall consist of three members from each District, to be chosen by the qualified electors of their respective Districts for two years; and the elections to be held in every District on the first Monday in August for the year 1828, and every succeeding two years thereafter; and the General Council shall be held once a year, to be convened on the second Monday of October in each year, at New Echota.

Sec. 4. No person shall be eligible to a seat on the General Council, but a free Cherokee Male citizen, who shall have attained to the age of twenty-five years. The descendants of Cherokee men by all free women, except the African race, whose parents may be or have been living together as man and wife, according to the customs and laws of this Nation, shall be entitled to all the rights and privileges of this Nation, as well as the posterity of Cherokee women by all free men. No person who is of negro or mulatto parentage, either by the father or mother side, shall be eligible to hold any office of profit, honor or trust, under this Government.

Sec. 5. The Electors, and members of the General Council shall, in all cases except those of treason, felony, or breach of peace, be privileged from arrest during their attendance at election, and at the General Council, and in going to, and returning from the same.

Sec. 6. In all elections by the people, the electors shall vote viva voce. Electors for members to the General Council for 1828 shall be held at the places of holding the several courts, and at the other two precincts in each District which are designated by the law under which the members of this convention were elected; and the District Judges shall superintend the elections within the precincts of their respective Court Houses, and the Marshals & Sheriffs shall superintend within the precincts which may be assigned them by the Circuit Judges of their respective Districts, together with one other person, who shall be appointed by the Circuit Judges for each precinct within their respective Districts, and the Circuit Judges shall also appoint a clerk to each precinct. The superintendents and clerks shall on the Wednesday morning succeeding the election assemble at their respective Court Houses and proceed to examine and ascertain the true state of the polls, and shall issue to each member, duly elected, a certificate; and also make an official return of the state of the polls of election to the principal chief, and it shall be the duty of the Sheriffs to deliver the same to the Executive Office; Provided nevertheless, The General Council shall have power, after the election of 1828 to regulate by law the precincts and superintendents and clerks of elections in the several Districts.

Sec. 7. All free male citizens (except negroes, and descendants of white and Indian men by negro women, who may have been set free,) who shall have attained to the age of eighteen years, shall be equally entitled in vote at all public elections.

Sec. 8. Each House of the General Council shall judge of the qualifications, elections, and returns of its own members.

Sec. 9. Each House of the General Council may determine the rules of its proceedings, punish a member for disorderly behavior, and with the concurrence of two thirds, expel a member; but not a second time for the same cause.

Sec. 10. Each house of the General Council, when assembled, shall choose its own officers; a majority of each house shall constitute a quorum to do business, but a smaller number may adjourn from day to day, and compel the attendance of absent members in such manner and under such penalty, as each house may prescribe.

Sec. 11. The members of the committee shall each receive from the public Treasury a compensation for their services, which shall be two dollars and fifty cents per day during their attendance at the General Council; and the members of the Council shall each receive two dollars per day, for their services during their attendance at the General Councils Provided, That the same may be increased or diminished by law, but no alteration shall take effect during the period of service of the members of the General Council, by whom such alteration shall have been made.

Sec. 12. The General Council shall regulate by law, by whom and in what manner, writs of elections shall be issued to fill the vacancies which may happen in either branch thereof.

Sec. 13. Each member of the General Council, before he takes his seat, shall take the following oath of affirmation; to wit:

"I A, B, do solemnly swear (or affirm as the case may be) that I have not obtained my election by Bribery, Threats, or any undue and unlawful means used by himself, or others by my desire or approbation, for that purpose; that I consider myself Constitutionally qualified as a member of _____,; and that, on all questions and measures which may come before me, I will so give my vote, and so conduct myself, as may, in my judgment, appear most conducive to the interest and prosperity of this Nation; and that I will bear true faith and allegiance to the same, and to the utmost of my ability and power observe conform to, support, and defend the Constitution thereof."

Sec. 14. No person who may be convicted of felony before any court of this Nation shall be eligible to any office or appointment of honor, profit, or trust, within this Nation.

Sec. 15. The General Council shall have power to make all laws and regulations, which they shall deem necessary and proper for the good of the Nation, which shall not be contrary to this Constitution.

Sec. 16. It shall be the duty of the General Council to pass such laws as may be necessary and proper, to decide differences by arbitrators to be appointed by the parties; who may choose that summary mode of adjustment.

Sec. 17. No power of suspending the laws of this Nation shall be exercised unless by the Legislature or its authority.

Sec. 18. No respective law, nor any law impairing the obligations of contracts shall be passed.

Sec. 19. The Legislature shall have power to make laws for laying and collecting taxes, for the purpose of raising revenue.

Sec. 20. All bills making appropriations shall originate in the Committee, but the Council may propose amendments or reject the same.

Sec. 21. All other bills may originate in either house, subject to the concurrence or rejection of the other.

Sec. 22. All acknowledged Treaties shall be the Supreme Law of the land.

Sec. 23. The General Council shall have the sole power of deciding on the construction of all Treaty stipulations.

Sec. 24. The Council shall have the sole power of impeaching.

Sec. 25. All impeachments shall be tried by the Committee; when sitting for that purpose, the members shall be upon oath or affirmation; and no person shall be convicted without the concurrence of two thirds of the members present.

Sec. 26. The Principal Chief, assistant principal Chief, and all civil officers, under this nation shall be liable to impeachment for any misdemeanor in office, but Judgment in such cases shall not extend further that removal from office, and disqualification to hold office of honor, trust or profit, under this Nation. The party, whether convicted or acquitted shall, nevertheless, be liable to indictment, trial, judgment and punishment according to law.

ARTICLE IV

Sec. 1. The Supreme Executive power of this Nation shall be vested in a Principal Chief, who shall be chosen by the General Council, and shall hold his office four years; to be elected as follows.—The General Council, by a joint vote, shall, at their second annual session, after the rising of this Convention, and at every fourth annual session thereafter, on the second day after the Houses shall be organized, and competent to proceed to business, elect a Principal Chief.

Sec. 2. No person except a natural born citizen shall be eligible to the office of Principal Chief; neither shall any person be eligible to that office, who shall not have attained to the age of thirty-five years.

Sec. 3. There shall also be chosen at the same time, by the General Council, in the same manner, for four years, an assistant Principal Chief.

Sec. 4. In case of the removal of the Principal Chief from office, or of his death, resignation, or inability to discharge the powers and duties of the said office, the same shall devolve on the Assistant Principal Chief, until the inability be removed or the vacancy filled by the General Council.

Sec. 5. The General Council may, by law, provide for the case of removal, death, resignation or inability of both the Principal and assistant Principal Chiefs, declaring what officer shall then act as Principal Chief, until the disability be removed, or a Principal Chief shall be elected.

Sec. 6. The Principal Chief and assistant Principal Chief, shall at stated times, receive for their services a compensation, which shall neither be increased nor diminished during the period for which they shall have been elected; and they shall not receive, within that period, any other emolument from the Cherokee Nation, or any other government.

Sec. 7. Before the Principal Chief enters on the execution of his office, he shall take the following oath, or affirmation; I do solemnly swear (or affirm) that I will faithfully execute the office of Principal Chief of the Cherokee Nation, and will, to the best of my ability, preserve, protect, and defend the Constitution of the Cherokee Nation."

Sec. 8. He may, on extraordinary occasions, convene the General Council at the Seat of Government.

Sec. 9. He shall from time to time give to the General council information of the State of the Government, and recommend to their consideration such measures as he may think expedient.

Sec. 10. He shall take care that the laws be faithfully executed.

Sec. 11. It shall be his duty to visit the different districts, at least once in two years, to inform himself of the general condition of the Country.

Sec. 12. The Assistant Principal Chief shall, by virtue of his office, aid and advise the Principal Chief in the Administration of the Government, at all times during his continuance in office.

Sec. 13. Vacancies that may happen in offices, the appointment of which is vested in the General Council, shall be filled by the Principal Chief, during the recess of the General Council, by granting Commissions which shall expire at the end of the next Session.

Sec. 14. Every Bill which shall have passed both Houses of the General Council shall, before it becomes a law, be presented to the Principal Chief of the Cherokee Nation. If he approve, he shall sign it, but if not, he shall return it, with his objections to that house in which it shall have originated, who shall enter the objections at large on their journals, and precede to reconsider it. If, after such reconsideration, two thirds of that House shall agree to pass the bill, it shall be sent, together with the objections to the other house, by which it shall likewise be reconsidered, and if approved by two-thirds of that house, it shall become a law. If any bill shall not be returned by the Principal Chief within five days (Sundays excepted) after it shall have been presented to him, the same shall be a law, in like manner as if he had signed it; unless the General Council by their adjournment prevent its return, in which case it shall be a law, unless sent back within three days after their next meeting.

Sec. 15. Members of the General Council and all officers, Executive and Judicial, shall be bound by oath to support the Constitution of this Nation, and to perform the duties of their respective offices, with fidelity.

Sec. 16. In case of disagreement between the two houses with respect to the time of adjournment, the Principal Chief shall have power to adjourn the General Council to such a time as he thinks proper, provided it be not to a period beyond the next Constitutional meeting of the same.

Sec. 17. The Principal Chief shall, during the sitting of the General Council, attend at the Seat of Government.

Sec. 18. There shall be a Council to consist of three men to be appointed by the joint vote of both Houses, to advise the Principal Chief in the Executive part of the Government, whom the Principal Chief shall have full power, at his discretion, to assemble; and he, together with the assistant Principal Chief, and the counsellors, or a majority of them may, from time to time, hold and keep a Council for ordering and directing the affairs of the Nation according to law.

Sec. 19. The members of the Council shall be chosen for the term of one year.

Sec. 20. The resolutions and advice of the Council shall be recorded in a register and signed by the members agreeing thereto, which may be called for by either house of the General Council; and any counsellor may enter his dissent to the resolution of the majority.

Sec. 21. The Treasurer of the Cherokee Nation shall be chosen by the joint vote of both Houses of the General Council for the term of two years.

Sec. 22. The Treasurer shall, before entering on the duties of his office, give bond to the Nation with sureties to the satisfaction of the Legislature, for the faithful discharge of his trust.

Sec. 23. No money shall be drawn from the Treasury, but by warrant from the Principal Chief, and in consequence of appropriations made by law.

Sec. 25 [sic]. It shall be the duty of the Treasurer to receive all public moneys, and to make a regular statement and account of the receipts and expenditures of all public moneys to the annual Session of the General Council.

ARTICLE V

Sec. 1. The Judicial Powers shall be vested in the Supreme Court, and such Circuit and Inferior Courts, as the General Council may, from time to time, ordain and establish.

Sec. 2. The Supreme Court shall consist of three Judges, any two of whom shall be a quorum.

Sec. 3. The two Judges of each shall hold their Commission four years, but any of them may be removed from office on the address of two thirds of each house of the General Council to the Principal Chief, for that purpose.

Sec. 4. The Judges of the Supreme and Circuit Courts shall at stated times, receive a compensation, which shall not be diminished during their continuance in office, but they shall receive no fees or perquisites of office, nor hold any other office of profit or trust, under this Nation or any other power.

Sec. 5. No person shall be appointed a Judge of any of the Courts before he shall have attained to the age of thirty years, nor shall any person continue to execute the duties of any of the said offices after he shall have attained to the age of seventy years.

Sec. 6. The Judges of the Supreme and Circuit Courts shall be appointed by a joint vote of both houses of the General Council.

Sec. 7. There shall be appointed in each District, under the Legislative authority, as many Justices of the Peace as it may be deemed the public good requires, whose powers, duties, and duration in office, shall be clearly designated.

Sec. 8. The Judges of the Supreme Court and Circuit Courts shall have complete criminal Jurisdiction in such cases & in such manner as may be pointed out by law.

Each Court shall choose its own Clerks for the term of four years; but such Clerks shall not be continued in office unless their qualifications shall be adjudged and approved of, by the Judges of the Supreme Court and they shall be removable for breach of good behavior at anytime, by the Judges of their respective courts.

Sec. 10. No Judge shall sit on trial of any cause, where the parties shall be connected with him by affinity or consanguinity, except by consent of the parties. In case all the Judges of the Supreme Court shall be interested in the event of any cause, or related to all, or either, of the parties, the Legislature may provide by law for the selection of three men of good character and knowledge, for the determination thereof, who shall be specially commissioned by the Principal Chief for the case.

Sec. 11. All writs and other process shall run, in the name of the Cherokee Nation, and bear test, and be signed by the respective clerks.

Sec. 12. Indictments shall conclude, "against the peace & dignity of the Cherokee Nation."

Sec. 13. The Supreme Court shall hold its session annually at the Seat of Government to be convened on the second Monday of October in each year.

Sec. 14. In all criminal prosecutions, the accused shall have the right of being heard, of demanding the nature and cause of the accusation against him, of meeting the witnesses face to face, of having compulsory process for obtaining witness in his favor, and in prosecution by indictment or information, a speedy public trial by an impartial jury of the vicinage; nor shall he be compelled to give evidence against himself.

Sec. 15. The people shall be secure in their persons, houses, papers, and possessions from unreasonable seizures, and searches, and no warrant to search any place or to seize any person or things, shall issue without describing them as nearly as may be, nor without good cause, supported by oath or affirmation. All prisoners shall be bailable by sufficient securities, unless for capital offenses, where the proof is evident, or presumption great.

ARTICLE VI

Sec. 1. Whereas the ministers of the Gospel are, by their profession dedicated to the service of God and the care of souls, and ought not to be diverted from the great duty of their function, therefore, no minister of the Gospel, or public preacher, of any religious persuasion whilst he continues in the exercises of his pastoral functions, shall be eligible to the office of Principal Chief, or a seat on either house of the General Council.

Sec. 2. No person who denies the being of a God, or a future state of rewards & punishments shall hold any office in the civil department of this Nation.

Sec. 3. The free exercise of religious worship, and serving God without distinction, shall forever be allowed within this Nation Provided, That this liberty of conscience shall not be so construed as to excuse acts of licentiousness or justify practices inconsistent with the peace or safety of this Nation.

Sec. 4. Whenever the General Council shall determine the expediency of appointing delegates, or other public Agents, for the purpose of transacting business with the Government of the United States; the Principal Chief shall have power to recommend and by the advice and consent of the Committee, shall appoint and commission such delegates or Public Agents accordingly, and on all matters of interest touching the rights of the citizens of this Nation, which may require the attention of the United States Government, the Principal Chief shall keep up a friendly correspondence with that Government, through the medium of its proper officers.

Sec. 5. All commissions shall be in the name and by the authority of the Cherokee Nation, and be sealed with the Seal of the Nation, and be signed by the Principal Chief.

The Principal Chief shall make use of his private seal until a National Seal shall be provided.

Sec. 6. A sheriff shall be elected in each District by the qualified electors thereof, who shall hold his office for the term of two years, unless sooner removed. Should a vacancy occur subsequent to an election, it shall be filled by the Principal Chief as in other cases, and the person so appointed shall continue in office until the next General election, when such vacancy shall be filled by the qualified electors and the Sheriff then elected shall continue in office for two years.

Sec. 7. There shall be a Marshall appointed by a joint vote of both houses of the General Council for the term of four years, whose compensation and duties shall be regulated by law, & whose jurisdiction shall extend over the Cherokee Nation.

Sec. 8. No person shall for the same offence be twice put in jeopardy of life, or limb, nor shall any person's property be taken or applied to public use without his consent; Provided, that nothing in this clause shall be so construed as to impair the right and power of the General council to lay and collect Taxes. All courts shall be open, and every person for an injury done him in his property, person, or reputation, shall have remedy by due course of law.

Sec. 9 The right of trial by jury shall remain inviolate.

Sec. 10. Religion, morality, and knowledge being necessary to good Government, the preservation of liberty, and the happiness of mankind, Schools and the means of education shall forever be encouraged in this Nation.

Sec. 11. The appointment of all officers, not otherwise directed by this Constitution shall be vested in the legislature.

Sec. 12. All laws in force in this nation, at the passing of this Constitution shall so continue until altered or repealed by the legislature, except where they are temporary, in which case they shall expire at the times respectively limited for their duration; if not continued by act of the legislature.

Sec. 13. The General Council may at any time propose such amendments to this Constitution as two thirds of each house shall deem expedient; and the Principal Chief shall issue a proclamation, directing all the civil officers of the several Districts to promulgate the same as extensively as possible within their respective Districts, at least nine months previous to the next General election; and if at the first session of the General Council after such General election, two thirds of each house shall by yeas and nays ratify such proposed amendments, they shall be valid to all intents and purposes, as parts of this Constitution; Provided, That such proposed amendments shall be read on three several days in each house, as well when the same are proposed, as when they are finally ratified.

Done in Convention at New Echota, this twenty-sixth day of July, in the year of our Lord one thousand eight hundred and twenty seven. In testimony, whereof, we have each of us, here unto subscribed our names.

Cherokee Phoenix, vol. I, no. 1, February 21, 1828; vol. I, no. 2, February 28, 1828; vol. I, no. 3, March 6, 1828. Full text is available online at http://library.wcu.edu/CherokeePhoenix.

Cherokee Phoenix,
Statement of Purpose, 1828

Another significant emblem of acculturation in the Cherokee Nation was the first American Indian newspaper, the Cherokee Phoenix. *First published at the Cherokee capital of New Echota in 1828, the paper was made possible by Sequoyah's invention of a Cherokee alphabet, the sponsorship of the Cherokee National Council (for which the paper served as official spokesperson), and assistance from the American Board of Commissioners for Foreign Missions. Its first editor was Elias Boudinot, an erudite, New England–educated Cherokee, and its first issue carried the following statement of purpose, a learned and honorable sentiment that hardly squared with Georgia's depiction of these Indians as uneducable savages, a view that was symptomatic of the entire problem with the Cherokees, as far as removal proponents were concerned.*

NEW ECHOTA
Thursday, February 21, 1828
To The Public

We are happy in being able, at length, to issue the first number of our paper, although after a longer delay than we anticipated. This delay has been owing to unavoidable circumstances, which, we think, will be sufficient to acquit us, and though our readers and patrons may be wearied in the expectation of gratifying their eyes on this paper of no ordinary novelty, yet we hope their patience will not be so exhausted, but that they will give it a calm perusal, and pass upon it a candid judgment. It is far from our expectation that it will meet with entire and universal approbation, particularly from those who consider learning and science necessary to the merits of newspapers. Such must not expect to be gratified here, for the merits, (if merits they can be called,) on which our paper is expected to exist, are not alike with those which keep alive the political and religious papers of the day. We lay no claim to extensive information; and we sincerely hope, this public disclosure will save us from the severe criticisms, to which our ignorance of many things, will frequently expose us, in the future course of our editorial labors. Let the public but consider our motives, and the design of this paper, which is, the benefit of the Cherokees, and we are sure, those who wish well to the Indian race, will keep out of view all the failings and deficiencies of the Editor, and give a prompt support to the first paper ever published in the Indian country, and under the direction of some of the remnants of those, who by the most mysterious course of providence, have dwindled into oblivion. To prevent us from the like destiny, is certainly a laudable undertaking, which the Christian, the Patriot, and the Philanthropist will not be ashamed to aid. Many are now engaged, by various means and with various success, in attempting to rescue, not only us, but all our kindred tribes, from the impending danger which has been so fatal to our fore-fathers; and we are happy to be in a situation to tender them our public acknowledgements for their unwearied efforts. Our present undertaking is intended to be nothing more than a feeble auxiliary to these efforts. Those therefore, who are engaged for the good of the Indians of every tribe, and who pray that salvation, peace, and the comforts of civilized life may be extended to every Indian fire side on this continent, will consider us as co-workers together in their benevolent labors. To them we make our appeal for patronage, and pledge ourselves to encourage and assist them, in whatever appears to be for the benefit of the Aborigines.

In the commencement of our labours, it is due to our readers that we should acquaint them with the general principles, which we have prescribed to ourselves as rules in conducting this paper. These principles we shall accordingly state briefly. It may, however, be proper to observe that the establishment which has been lately purchased, principally with the charities of our white brethren is the property of the Nation and that the paper, which is now offered to the public, is patronized by, and under the direction of, the Cherokee Legislature, as will be seen in the Prospectus already before the public. As servants we are bound to that body, from which, however, we have not received any instructions, but are left at liberty to form such regulations for our conduct as will appear to us most conducive to the interests of the people, for whose benefit, this paper has been established.

As the Phoenix is a national paper, we shall feel ourselves bound to devote it to national purposes. "The laws and public documents of the Nation," and matters relating to the welfare and condition of the Cherokees as a people, will be faithfully published in English and Cherokee.

As the liberty of the press is so essential to the improvement of the mind, we shall consider our paper, a free paper, with, however, proper and usual restrictions. We shall reserve to ourselves the liberty of rejecting such communications as tend to evil, and such as are too intemperate and too personal. But the columns of this paper shall always be open to free and temperate discussions on matters of politics, religion, &c.

We shall avoid as much as possible, controversy on disputed doctrinal points in religion. Though we have our particular belief on this important subject, and perhaps are as strenuous upon it, as some of our brethren of a different faith, yet we conscientiously think, & in this thought we are supported by men of judgment that it would be injudicious, perhaps highly pernicious, to introduce to this people, the various minor differences of Christians. Our object is not sectarian; and if we had a wish to support, in our paper, the denomination with which we have the honor and privilege of being connected, yet we know our incompetency for the task.

We will not unnecessarily intermeddle with the politics and affairs of our neighbors. As we have no particular interest in the concerns of the surrounding states, we shall only expose ourselves to contempt and ridicule by improper intrusion. And though at times, we should do ourselves injustice, to be silent, on matters of great interest to the Cherokees, yet we will not return railing for railing, but consult mildness, for we have been taught to believe, that "A soft answer turneth away wrath; but grievous words stir up anger." The unpleasant controversy existing with the state of Georgia, of which many of our readers are aware, will frequently make our situation trying, by having hard sayings and threatenings thrown out against us, a specimen of which will be found in our next. We pray God that we may be delivered from such spirit.

In regard to the controversy with Georgia, and the present policy of the General Government, in removing, and concentrating the Indians, out of the limits of any state, which, by the way, appears to be gaining strength, we will invariably and faithfully state the feelings of the majority of our people. Our views, as a people, on this subject, have been most sadly misrepresented. These views we do not wish to conceal, but are willing that the public should know what we think of this policy, which, in our opinion, if carried into effect, will prove pernicious to us.

We have been asked which side of the Presidential question we should take. Our answer is, we think best to take a neutral stand, and we know that such a course is most prudent, as we have no vote on the question, and although we have our individual choice, yet it would be folly for us to spend words and time on a subject, which has engrossed very much, the attention of the public already.

In fine, we shall pay a sacred regard to truth, and avoid, as much as possible, that partiality to which we shall be exposed.—In relating facts of a local nature, whether political, moral, or religious, we shall take care that exaggeration shall not be our crime. We shall also feel ourselves bound to correct all mistatements, relating to the present conditions of the Cherokees.

How far we shall be successful in advancing the improvement of our people, is not now for us to decide. We hope, however, our efforts will not be altogether in vain.—Now is the moment when mere speculation on the practicability of civilizing us is out of the question. Sufficient and repeated evidence has been given, that Indians can be reclaimed from a savage state, and that with proper advantages, they are as capable of improvement in mind as any other people; and let it be remembered, notwithstanding the assertions of those who talk to the contrary, that this improvement can be made, not only by the Cherokees, but by all the Indians, in their present locations. We are rendered bold in making this assertion by considering the history of our people within the last fifteen years. There was a time within our remembrance, when darkness was sadly prevalent, and ignorance abounded amongst us—when strong and deep rooted prejudices were directed against many things relating to civilized (word unclear) had when it was thought a disgrace for a Cherokee to appear in the costume of a white man. We mention these things not by way of boasting, but to show to our readers that it is not a visionary thing to attempt to civilize and Christianize all the Indians, but highly practicable.

It is necessary for our white patrons to know that this paper is not intended to be a source of profit, and that its continuance must depend, in a great measure, on the liberal support which they may be pleased to grant us. Though our object is not gain, yet we with as much patronage, as will enable us to support the establishment without subjecting it to pecuniary difficulties. Those of our friends, who have done so much already for us by instructing us in the arts of civilized life, and enabling us to enjoy the blessings of education, and the comforts of religion, and to those exertions may be attributed the present means of improvement in this Nation, will not think it a hard matter that their aid should now be respectfully requested. In order that our paper may have an extensive circulation in this Nation and out of it, we have fixed upon the most liberal terms possible; such, in our opinion, as will render it as cheap as most of the Southern papers; and in order that our subscribers may be prompt in their remittances, we have made considerable difference between the first and the last payments. Those who have any experience in the management of periodicals will be sensible how important it is, that the payments of subscribers should be prompt and regular, particularly where the existence of a paper depends upon its own income. We sincerely hope that we shall never have any occasion to complain of the delinquency of any of our patrons.

We would now commit our feeble efforts to the good will and indulgence of the public, praying that God will attend them with his blessing, and hoping for that happy period, when all the Indian tribes of America shall arise, Phoenix like, from their ashes, and when the terms, "Indian depredation," "war whoop," "scalping knife" and the like, shall become obsolete, and for ever be "buried deep under ground."

Cherokee Phoenix, vol. I, no. 1, February 21, 1828. Full text is available online at http://library.wcu.edu/CherokeePhoenix.

First Blood Shed by the Georgians, 1830

White interlopers were more an annoyance than a problem for the Cherokees until the discovery of gold in the mountains of north Georgia in 1829. When unsavory whites poured in to hunt for gold, they also preyed on Cherokee homes and farms. Georgia authorities appeared indifferent. Tensions were thus running high when Cherokees complained about white squatters occupying their lands near the Alabama border, lands recognized as Cherokee by the federal government.

FIGURE 5

John Ross—Ross was principal chief of the Cherokee Nation and became
an eloquent opponent of removal. Under his guidance, Cherokees had
embraced many aspects of white culture, including their form of government, their participation in a market economy, and the publication of a
newspaper. Confronted with pressure for removal, Ross battled compliant
factions within his own tribe and sought relief from the U.S. judiciary but
was ultimately unsuccessful in all his efforts. *(Library of Congress)*

*Although the government sustained the Cherokee title, it refused to evict the squat-
ters, insisting it was the Cherokee's responsibility to police their own nation.
Accordingly, principal chief John Ross ordered it done. The subsequent evictions
immediately became a source of considerable controversy, especially when Cherokees were beaten or killed by angry whites in the aftermath. The* Cherokee
Phoenix and Indian Advocate *(by 1830 the newspaper had taken up the
cause of all Indians) weighed in on the matter: It urged calm and made clear that
Cherokees had every right to defend themselves and their property.*

Since writing the above, we have been told by a gentleman who
passed this place as an express to the agent, from the principal
chief, that a Cherokee has, at last, been killed by the intruders, and
three more taken bound into Georgia! We are not prepared this
week to give the public any particulars respecting this unpleasant
affair. The general facts are, however, these, the particulars of

which will be given in our next. A company of Cherokees, among whom were some of our most respectable citizens, constrained by the repeated aggressions and insults of a number of intruders, who had settled themselves far in the country, & likewise by the frequent losses sustained by many of our citizens in cattle and horses from their own countrymen, who are leagued in wickedness with our civilized brothers, started the other day, under the authority of the Principal Chief to correct, at least part of the evil. They were out two days, in which time they arrested four Cherokee horse-thieves. These received exemplary punishment. They found also 17 families of intruders, living, we believe, in Cherokee houses. These they ordered out and after safely taking out their beddings, chairs, &c. the houses were set on fire. In no instance was the least violence used on the part of the Cherokees. When the company returned home, five of them tarried on the way, who, we are sorry to say, had become intoxicated. In this situation, they were found by a company of intruders, twenty five in number.—One was killed, & three taken into Georgia.

Thus a circumstance, which we have for a long time dreaded, and which has been brought about by the neglect of the executive to remove the great nuisance to the Cherokees; has happened. We are nevertheless, glad, that the injury received is on the side of this nation. It has been the desire of our enemies that the Cherokees may be urged to some desperate act—thus far this desire has never been realized, and we hope, notwithstanding the great injury now sustained, their wanted forbearance will be continued. If our word will have any weight with our countrymen in this very trying time, we would say: forbear, forbear—revenge not, but leave vengeance to him "to whom vengeance belongeth."

P. S. On last Saturday, it was reported, that a large company of Georgians were on their way to arrest Mr. Ross and Major Ridge. We think it not improbable that an attempt of that kind will be made. If so, self defence, on the part of the Cherokees, many of whom, we understand, were at Ross's and Ridge's would undoubtedly be justifiable.

Cherokee Phoenix and Indians' Advocate, vol. II, no. 43, February 10, 1830. Full text available online at http://library.wcu.edu/CherokeePhoenix.

A Seminole Describes
White-Indian Relations, 1841

*Captured near the close of the Second Seminole War, the warrior-leader Coa-
cooche was brought to Colonel William Worth with the purpose of having the
Seminole leader persuade other Seminoles to lay down arms. He did convince
other Seminoles to surrender, but not before describing his perception of whites
and Seminole relations with them. The obvious bitterness of Coacooche's words
could not mask their poignancy, and his sentiments could have been uttered by
any Indian of his generation.*

Coacooche rose, evidently struggling to suppress a feeling which
made his manly form quiver with excitement: "I was once a boy,"
said he, in a subdued tone; "then I saw the white man afar off. I
hunted in these woods, first with a bow and arrow; then with a
rifle. I saw the white man, and was told he was my enemy. I could
not shoot him as I would a wolf or a bear; yet like these he came
upon me; horses, cattle, and fields, he took from me. He said he was
my friend; he abused our women and children, and told us to go
from the land. Still he gave me his hand in friendship; we took it;
whilst taking it, he had a snake in the other; his tongue was forked;
he lied, and stung us. I asked but for a small piece of these lands,
enough to plant and to live upon, far south, a spot where I could
place the ashes of my kindred, a spot only sufficient upon which I
could lay my wife and child. This was not granted me."

Wayne Moquin and Charles Van Coren, eds., *Great Documents in American Indian
History* (New York: Praeger, 1973), p. 156.

IV

Public Statements
and Government Policy

T *he U.S. attempt to integrate Indians into white society sometimes thrived, as the example of the Cherokees showed, but acculturation more often foundered because of Indian opposition. When whites wanted Indian lands, the most successful acculturation provided no defense, and the legal system ultimately proved impotent, realities that the Cherokees discovered in one of the most disgraceful incidents of removal.*

As early as 1804, removal was being considered—at least in theory— as a solution to Indian resistance to acculturation, and Thomas Jefferson suggested that part of the Louisiana Purchase could be set aside for an Indian enclave. But removal did not become policy until after the War of 1812, when white settlers began eyeing Indian lands. In 1825, President James Monroe officially sanctioned removal, and federal negotiators began formally broaching it with Indians. Five years later, Congress institutionalized the policy in the Indian Removal Act.

Indians, however, agreed to removal infrequently, always grudgingly at best and under some degree of coercion. Many Indians resolutely refused to consider it. The general public also found the idea of uprooting large populations from their homelands vaguely distasteful, and some condemned the policy as barbarous and degrading to a great nation.

In the documents that follow, we will see removal from four different perspectives: practical, moral, legislative, and legal. The first selection is an excerpt from the 1829 report submitted by Thomas L. McKenney, whom Andrew Jackson enlisted to promote removal as a humane way to preserve Indian cultures. McKenney had earlier supervised Indian trade for the government and since 1824 had been in the War Department over-seeing general Indian affairs (as the head of a bureau on Indian affairs, an entity created by Secretary of War John C. Calhoun). McKenney addressed the problem of Indian resistance to removal as a practical matter, and though he knew Indians well, he was willing to attribute their reluctance to relocate as self-interested tactics of jealous chiefs eager to hold on to their power. McKenney's perspective could be quite persuasive for those uncertain about the morality of Indian removal.

Thomas L. McKenney's Annual Report, November 17, 1829

ON THE 30TH MAY last, General Carroll, of Tennessee, was appointed Commissioner, to go among the Cherokee and Creek Indians, and hold conferences with them on the subject of emigration. On the 8th July following, General Coffee was united in the same commission. . . .

Meanwhile, Col. Montgomery, the Agent for the Cherokees, was acting under instructions growing out of the provisions of the treaty of Washington, of 6th May, 1828, and the Creek Agent, Col. Crowell, under the act of Congress of 20th May, 1826, to aid certain Indians of the Creek nation in their removal West of the Mississippi, and a subsequent act of 9th May, 1828, appropriating $50,000 with a view to the same object.

Under the treaty, of the 6th May, 1828, and with the means provided by Congress to carry the same into effect, Col. Montgomery has enrolled and sent off 510 souls, of whom 431 are Cherokees, and 79 blacks; and Col. Crowell has sent off 1200 Creeks. The evidence furnished the Department, as to the disposition of both those tribes to remove, is demonstrative of their willingness to go; but they are held in check by their chiefs and others, whose interest it is to keep them where they are. Among the Creeks, especially, the most severe punishments have been inflicted, by mutilating, and otherwise, those who had enrolled to go, and while in their camp, and where they supposed they would be protected. Such is the dread of these people of the violence of their chiefs, that they are afraid to express their wishes on this subject, except in whispers, and then only to those in whom they have entire confidence. It will be seen from Gen. Coffee's report . . . that a like terror is exercised over the Cherokees. It is by no means unnatural for the chiefs of those tribes to oppose the going away of their people. It would be unnatural if they did not. In proportion to the reduction of their numbers does their power decrease; and their love of power is not less strong than other people's. It confers distinctions, not only among themselves, but in relation, also, to neighboring tribes. And to this feeling may be superadded the uncertainty which rests upon the future, drawn from the lessons of the past. But there are, I respectfully suggest, remedies for both, and the Federal Government has the power to apply them. The presence of an armed force would effectually relieve the first; and the adoption of a system for their security, and preservation, and future happiness, that should be as effective and ample as it ought to be permanent, would relieve the last. I would not be mistaken as to the use that should be made of the military. Its presence should be preceded by the solemn declaration that it was coming not to compel a single Indian to quit the place of his choice, but only to protect those who desire to better their condition, and in the exercise of their wish to do so. Humanity seems to require this, and, if this measure had been adopted sooner, many who now smart under the lash of their chiefs, and who are doomed to pass the remainder of their lives with mutilated bodies, would be free from the one, and not have to endure the suffering and disgrace of the other.

Surely when States, in the exercise of their sovereignty, are extending their laws over a people whose chiefs admit (I refer to the Cherokees) that such a measure would "seal their destruction," and when every circumstance appears to have combined to render the great body of our Indians within the limits of States unhappy, and to impoverish and destroy them, something ought to be done for their relief. Justice demands it, and Humanity pleads for these people. The public sympathy is strongly excited.

The Florida Indians, there is little doubt, are willing to join the Creeks; and the dispositions of the Chickasaws are indicated by the extract herewith submitted, on the subject of their recent visit to seek a country. The Indians in Ohio, especially the Senecas and Delawares, seek to go. I submit a talk of the chiefs of the former, addressed to the President on this subject. The Agent, Col. M'Elvaine, is of opinion that, in five years, with the means to effect their removal; there will remain no Indians in Ohio.

* * *

In reference to emigration, and to the means necessary for its accomplishment, I beg leave respectfully to add, that, in lieu of the usual mode of estimating, for all the different branches of expenditure, upon the basis of numbers, for rations, transportation, &c., &c., which can never be done with certainty, (if not being possible to know beforehand how many will go,) a sum be appropriated and made applicable to emigration generally, and to compensation for improvements, and placed at the disposal of the Executive; and for this object I recommend the sum of $300,000. It is my opinion, also, that a great saving might be effected by changing the agencies for emigration from the local agents to contractors. I have seen nothing to induce a belief that the Agents employed among the Cherokees and Creeks have not been zealous; but it does appear to me that a saving of more than one-third of the cost of each emigrant could be realized upon contract. The Agents might be well employed, and usefully and abundantly, in cooperating, and especially in seeing that all the terms of the contracts in which the comfort, and health, &c., of the emigrants were concerned, were faithfully executed.

But it does appear to me as indispensable, that, as a first step in any great movement of the sort, the country on which it is proposed to place these people at rest, and forever, should be clearly defined, and nothing left unprovided for by the Government, that concerns either their security, preservation, or improvement. Nor should the emigrants be sent off to settle where and how they might list: but the whole business should, I respectfully submit, be conducted upon one regular and systematic plan: and what may be done in reference to the whole of it ought to be done with a view to their solid and lasting welfare.

Wilcomb E. Washburn, *The American Indian and the United States, A Documentary History— Volume 1* (New York: Random House, 1973), 11–13.

John Eaton and the Cherokees, 1829

It was clear from the start that fundamentally altering Indian relations would be a priority for Andrew Jackson's presidency. The administration had been in office only a few weeks when John Eaton, Jackson's secretary of war, scolded a Cherokee delegation led by John Ross for opposing removal. In counseling removal as a solution to Cherokee difficulties in Georgia, Eaton revealed more than an obvious break with the civilization program; his was an ominous warning that under Jackson, the government's patience would be thin and brittle, and its posture toward aggressive anti-Indian measures by state governments would be passive at best.

April 18, 1829

Friends and Brothers,

Your letter of the 17th of February, addressed to the late Secretary of War, has been brought to the notice of this Department, since the communication made to you on the 11th Instant; and having conversed freely and fully with the President of the United States, I am directed by him to submit the following as the views which are entertained, in reference to the subjects which you have submitted for consideration.

You state that "the Legislature of Georgia in defiance of the laws of the United States, and the most solemn Treaties existing," have extended a jurisdiction over your Nation to take effect in June 1830. That "your nation had no voice in the formation of the confederacy of the Union, and has ever been unshackled with the laws of individual states because independent of them"; and that consequently this act of Georgia is to be viewed, "in no other light, than a wanton usurpation of power, guaranteed to no State, neither by the common law of the land, nor by the laws of nature."

To all this, there is a plain and obvious answer, deducible from the known history of the Country. During the War of the Revolution, your nation was the friend and ally of Great Britain; a power which then claimed entire sovereignty, within the limits of what constituted the thirteen United States. By the declaration of Independence and subsequently the Treaty of 17 all the rights of sovereignty pertaining to Great Britain, became vested respectively in the original States, of this union, including North Carolina and Georgia, within whose territorial limits, as defined and known, your nation was then situated. If, as is the case, you have been permitted to abide on your lands from that period to the present, enjoying the right of soil, and privilege to hunt, it is not thence to be inferr'd, that this was anything more than a permission growing out of compacts with your nation; nor is it a circumstance whence, now to deny to those States, the exercise of their original Sovereignty.

In the year 1785, three years after the Independence of the States, which compose this union, had been acknowledged by Great Britain, a treaty, at Hopewell, was concluded with your nation by the United States. The emphatic language it contains cannot be mistaken, commencing as follows—

"The Commissioners plenipotentiaries of the United States in Congress assembled, give peace to all the Cherokees, and receive them into favor and protection of the United States of America." It proceeds then to allot, and to define your limits and your hunting grounds. You were secured, in the privilege of pursuing the game; and from encroachment by the whites. NO right however, save a mere possessory one, is by the provisions of the treaty of Hopewell conceded to your nation. The soil, and the use of it, were suffered to remain with you, while the Sovereignty abided, precisely where it did before, in those states within whose limits you were situated.

Subsequent to this, your people were at enmity with the United States, and waged war upon our frontier settlements; a desirable peace was not entered into with you, until 1791. At that period a good understanding obtained, hostilities ceased, and by the Treaty made and concluded, your nation was placed under the protection of our Government, and a guarantee given, favorable to the occupancy and possession of Your Country. But the United States, always mindful of the authority of the States, even when treating, for what was so much desired, peace with their red brothers, forbore to offer a guarantee adverse to the sovereignty of Georgia. They could not do so; they had not the power.

At a more recent period, to wit, in 1802, the State of Georgia, defining her own proper limits, ceded to the United States, all her western territory upon a condition which was accepted, "that the

United States shall, at their own expense, extinguish for the use of Georgia as early as the same can be peaceably obtained on reasonable terms, the Indian title, to all the lands within the State of Georgia." She did not ask the military arm of the Government to be employed, but in her mildness and forbearance, only, that the soil might be yielded to her, as soon as it could peaceably be obtained, and on reasonable terms. In relation to Sovereignty nothing is said, or hinted at in the compact; nor was it necessary or even proper, as both the parties to the agreement well knew that it was a right which already existed in the state in virtue of the declaration of our independence, and of the Treaty of 1783, afterwards concluded.

These things have been made known to you frankly, and after the most friendly manner; and particularly at the making of the treaty with your nation in 1817, when a portion of your people stipulated to remove to the West of the Mississippi; and yet it is alleged in your communication to this Department, that you have "been unshackled with the laws of individual States, because independent of them."

The course you have pursued of establishing an independent, substantive, government, within the territorial limits of the State of Georgia, adverse to her will, and contrary to her consent, has been the immediate cause, which has induced her, to depart from the forbearance, she has so long practiced; and in virtue of her authority, as a Sovereign, Independent State, to extend over your country, her Legislative enactments, which she and every other state embraced in the confederacy, from 1783 to the present time, when their independence was acknowledged and admitted, possessed the power to do, apart from any authority or opposing interference by the general government.

But suppose, and it is suggested, merely for the purpose of awakening your better judgment, that Georgia cannot, and ought not, to claim the exercise of such power. What alternative is then presented? In reply allow me to call your attention for a moment to the grave character of the course, which under a mistaken view of your own rights, you desire this Government to adopt. It is no less than an invitation, that she shall step forward to arrest the constitutional act of an independent State, exercised within her own limits. Should this be done, and Georgia persist in the maintenance of her rights, and her authority, the consequences might be, that the act would prove injurious to us, and in all probability ruinous to you. The sword might be looked to as the arbiter in such an interference. But this can never be done. The President cannot, and will not, beguile you with such an expectation. The arms of this country can never be employed, to stay any state of this Union from the exercise of those legitimate powers which attach, and belong to their sovereign character. An interference to the extent of affording you protection, and the occupancy of your soil is what is demanded of the justice of this Country and will not be withheld, yet in doing this, the right of permitting to You the enjoyment of a separate government, within the limits of a State, and denying the exercise of Sovereignty to that State, within her own limits, cannot be admitted. It is not within the range of powers granted by the states to the general government, and therefore not within its competency to be exercised.

In this view of the circumstances connected with your application, it becomes proper to remark that no remedy can be perceived, except that which frequently, heretofore has been submitted for your consideration, a removal beyond the Mississippi, where, alone, can be assured to you protection and peace. It must be obvious to you, and the President has instructed me again to bring it to your candid and serious consideration, that to continue where you are, within the territorial limits of an independent state, can promise you nothing but interruption and disquietude. Beyond the Mississippi your prospects will be different. There you will find no conflicting interests. The United States power and sovereignty, uncontrolled by the high authority of state jurisdiction, and resting on its own energies, will be able to say to you, in the language of your own nation, the soil shall be yours while the trees grow, or the streams run. But situated where you now are, he cannot hold to you such language, or consent to beguile you, by inspiring in your bosoms hopes and expectations, which cannot be realized. Justice and friendly feelings cherished towards our red brothers of the forest, demand that in all our intercourse, frankness should be maintained.

The President desires me to say, that the feelings entertained by him towards your people, are of the most friendly kind; and that in the intercourse heretofore, in past times, so frequently had with the Chiefs of your nation, he failed not to warn them of the consequences which would result to them from residing within the limits of

Sovereign States. He holds to them, now, no other language, than that which he has heretofore employed; and in doing so, feels convinced that he is pointing out that course which humanity and a just regard for the interest of the Indian will be found to sanction. In the view entertained by him of this important matter, there is but a single alternative, to yield to the operation of those laws, which Georgia claims, and has a right to extend throughout her own limits, or to remove, and by associating with your brothers beyond the Mississippi to become again united as one Nation, carving along with you that protection, which, there situated, it will be in the power of the government to extend. The Indians being thus brought together at a distance from their brothers, will be relieved from very many of those interruptions, which, situated as they are at present, are without a remedy. The Government of the United States will then be able to exercise over them a paternal, and superintending care to happier advantage, to stay encroachments, and preserve them in peace and amity with each other; while with the aid of schools a hope may be indulged, that ere long industry and refinement, will take the place of those wandering habits now so peculiar to the Indian character, the tendency of which is to impede them in their march to civilization.

Respecting the intrusions on your lands, submitted also for consideration, it is sufficient to remark, that of these the Department had already been advised, and instructions have been forwarded to the agent of the Cherokees directing him to cause their removal; and it is earnestly hoped, that on this matter, all cause for future complaint will cease, and the order prove effectual.

Francis Paul Prucha, ed., *Documents of United States Indian Policy* (Lincoln: University of Nebraska Press, 2000), 44–46.

Andrew Jackson Calls for Removal, 1829

Andrew Jackson's first Annual Message included a section that addressed the circumstance of eastern Indians and concluded that their removal was in the best interests of everyone, the Indians included. He couched his recommendation in

FIGURE 6

Andrew Jackson—His iron resolve and overwhelming political popularity made it impossible to resist President Jackson's push for legislation that would authorize the government to negotiate removal treaties and to fund transportation for evicted Indians. His claim that the removal policy was the most humane one for Indians would have been more persuasive if the policy had been humanely administered. *(Library of Congress)*

humanitarian terms that spoke of voluntary removal, but he also was clear that Indians who chose to remain by "the graves of their fathers" did so at the pleasure of the states and, by implication, at their own peril.

The condition and ulterior destiny of the Indian tribes within the limits of some of our States have become objects of much interest and importance. It has long been the policy of Government to introduce among them the arts of civilization, in the hope of gradually reclaiming them from a wandering life. This policy has, however, been coupled with another wholly incompatible with its success. Professing a desire to civilize and settle them, we have at the same time lost no opportunity to purchase their lands and thrust them farther into the wilderness. By this means they have not only been kept in a wandering state, but been led to look upon us as unjust and indifferent to their fate. Thus, though lavish in its expenditures upon the subject, Government has constantly defeated its own policy, and the Indians in general, receding farther and farther to the west, have retained their savage habits. A portion, however, of the Southern tribes, having mingled much with the whites and made some progress in the arts of civilized life, have lately attempted to erect an independent government within the limits of Georgia and Alabama. These States, claiming to be the only sovereigns within their territories, extended their laws over the Indians, which induced the latter to call upon the United States for protection.

Under these circumstances the question presented was whether the General Government had a right to sustain those people in their pretensions. The Constitution declares that "no new State shall be formed or erected within the jurisdiction of any other State" without the consent of its legislature. If the General Government is not permitted to tolerate the erection of a confederate State within the territory of one of the members of this Union against her consent, much less could it allow a foreign and independent government to establish itself there. Georgia became a member of the Confederacy which eventuated in our Federal Union as a sovereign State, always asserting her claim to certain limits, which, having been originally defined in her colonial charter and subsequently recognized in the treaty of peace, she has ever since continued to enjoy, except as they have been circumscribed by her own voluntary transfer of a portion of her territory to the United States in the articles of cession of 1802. Alabama was admitted into the Union on the same footing with the original States, with boundaries which were prescribed by Congress. There is no constitutional, conventional, or legal provision which allows them less power over the Indians within their borders than is possessed by Maine or New York. Would the people of Maine permit the Penobscot tribe to erect an independent government within their State? And unless they did would it not be the duty of the General Government to support them in resisting such a measure? Would the people of New York permit each remnant of the Six Nations within her borders to declare itself an independent people under the protection of the United States? Could the Indians establish a separate republic on each of their reservations in Ohio? And if they were so disposed would it be the duty of this Government to protect them in the attempt? If the principle involved in the obvious answer to these questions be abandoned, it will follow that the objects of this Government are reversed, and that it has become a part of its duty to aid in destroying the States which it was established to protect.

Actuated by this view of the subject, I informed the Indians inhabiting parts of Georgia and Alabama that their attempt to establish an independent government would not be countenanced by the Executive of the United States, and advised them to emigrate beyond the Mississippi or submit to the laws of those States.

Our conduct toward these people is deeply interesting to our national character. Their present condition, contrasted with what they once were, makes a most powerful appeal to our sympathies. Our ancestors found them the uncontrolled possessors of these vast regions. By persuasion and force they have been made to retire from river to river and from mountain to mountain, until some of the tribes have become extinct and others have left but remnants to preserve for awhile their once terrible names. Surrounded by the whites with their arts of civilization, which by destroying the resources of the savage doom him to weakness and decay, the fate of the Mohegan, the Narragansett, and the Delaware is fast overtaking the Choctaw, the Cherokee, and the Creek. That this fate surely awaits them if they remain within the limits of the States does not admit of a doubt. Humanity and national honor demand that every effort should be made to avert so great a calamity. It is too late to inquire whether it was just in the United States to include them and their territory within the bounds of new States, whose limits they could control. That step can not be retraced. A State can not be dismembered by Congress or restricted in the exercise of her constitutional power. But the people of those States and of every State, actuated by feelings of justice and a regard for our national honor, submit to you the interesting question whether something can not be done, consistently with the rights of the States, to preserve this much-injured race.

As a means of effecting this end I suggest for your consideration the propriety of setting apart an ample district west of the Mississippi, and without the limits of any State or Territory now formed, to be guaranteed to the Indian tribes as long as they shall occupy it, each tribe having a distinct control over the portion designated for its use. There they may be secured in the enjoyment of governments of their own choice, subject to no other control from the United States than such as may be necessary to preserve peace on the frontier and between the several tribes. There the benevolent may endeavor to teach them the arts of civilization, and, by promoting union and harmony among them, to raise up an interesting commonwealth, destined to perpetuate the race and to attest the humanity and justice of this Government.

This emigration should be voluntary, for it would be as cruel as unjust to compel the aborigines to abandon the graves of their fathers and seek a home in a distant land. But they should be distinctly informed that if they remain within the limits of the States they must be subject to their laws. In return for their obedience as individuals they will without doubt be protected in the enjoyment of those possessions which they have improved by their industry. But it seems to me visionary to suppose that in this state of things claims can be allowed on tracts of country on which they have neither dwelt nor made improvements, merely because they have seen them from the mountain or passed them in the chase. Submitting to the laws of the States, and receiving, like other citizens, protection in their persons and property, they will ere long become merged in the mass of our population.

James D. Richardson, comp., *A Compilation of the Messages and Papers of the Presidents, 1789–1908,* vol. 2 (Washington, DC: Bureau of National Literature and Art, 1908), 456–59.

Jackson's wishes were soon translated into an Indian removal bill that caused prolonged and heated debate in Congress during the spring of 1830. The following two selections provide a characteristic sample of opposition to and advocacy for the measure.

FIGURE 7

An Indian Town—Andrew Jackson depicted all Indians as roving savages, but he was aware of the existence of such settlements as depicted here: stationary towns where Indians resided in dwellings surrounded by croplands and pastures. This type of town was typical of southeastern Indians, collectively known as the Five Civilized Tribes. *(Library of Congress)*

Edward Everett Opposes
Indian Removal, 1830

Representative Edward Everett of Massachusetts had already distinguished himself in public life at the time of the debates, and his condemnation of the proposed legislation was an eloquent appeal to common sense, fair play, and the preservation of American honor.

19 May 1830

Such is the bill of which we are told that there is nothing in it objectionable, that it contemplates nothing compulsory. This is the removal which is said to be voluntary. These are the laws which are said to have no connection with the subject; into which we have been told it is irrelevant and idle to inquire.

Nothing to do with the subject! Take the bill as it is! Not to presume that Georgia, Alabama, or Mississippi has passed, or can pass,
any law that varies this question! Why, it is the very point on which
the rightfulness of the measure turns. Here is wrapped up the great
objection to the removal, that it is compulsory; an objection which
we published ten thousand copies of the report of the Indian committee to obviate; and which is not touched, I believe, in that report.
The State laws [have] nothing to do with our legislation! Why, they
are the very means on which our agents rely to move the Indians.
It is the argument first and last on their tongues. The President uses
it; the Secretary uses it; the commissioners use it. The States have
passed the laws. You cannot live under them. We cannot and shall
not protect you from them. We advise you, as you would save your
dear lives from destruction, to go.

I appeal to the House if I overstate this point.

The question, then, is, shall we nerve the arm of this State legislation, which is put forth forcibly to remove the Indians? That is the
question for us to decide. It is the only question, and we are the only
authority. This Congress is the only tribunal clothed with power to
decide it. It depends on our vote; and it depends on nothing else. It
is the business of the President to enforce our laws, not the laws of
the States. He is solemnly sworn, to the best of his ability, to "preserve, protect, and defend the constitution of the United States," to
take care that the laws we pass are faithfully executed; and "this constitution and the laws of the United States made in pursuance thereof,
and all treaties made, or which shall be made, under the authority
of the United States, shall be the supreme law of the land, and the
judges in every State shall be bound thereby, any thing in the constitution or laws of any State to the contrary notwithstanding."

The President, then, has no power in this matter but to execute
the laws and treaties of the United States. The great question is to
be settled by us. We are to protect the Indians from this legislation,
or abandon them to it. No other power on earth can do it.

Sir, it is force. The President himself authorizes us to call it force.
In his message, at the opening of the session, he says: "By persuasion and force they have been made to retire from river to river, and
from mountain to mountain." When were any means employed to
detrude the Indians; better entitled than these laws to the name of
force? He does not probably refer to open wars against hostile

nations, in which he has been himself, so beneficially for his country, and so much to his own fame, distinguished. No. I take the message to intend legislative force, moral force, duress; the untiring power of civilized man pushing his uncivilized neighbor farther and farther into the woods. This I take to be the force to which the President alludes. And if this kind of action, unavoidably incident to the contiguity of the two races, be justly called force, how much more so the legislation of which the Indians complain, avowedly instituted to effect their removal, and confessedly insupportable in its nature!

Sir, it is force. It is because it is force that our interference for protection is invoked. I know it comes in the form of law; but is not the law force? Suppose the Indians disobey the laws, (and they are no more bound to obey them than the Mexicans are,) is there no force then? Are not the sheriff, the constable; the jailor, the executioner, ministers of force? No force? A law passed over my head by a power which I cannot resist, a law intended to make me fly the country, because I cannot live under it, and I not forced to go?

* * *

[The policy of removal] has proved utterly abortive, so long as it was conducted on the only rightful and equitable principle, that of the free consent of the Indians. It is because their free consent could not be obtained; it is because it is well known that voluntarily they would never go, that the States have extended over them a coercive legislation, under which it is avowed that they cannot and will not live; and now we are asked to furnish the means to effect their voluntary removal.

* * *

Such are the people we are going to remove from their homes: people, living, as we do, by husbandry, and the mechanic arts, and the industrious trades; and so much the more interesting, as they present the experiment of a people rising from barbarity into civilization. We are going to remove them from these their homes to a distant wilderness. Whoever heard of such a thing before? Whoever read of such a project? Ten or fifteen thousand families, to be rooted up, and carried hundreds, aye, a thousand of miles into the wilderness! There is not such a thing in the annals of mankind. It was the practice—the barbarous and truly savage practice—of the

polished nations of antiquity to bring home a part of the population of conquered countries as slaves. It was a cruel exercise of the
rights of the conqueror, as then understood, and in turn practised,
by all nations. But in time of peace, toward unoffending communities, subject to our sovereignty indeed, but possessing rights guarantied to them by more than one hundred treaties, to remove them,
against their will, by thousands, to a distant and a different country,
where they must lead a new life, and form other habits, and
encounter the perils and hardships of a wilderness: sir, I never
heard of such a thing; it is an experiment on human life and
human happiness of perilous novelty. Gentlemen, who favor the
project, cannot have viewed it as it is. They think of a march of
Indian warriors, penetrating, with their accustomed vigor, the forest or the cane brake—they think of the youthful Indian hunter,
going forth exultingly to the chase. Sir, it is no such thing. This is all
past; it is a matter of distant tradition, and poetical fancy. They
have nothing now left of the Indian, but his social and political
inferiority. They are to go in families, the old and the young, wives
and children, the feeble, the sick. And how are they to go? Not in
luxurious carriages; they are poor. Not in stage coaches; they go to
a region where there are none. Not even in wagons, nor on horse-
back, for they are to go in the least expensive manner possible.
They are to go on foot; nay, they are to be driven by contract. The
price has been reduced, and is still further to be reduced, and it is
to be reduced, by sending them by contract. It is to be screwed
down to the least farthing, to eight dollars per head. A community
of civilized people, of all ages, sexes, and conditions of bodily
health, are to be dragged hundreds of miles, over mountains, rivers,
and deserts, where there are no roads, no bridges, no habitations,
and this is to be done for eight dollars a head; and done by contract.
The question is to be, what is the least for which you will take so
many hundred families, averaging so many infirm old men, so
many little children, so many lame, feeble, and sick? What will you
contract for? The imagination sickens at the thought of what will
happen to a company of these emigrants, which may prove less
strong, less able to pursue the journey than was anticipated. Will
the contractor stop for the old men to rest, for the sick to get well,
for the fainting women and children to revive? He will not; he cannot afford to. And this process is to be extended to every family, in

a population of seventy-five thousand souls. This is what we call the removal of the Indians!

It is very easy to talk of this subject, reposing on these luxurious chairs, and protected by these massy walls, and this gorgeous canopy, from the power of the elements. Removal is a soft word, and words are delusive. But let gentlemen take the matter home to themselves and their neighbors. There are seventy-five thousand Indians to be removed.

* * *

Sir, this policy cannot come to good. It cannot, as it professes, elevate the Indian. It must and will dishearten, depress, and crush him. If he has within him a spark of that pride, without which there can be no rational improvement, this gloomy policy would subdue it. I have labored hard to take an opposite view of the subject; but there is no bright side to it. It is all unmingled, unmitigated evil. There is evil on the other side, but none commensurate with that of this compulsory removal.

There, sir, I set my foot; it is compulsory. If you will treat the Indians as free agents; if you will withdraw your legal duress; if they are willing, after exploring the country, to go, I am willing they should, and will join in making the appropriation. But while the laws exist, beneath which they cannot live, it is in vain to tell me they are willing to go. How do you know it? Do you tell me a man, locked up in prison, does not wish to come out! How do you know it? Unlock the prison doors, and then you can tell.

* * *

The evil, sir, is enormous; the violence is extreme; the breach of public faith deplorable; the inevitable suffering incalculable. Do not stain the fair fame of the country: it has been justly said, it is in the keeping of Congress, on this subject. It is more wrapped up in this policy, in the estimation of the civilized world, than in all your other doings. Its elements are plain, and tangible, and few. Nations of dependent Indians, against their will, under color of law, are driven from their homes into the wilderness. You cannot explain it, you cannot reason it away. The subtleties, which satisfy you, will not satisfy the severe judgment of enlightened Europe. Our friends there will view this measure with sorrow, and our enemies alone with joy.

And we ourselves, sir, when the interests and passions of the day are past, will look back upon it, I fear, with self-reproach, and a regret as bitter as unavailing.

Congressional Debates, 27th Cong., 1st sess., 1061, 1063, 1068, 1070, 1079.

Henry G. Lamar Supports Indian Removal, 1830

On the other side, Henry G. Lamar just as fervently supported removal, doubtless because he was an avid follower of Andrew Jackson's and because he was from Georgia, the state most resolutely committed to the complete expulsion of its Indian population. Lamar emphasized as the overarching consideration the federal government's obligation to fulfill its promises and challenged assertions that removal was either compulsory for or injurious to Indians.

May 19, 1830

Sir, it is unnecessary to further scan the course of policy pursued by other States. Georgia would disdain to exercise the authority if derived from precedents only. Let us proceed to inquire into the expediency of this Government extending its aid in the exertion of all honorable and necessary means to the effectuation of their [the Indians] removal and colonization. It is due to Georgia as a right, it is necessary to preserve the plighted faith of the United States, and will meliorate the condition of the Indians themselves. The State of Georgia and the United States, since 1802, have occupied the attitude of creditor and debtor, without the benefit of an appeal to any tribunal or umpire to enforce the obligation, or to determine whether or not the debtor has acted in good faith. This perplexing and unpleasant situation, as might have been expected, has been the fruitful source of controversy between the State and the Federal Governments. It should be desirable to all to remove the cause, and, by so doing, put a termination to their well founded complaints. By the compact, the United States, so soon as it could be done "peaceably, and on reasonable terms," was bound to extinguish, for the use of Georgia, the possessory right of the Indians to all the lands within the limits of that State. Twenty-seven years have elapsed since the fulfilment of this promise was assumed. Two new and flourishing States, rising with Georgia in population and wealth, have been erected out of the territory she parted with as the consideration of this undertaking; and, in apparent disregard of the conditions of the compact, titles have been extinguished for other States (where there was no such obligation) to Cherokee lands, equal, if not greater than that claimed by Georgia. It is a maxim which the law enforces between individuals, that they must be just before they can be generous. It is equally correct in its application to communities or Governments; and had the United States acted in conformity to this principle, Georgia would have had no just grounds of complaint.

But a different course has been pursued, and the consequences are, that that State has an Indian population of five thousand souls, quartered upon five million two hundred and sixty-nine thousand one hundred and sixty acres of land within her limits, if we include in the estimate the disputed territory; nor is this all: not content with the rights of occupancy, they have erected within her bosom an independent Government, and claim the right of enforcing upon her citizens their bloody code. Under these circumstances, the alternative was presented, either to acquiesce, and tacitly admit the lawfulness of their pretensions to an independent Government, or, by an exertion of her sovereign authority, to prostrate all hopes to it. She chose the latter course; and there is sufficient moral firmness in that State to execute her lawful purposes, to disregard unjust censure, the cant of hypocrisy, or the movement of a political party, however masked under the imposing garb of philanthropy. But from this unpleasant situation it is desirable to be relieved; and is it not due to her, that the United States should act with becoming liberality, not with the view only of their transmigration beyond the Mississippi, but to fulfil her engagements with Georgia, and meet the expectations which her Citizens reposed in the justice and integrity of this Government? There is no real or imaginary evil in voting for an appropriation, however large; no force is to be employed, no coercion contemplated. They will be left to their own judgment, and the adoption of their own course, uncontrolled by the restraints or exactions of this Government. If, in the full exercise of this discretion, they should prefer to emigrate, sooner than to remain subject to the authority of the States, affording the means to them to do so is only a compliance, so far as the Cherokees are concerned, with the obligations of the United States to Georgia. Should they decline an exchange of situation, no difficulty can occur. It will not be one of those fatal delusions where the error of misguided policy shall have compromitted the interest of the Government beyond the hope of avoidance or escape. For, should the attempt be abortive, the appropriation, to the extent it shall not have accomplished its purpose, will remain unexpended. If successful, the United States will be reimbursed in the sale of the lands occupied by the Creeks, Choctaws, and that portion of the lands occupied by the Cherokees in the State of Alabama. Sir, if gentlemen are sincere in their regard for the future condition and welfare of the Indians; if feelings of disinterested benevolence are indulged for them; let past experience be the guide to direct, and the remnants of other tribes serve as beacons to admonish against the causes of their extermination: whether they have been of a moral, physical, or political character, it matters not. Should they remain where they are, as certain as a like cause produces the same effect, they will inevitably experience the same fate. It is admitted that they, in common with the human family, indulge their local attachments; and, unless inducements are offered, or there is a hope of bettering their condition, that they will reluctantly abandon their present habitation. But it cannot be denied but that there are countervailing considerations to induce a removal. Their game is destroyed. They are unfavorably situated to advance one grade above the wandering savage, to the life of herdsmen, which is the natural progress of society. A sudden transition from the former to the husbandman, is too great to be voluntarily adopted. It will not be until every other expedient is exhausted and necessity forces it on them. It is incompatible with their inclinations and habits of indolence. The country to which they are invited is favorable in this point of view. Their relations and friends who have gone before them, have experienced the advantages of this change. Instead (as has been stated in debate) of their sending back their curses on us, they are soliciting their tribes to follow their example. Pass the bill on your table, and there is no doubt but that a part will go at once, and ultimately the balance could not be restrained—go they will.

Sir, we have had the most favorable representation given the increasing improvement and comforts of the southern Indians, and that urged as an objection to their removal. It may be the case with a few chiefs and half breeds; but those best acquainted with the mass of their population, deny that it is so with them. Whoever has witnessed the progress of civilization, cannot be insensible of the great disparity which it produces in their situation. Its advancement is slow, and confined to a few. It elevates their standing, and acquires for them a controlling Influence, which is directed to the advancement of their own interest, and that of their immediate connexions. The notions of separate property, which it begets, engenders feelings of avarice, and their intellectual superiority enables them to gratify this propensity. The consequence is, that the property of the nation is concentrated in the hands of few, while nine-tenths of them are proportionably miserably poor, abject, servile, and degraded. I care not to which tribe your attention may be directed, to the Creeks or the Cherokees; the rapacity of the chiefs has reduced them to this state of poverty and degradation.

Congressional Debates, 27th Cong., 1st sess., 1119–20.

Indian Removal Act of 1830

At the close of the congressional debate, opponents of removal had made persuasive arguments, but in many respects the conclusion of the process was foreordained by Jackson's popularity and the temptation posed by vast tracts of land to be made available for white settlement. Indian removal did not pass with overwhelming majorities, but it did not need to. While the law did not specifically empower the government to remove Indians by force, it provided the means to do so in the hands of men willing to use it. As of May 28, 1830, the days of eastern Indians residing unmolested on their lands were numbered.

An Act to provide for an exchange of lands with the Indians residing in any of the states or territories, and for their removal west of the river Mississippi.

FIGURE 8

The Grand National Caravan Moving East—Shortly after beginning his second term, Jackson toured New England, and this political cartoon of the time lampoons Jackson's popularity while providing a sardonic commentary on Indian removal. *(Library of Congress)*

Be it enacted by the Senate and House of Representatives of the United States of America, in Congress assembled, That it shall and may be lawful for the President of the United States to cause so much of any territory belonging to the United States, west of the river Mississippi, not included in any state or organized territory, and to which the Indian title has been extinguished, as he may judge necessary, to be divided into a suitable number of districts, for the reception of such tribes or nations of Indians as may choose to exchange the lands where they now reside, and remove there; and to cause each of said districts to be so described by natural or artificial marks, as to be easily distinguished *from* every other.

SEC. 2. *And be it further enacted,* That it shall and may be lawful *for* the President to exchange any or all of such districts, so to be laid off and described, with any tribe or nation of Indians now residing within the limits of any of the states or territories, and with which the United States have existing treaties, for the whole or any part or portion of the territory claimed and occupied by such tribe or nation, within the bounds of any one or more of the states or territories, where the land claimed and occupied by the Indians, is owned by the United States, or the United States are bound to the state within which it lies to extinguish the Indian claim thereto.

SEC. 3. *And be it further enacted,* That in the making of any such exchange or exchanges, it shall and may be lawful for the President solemnly to assure the tribe or nation with which the exchange is made, that the United States will forever secure and guaranty to them, and their heirs or successors, the country so exchanged with them; and if they prefer it, that the United States will cause a patent or grant to be made and executed to them for the same: *Provided always,* That such lands shall revert to the United States, if the Indians become extinct, or abandon the same.

SEC. 4. *And be it further enacted,* That if, upon any of the lands now occupied by the Indians, and to be exchanged for, there should be such improvements as add value to the land claimed by any individual or individuals of such tribes or nations, it shall and may be lawful for the President to cause such value to be ascertained by appraisement or otherwise, and to cause such ascertained value to be paid to the person or persons rightfully claiming such improvements. And upon the payment of such valuation, the improvements so valued and paid for, shall pass to the United States, and possession shall not afterwards be permitted to any of the same tribe.

SEC. 5. *And be it further enacted,* That upon the making of any such exchange as is contemplated by this act, it shall and may be lawful for the President to cause such aid and assistance to be furnished to the emigrants as may be necessary and proper to enable them to remove to, and settle in, the country for which they may have exchanged; and also, to give them such aid and assistance as may be necessary for their support and subsistence for the first year after their removal.

SEC. 6. *And be it further enacted,* That it shall and may be lawful for the President to cause such tribe or nation to be protected, at their new residence, against all interruption or disturbance from any other tribe or nation of Indians, or from any other person or persons whatever.

SEC. 7. *And be it further enacted,* That it shall and may be lawful for the President to have the same superintendence and care over any tribe or nation in the country to which they may remove, as contemplated by this act, that he is now authorized to have over them at their present places of residence: *Provided,* That nothing in this act contained shall be construed as authorizing or directing the violation of any existing treaty between the United States and any of the Indian tribes.

SEC. 8. *And be it further enacted,* That for the purpose of giving effect to the provisions of this act, the sum of five hundred thousand dollars is hereby appropriated, to be paid out of any money in the treasury, not otherwise appropriated.

APPROVED, May 28, 1830.

Statutes at Large of the United States of America, 1789–1873, vol. 4 (Washington, DC, 1846), 411–12.

Commissioner of Indian Affairs Elbert Herring Describes Removal as Humane, 1831

In 1831, Congress authorized the president to appoint a Commissioner of Indian Affairs within the War Department at an annual salary of $3,000. For most of Andrew Jackson's presidency, the commissioner was Elbert Herring, a New England lawyer and an accomplished bureaucrat. Herring's report in the year after removal's enactment painted a rosy picture of the developing process, although close observers knew that often removal negotiations were dubious and that dire problems plagued the westward journeys. Herring did note, however, that Cherokee chiefs were proving stubbornly resistant to removal, a stance he claimed did not represent the wishes of the Cherokee Nation. Believing in that claim, unabashedly set forth in an official government document, made it easier for Herring to dismiss resistant Cherokee chiefs as counterfeits and to treat a compliant minority as bona fide, precisely what happened at New Echota four years later.

November 19, 1831

The humane policy, exemplified in the system adopted by the Government with respect to the Indian tribes residing within the limits of the United States, which is now in operation, is progressively developing its good effects: and, it is confidently trusted, will at no distant day, be crowned with complete success. Gradually diminishing in numbers and deteriorating in condition; incapable of coping with the superior intelligence of the white man, ready to fall into the vices, but unapt to appropriate the benefits of the social state: the increasing tide of white population threatened soon to engulf them, and finally to cause their total extinction. The progress is slow but sure; the cause is inherent in the nature of things; tribes numerous and powerful have disappeared from among us in a ratio of decrease, ominous to the existence of those that still remain, unless counteracted by the substitution of some principle sufficiently potent to check the tendencies to decay and dissolution. This salutary principle exists in the system of removal; of change of residence; of salutary principle in territories exclusively their own, and under the protection of the United States; connected with the benign influences of education and instruction in agriculture and the several mechanic arts, whereby social is distinguished from savage life.

In pursuance of this policy, the necessary measures have been taken for the execution of the Choctaw treaty ratified at the last session of Congress, and the Indians of that tribe are now in motion. It is presumed that about 5000 will emigrate west of the Mississippi before the winter sets in; and there are the best grounds for believing, that a much greater number will go over in the course of the ensuing year. Sanguine expectations may thus be indulged, that the whole nation will be moved within the time (three years) prescribed by the treaty.

The Chickasaw Indians who are disposed to follow their friends and neighbors, the Choctaws, and to reside near them, have not yet been provided with suitable lands. For the purpose of procuring such for their accommodation, it became necessary to effect an arrangement with the Choctaws for a cession of a portion of their country in the west. Major John H. Eaton and General John Coffee have accordingly been constituted commissioners to treat with the Choctaws for this object. In the event of a successful issue of their negotiation, the removal of the Chickasaws will probably take place before the termination of another year,

The chiefs of the Cherokees have given, as yet, no evidence of a relinquishment of their determination not to accept the propositions of the Government, so cordially embraced by the tribes beforementioned for an exchange of lands and residence. The influence of the Indian chief is of a nature to overrule the general wish, which, if allowed to express itself freely might be favorable to removal. Being induced to believe, from information to be relied on, that a number of the tribe would emigrate, if encouraged and aided by the Government, the department endeavored to revive emigration under the provisions of the treaty of 1828. The plan is in operation, but is of too recent date to admit of calculating the probability and extent of its success.

The Creek Indians are in the same predicament—their position having been unaltered through the past year. Involved in difficulties, they have shown no inclination to relieve themselves from the embarrassment of their situation, by accepting the liberal and often-repeated propositions of the Government. It is to be hoped that the time will shortly come, when better counsels will prevail, and a juster appreciation of the benefits submitted to their choice, open their eyes to a sense of their real interests.

Wilcomb E. Washburn, *The American Indian and the United States, A Documentary History—Volume 1* (New York: Random House, 1973), 18–19.

Cherokee Nation v. *State of Georgia,* 1831

Beset by Georgia's effort to extend state law into the Cherokee Nation, Cherokees sought relief from the U.S. Supreme Court. In 1831, in the case of Cherokee Nation v. State of Georgia, *Chief Justice John Marshall handed down a lengthy ruling that clearly sympathized with the Indians but asserted that the Court did not have jurisdiction. Because Indians constituted "domestic dependent nations" instead of foreign nations with rights of sovereignty, the Court did not have the authority to intervene. The decision understandably disappointed and disillusioned the Cherokees who were thus left helpless before Georgia's relentless program of harassment.*

Mr Chief Justice MARSHALL delivered the opinion of the Court.

This bill is brought by the Cherokee nation, praying an injunction to restrain the state of Georgia from the execution of certain laws of that state, which, as is alleged, go directly to annihilate the Cherokees as a political society, and to seize, for the use of Georgia, the lands of the nation which have been assured to them by the United States in solemn treaties repeatedly made and still in force.

If courts were permitted to indulge their sympathies, a case better calculated to excite them can scarcely be imagined. A people once numerous, powerful, and truly independent, found by our ancestors in the quiet and uncontrolled possession of an ample domain, gradually sinking beneath our superior policy, our arts and our arms, have yielded their lands by successive treaties, each of which contains a solemn guarantee of the residue, until they retain no more of their formerly extensive territory than is deemed necessary to their comfortable subsistence. To preserve this remnant, the present application is made.

Before we can look into the merits of the case, a preliminary inquiry presents itself. Has this court jurisdiction of the cause?

The third article of the constitution describes the extent of the judicial power. The second section closes an enumeration of the cases to which it is extended, with 'controversies' 'between a state or the citizens thereof, and foreign states, citizens, or subjects.' A subsequent clause of the same section gives the supreme court original jurisdiction in all cases in which a state shall be a party. The party defendant may then unquestionably be sued in this court. May the plaintiff sue in it? Is the Cherokee nation a foreign state in the sense in which that term is used in the constitution?

The counsel for the plaintiffs have maintained the affirmative of this proposition with great earnestness and ability. So much of the argument as was intended to prove the character of the Cherokees as a state, as a distinct political society, separated from others, capable of managing its own affairs and governing itself, has, in the opinion of a majority of the judges, been completely successful.

They have been uniformly treated as a state from the settlement of our country. The numerous treaties made with them by the United States recognize them as a people capable of maintaining the relations of peace and war, of being responsible in their political character for any violation of their engagements, or for any aggression committed on the citizens of the United States by any individual of their community. Laws have been enacted in the spirit of these treaties. The acts of our government plainly recognize the Cherokee nation as a state, and the courts are bound by those acts.

A question of much more difficulty remains. Do the Cherokees constitute a foreign state in the sense of the constitution?

The counsel have shown conclusively that they are not a state of the union, and have insisted that individually they are aliens, not owing allegiance to the United States. An aggregate of aliens composing a state must, they say, be a foreign state. Each individual being foreign, the whole must be foreign.

* * *

Though the Indians are acknowledged to have an unquestionable, and, heretofore, unquestioned right to the lands they occupy, until that right shall be extinguished by a voluntary cession to our government; yet it may well be doubted whether those tribes which reside within the acknowledged boundaries of the United States can, with strict accuracy, be denominated foreign nations. They may, more correctly, perhaps, be denominated domestic dependent nations. They occupy a territory to which we assert a title independent of their will, which must take effect in point of possession when their right of possession ceases. Meanwhile they are in a state of pupilage. Their relation to the United States resembles that of a ward to his guardian.

They look to our government for protection; rely upon its kindness and its power; appeal to it for relief to their wants; and address the president as their great father. They and their country are considered by foreign nations, as well as by ourselves, as being so completely under the sovereignty and dominion of the United States, that any attempt to acquire their lands, or to form a political connexion with them, would be considered by all as an invasion of our territory, and an act of hostility.

* * *

The court has bestowed its best attention on this question, and, after mature deliberation, the majority is of opinion that an Indian tribe or nation within the United States is not a foreign state in the sense of the constitution, and cannot maintain an action in the courts of the United States.

* * *

If it be true that the Cherokee nation have rights, this is not the tribunal in which those rights are to be asserted. If it be true that wrongs have been inflicted, and that still greater are to be apprehended, this is not the tribunal which can redress the past or prevent the future.

The motion for an injunction is denied.

Full text is available online at http://laws.findlaw.com/us/30/1.html.

Worcester v. *State of Georgia,* 1832

As part of its program of legislative persecution and to impede missionaries from encouraging Indians, Georgia passed an act in 1831 that required white males residing among Indians to swear allegiance to the state. In September 1831, a Gwinnett County court indicted missionary Samuel A. Worcester (pronounced "Wooster") and other whites for violating this law. Worcester maintained that the Georgia statute violated the U.S. Constitution as well as a variety of treaties with the Cherokee Nation and the Trade and Intercourse Act. The Georgia court was unimpressed. It convicted Worcester and sentenced him to four years at hard labor in the state penitentiary, but he secured the services of William Wirt and appealed to the U.S. Supreme Court. When the Court handed down its decision the following year, it seemed a resounding victory for not only Worcester but the Cherokees as well. Speaking for the Court, Chief Justice John Marshall provided a voluminous review of American legal history and practices regarding colonial charters and state sovereignty. He finally concluded that Georgia had no right to extend its laws over the Cherokee Nation and consequently Samuel Worcester should be set free. But the Cherokee's judicial victory was rendered inconsequential when Georgia ignored the Court's decision and Andrew Jackson did not compel the state's submission to it. As for Worcester, he remained in custody until Georgia governor Wilson Lumpkin arranged his release in 1833. Greatly disheartened by the impotence of the federal courts and convinced that Cherokee removal was inevitable, he preceded them to the Indian Territory and remained there to ease their transition after removal and to help them revive their newspaper in their new lands.

Mr Chief Justice MARSHALL delivered the opinion of the Court.

This cause, in every point of view in which it can be placed, is of the deepest interest.

The defendant is a state, a member of the union, which has exercised the powers of government over a people who deny its jurisdiction, and are under the protection of the United States.

The plaintiff is a citizen of the state of Vermont, condemned to hard labour for four years in the penitentiary of Georgia; under colour of an act which he alleges to be repugnant to the constitution, laws, and treaties of the United States.

The legislative power of a state, the controlling power of the constitution and laws of the United States, the rights, if they have any, the political existence of a once numerous and powerful people, the personal liberty of a citizen, are all involved in the subject now to be considered.

* * *

The Cherokee nation, then, is a distinct community occupying its own territory, with boundaries accurately described, in which the laws of Georgia can have no force, and which the citizens of Georgia have no right to enter, but with the assent of the Cherokees themselves, or in conformity with treaties, and with the acts of congress. The whole intercourse between the United States and this nation, is, by our constitution and laws, vested in the government of the United States.

The act of the state of Georgia, under which the plaintiff in error was prosecuted, is consequently void, and the judgment a nullity. Can this court revise, and reverse it?

If the objection to the system of legislation, lately adopted by the legislature of Georgia, in relation to the Cherokee nation, was confined to its extra-territorial operation, the objection, though complete, so far as respected mere right, would give this court no power over the subject. But it goes much further. If the review which has been taken be correct, and we think it is, the acts of Georgia are repugnant to the constitution, laws, and treaties of the United States.

They interfere forcibly with the relations established between the United States and the Cherokee nation, the regulation of which, according to the settled principles of our constitution, are committed exclusively to the government of the union.

They are in direct hostility with treaties, repeated in a succession of years, which mark out the boundary that separates the Cherokee country from Georgia; guaranty to them all the land within their boundary; solemnly pledge the faith of the United States to restrain their citizens from trespassing on it; and recognize the pre-existing power of the nation to govern itself.

They are in equal hostility with the acts of congress for regulating this intercourse, and giving effect to the treaties.

The forcible seizure and abduction of the plaintiff in error, who was residing in the nation with its permission, and by authority of the president of the United States, is also a violation of the acts which authorise the chief magistrate to exercise this authority.

Will these powerful considerations avail the plaintiff in error? We think they will. He was seized, and forcibly carried away, while under guardianship of treaties guarantying the country in which he resided, and taking it under the protection of the United States. He was seized while performing, under the sanction of the chief magistrate of the union, those duties which the humane policy adopted by congress had recommended. He was apprehended, tried, and condemned, under colour of a law which has been shown to the repugnant to the constitution, laws, and treaties of the United States. Had a judgment, liable to the same objections, been rendered for property, none would question the jurisdiction of this court. It cannot be less clear when the judgment affects personal liberty, and inflicts disgraceful punishment, if punishment could disgrace when inflicted on innocence. The plaintiff in error is not less interested in the operation of this unconstitutional law than if it affected his property. He is not less entitled to the protection of the constitution, laws, and treaties of his country.

* * *

It is the opinion of this court that the judgment of the superior court for the county of Gwinnett, in the state of Georgia, condemning Samuel A. Worcester to hard labour, in the penitentiary of the state of Georgia, for four years, was pronounced by that court under colour of a law which is void, as being repugnant to the constitution, treaties, and laws of the United States, and ought, therefore, to be reversed and annulled.

Full text is available online at http://laws.findlaw.com/us/31/515.html.

V

The Ordeal of Removal

*T*he piecemeal and relatively voluntary process of Indian removal was quickly transformed by the passage of the Indian Removal Act in 1830. Afterward, as federal negotiators and state authorities worked in tacit cooperation to gain the consent of eastern Indians to give up their lands and move to the West, a sense of white urgency led to subtle and occasionally overt threats being leveled at reluctant tribes. Almost all Indians were understandably averse to uprooting their people and trekking to strange lands. In finally consenting to removal, for whatever reason, their worst fears were too often realized and sometimes exceeded. The process of departure was hurried by authorities and harried by criminals; the journey was beset by inadequate supplies, poor transportation, and lack of shelter; and unfriendly Indians already populated the destination.

In the gloomy time between the adoption of removal as a policy in 1825 and the institutionalization of it with legislation in 1830, Indians still believed they had a choice and sought to explain the logic of their positions. Kanakuk of the Kickapoo, a tribe that had settled in the Wabash region of Illinois and Indiana after the American Revolution, undertook one such effort. The Kickapoo had joined Tecumseh's confederation and had sided with the British in the War of 1812, actions for which they paid a heavy price in 1815 when the government extracted a large expanse of their Illinois lands. As pressure mounted in the ensuing years for the Kickapoo to relocate westward, many did, but others resisted because they were fearful of living close to hostile Indians in Missouri. In 1827, Kanakuk tried to explain why.

Indians Resolve to Remain
on Their Lands, 1827

I told you of all our troubles. I asked you to reflect on our situation and that we would come back to see you.

My father, you call all the redskins your children. When we have children, we treat them well. That is the reason I make this long talk to get you to take pity on us and let us remain where we are.

My father, I wish after my talk is over you would write to my Great Father, the president, that we have a desire to remain a little longer where we now are. I have explained to you that we have thrown all our badness away and keep the good path. I wish our Great Father could hear that. I will now talk to my Great Father, the president.

My Great Father, I don't know if you are the right chief, because I have heard some things go wrong. I wish you to reflect on our situation and let me know. I want to talk to you mildly and in peace, so that we may understand each other. When I saw the Great Spirit, he told me to throw all our bad acts away. We did so. Some of our chiefs said the land belonged to us, the Kickapoos; but this is not what the Great Spirit told me—the lands belong to him. The Great Spirit told me that no people owned the lands—that all was his, and not to forget to tell the white people that when we went into council. When I saw the Great Spirit, he told me, Mention all this to your Great Father. He will take pity on your situation and let you remain on the lands where you are for some years, when you will be able to get through all the bad places (the marks in the figure),[1] and where you will get to a clear piece of land where you will all live happy. When I talked to the Great Spirit, he told me to make my warriors throw their tomahawks in the bad place. I did so, and

---

[1] A reference to a drawing that depicted Kanakuk's concept of the path to Heaven.

every night and morning I raise my hands to the Great Spirit and pray to him to give us success. I expect, my father, that God has put me in a good way—that our children shall see their sisters and brothers and our women see their children. They will grow up and travel and see their totems. The Great Spirit told me, "Our old men had totems. They were good and had many totems. Now you have scarcely any. If you follow my advice, you will soon have totems again." Say this to my Great Father for me.

My father, since I talked with the Great Spirit, our women and children and ourselves, we have not such good clothes, but we don't mind that. We think of praying every day to the Great Spirit to get us safe to the good lands, where all will be peace and happiness.

My father, the Great Spirit holds all the world in his hands. I pray to him that we may not be removed from our land until we can see and talk to all our totems * * *

My father, when I left my women and children, they told me, "As you are going to see our Great Father, tell him to let us alone and let us eat our victuals with a good heart."

My father, since my talk with the Great Spirit we have nothing cooked until the middle of the day. The children get nothing in the morning to eat. We collect them all to pray to the Great Spirit to make our hearts pure, and then eat. We bring our children up to be good.

My father, I will tell you all I know. I will put nothing on my back. God told me, Whenever you make a talk, tell everything true. Keep nothing behind, and then you will find everything go right.

My father, when I talked with the Great Spirit, he did not tell me to sell my lands, because I did not know how much was a dollar's worth, or the game that run on it. If he told me so, I would tell you to-day.

My father, you have heard what I have said. I have represented to you our situation, and ask you to take pity on us and let us remain where we are * * *

My father, I have shown you in the lines I have made the bad places. Our warriors even are afraid of those dark places you see there. That is the reason they threw their tomahawks aside and put up their hands to the Great Spirit.

My father, every time we eat we raise our hands to the Great Spirit to give us success.

My father, we are sitting by each other here to tell the truth. If you write anything wrong, the Great Spirit will know it. If I say anything not true, the Great Spirit will hear it.

My father, you know how to write and can take down what is said for your satisfaction. I can not; all I do is through the Great Spirit for the benefit of my women and children.

My father, everything belongs to the Great Spirit. If he chooses to make the earth shake, or turn it over, all the skins, white and red, can not stop it. I have done. I trust to the Great Spirit.

Smithsonian Institution, Bureau of American Ethnology, *Fourteenth Annual Report of the Bureau of American Ethnology* (Washington, DC: GPO, 1896), part 2, 685–96.

Cherokee Anger, 1830

The disturbing consistency of white demands was not lost on Indians, but the new resolve to have those demands satisfied was an alarming acceleration of the process for targeted tribes. In 1830, Cherokees assessed the situation and weighed Andrew Jackson's recommendation that they give up their lands and leave the Southeast. In response, one of their number, Speckled Snake, indignantly traced a long history of white deceit and greed.

Brothers! We have heard the talk of our great father; it is very kind. He says he loves his red children. *Brothers!* When the white man first came to these shores, the Muscogees gave him land, and kindled him a fire to make him comfortable; and when the pale faces of the south made war on him, their young men drew the tomahawk, and protected his head from the scalping knife. But when the white man had warmed himself before the Indian's fire, and filled himself with the Indian's hominy, he became very large; he stopped not for the mountain tops, and his feet covered the plains and the valleys. His hands grasped the eastern and the western sea. Then he became our great father. He loved his red children; but said, "You must move a little farther, lest I should, by accident, tread on you." With one foot he pushed the red man over the Oconee, and with the other he trampled down the graves of his fathers. But our great father still loved his red children, and he soon made them another talk. He said much; but it all meant nothing, but "move a little farther; you are too near me." I have heard a great many talks from our great father, and they all begun and ended the same. *Brothers!* When he made us a talk on a former occasion, he said, "Get a little farther; go beyond the Oconee and the Oakmulgee: there is a pleasant country." He also said, "It shall be yours forever." Now he says, "The land you live on is not yours; go beyond the Mississippi; there is game; there you may remain while the grass grows or the water runs." *Brothers!* Will not our great father come there also? He loves his red children, and his tongue is not forked.

Samuel G. Drake, *The Aboriginal Races of North America*, 15th ed. (New York: Hurst & Company, 1880), 450.

Missionaries at Dancing Rabbit Creek, 1830

The Choctaws signed the first treaty negotiated under the Indian Removal Act of 1830, a treaty that relinquished all their remaining lands in Mississippi and placed them on an irreversible course for removal. As federal commissioners John Eaton and John Coffee prepared to open talks with Choctaws at Dancing Rabbit Creek, several white missionaries wanted to attend the negotiations. Describing the request as "strange," Eaton and Coffee refused to allow it; and though they did not say so, it was obvious they feared the missionaries would undermine arguments for removal. The missionaries tried again but were told again that they should "go away."

CAMP GROUND, *September* 18, 1830.

GENTLEMEN: We have just received your communication of this morning, and regret that our request of yesterday should have been considered "a strange one." We also regret that the impression should have been made that there was "a determination on the part of the missionaries to be present:" we assure you there was no such determination on our part.

As we are constrained to believe that our motives in coming to this place are not understood, we beg leave again respectfully to state that, as it respects any influence which we could, if disposed, exert, as to the result of the present negotiations, we should have had no motive to have left our homes on this occasion. We did think the request of the members of our church, that they might enjoy the privilege of religious instruction on the Sabbath a reasonable one, and that the commissioners, when they come to understand it, would not deny them this privilege. We did not suppose that this could, in the least, retard the business of the present meeting, or create the least possible expense.

Another reason for our being present on the occasion, and we believed would be deemed a valid one, was, that we, as the agents of the Choctaws, and of the American Board of Commissioners for Foreign Missions, have disbursed a large amount of money in the school and missionary operations this nation, and have now under our charge large and expensive establishments in different parts of it. We supposed it would not be considered improper for one or more persons, representing these interests, to be present on this occasion. At the treaty at Doak's stand in 1820, the superintendent of this mission was present, and received the most respectful treatment from the commissioners, and especially from the present Chief Magistrate of the United States.

It has been reported again and again to the Choctaws that no great men in the United States are religious, and that they are not in favor of the Choctaws becoming religious: if, while men of every other grade and color are permitted to be present, the missionaries alone are prohibited, we think it would tend greatly to confirm the above report. We cannot believe that the honorable the Secretary of War, and the Commissioner of the United States, now present, would willingly do any thing to confirm such an impression. It is doubtless known to the honorable the Secretary of War, and the Commissioner of the United States, that there are various reports in circulation among a portion of this nation, as well as among white people, prejudicial to the missionary character, representing us as speculators, &c. We did hope that the present would furnish us with a convenient and suitable opportunity of presenting correct and full information on the subject, and would result in such explanations and arrangements as the case might require. And we repeat the assurance, that the above were the motives, and the only motives, which brought us to this place.

With this explanation of our views, we comply with the injunction contained in your communication, and prepare to leave the ground immediately, unless we receive intimations to the contrary.

We have the honor to be, with respect,

Your obedient servants,

C. KINGSBURY.
CYRUS BYINGTON.
LOVING S. WILLIAMS.
COLVIN CUSHMAN.

September 18, 1830.

GENTLEMEN: We have received your joint letter. Business with the council prevented a reply until now. We cannot request your stay. We prefer that you should go away; and, in saying this, we intend nothing of disrespect to you, and most certainly nothing to the cause of religion. Our reason we have already offered—it is, that your labors here, under all the circumstances which are presented, cannot be profitably employed: of this you must yourselves be satisfied. A more unpropitious moment, and a place less promotive of religious results, could scarcely be dreamed of. Your absence may aid civil purposes greatly. Your presence cannot, we are persuaded, advance the cause of religion in the least. We must therefore insist upon it that you, and every other person engaged here in missionary purposes, leave the treaty ground; and, in saying this, we again beg to state that nothing disrespectful or unkind to any of you is intended. We request this to be received as our final answer on the subject.

J. H. EATON,
J. COFFEE.

U.S. Congress, *Correspondence on the Subject of the Emigration of Indians, 1831–1833,* 23rd Cong., 1st sess., 1833, S. Doc. 512, 2: 254–55.

A Choctaw Farewell, 1832

The wrenching decision of consenting to removal and the sad resignation that followed it are heartbreaking threads that run through the following narrative by George W. Harkins, a mixed-heritage Choctaw leader.

To the American People.

It is with considerable diffidence that I attempt to address the American people, knowing and feeling sensibly my incompetency; and believing that your highly and well improved minds could not be well entertained by the address of a Choctaw. But having determined to emigrate west of the Mississippi river this fall, I have thought proper in bidding you farewell, to make a few remarks of my views and the feelings that actuate me on the subject of our removal.

Believing that our all is at stake and knowing that you readily sympathize with the distressed of every country, I confidently throw myself on your indulgence and ask you to listen patiently. I do not arrogate to myself the prerogative of deciding upon the expediency of the late treaty, yet I feel bound as a Choctaw, to give a distinct expression of my feelings on that interesting, (and to the Choctaws) all important subject.

We were hedged in by two evils, and we chose that which we thought least. Yet we could not recognize the right that the state of Mississippi had assumed to legislate for us. Although the legislature of the state were qualified to make laws for their own citizens, that did not qualify them to become law makers to a people who were so dissimilar in manners and customs as the Choctaws are to the Mississippians. Admitting that they understood the people, could they remove that mountain of prejudice that has ever obstructed the streams of justice, and prevented their salutary influence from reaching my devoted countrymen? We as Choctaws rather chose to suffer and be free, than live under the degrading influence of laws, where our voice could not be heard in their formation.

Much as the state of Mississippi has wronged us, I cannot find in my heart any other sentiment than an ardent wish for her prosperity and happiness.

I could cheerfully hope that those of another age and generation may not feel the effects of those oppressive measures that have been so illiberally dealt out to us; and that peace and happiness may be their reward. Amid the gloom and honors of the present separation, we are cheered with a hope that ere long we shall reach our destined home, and that nothing short of the basest acts of treachery will ever be able to wrest it from us, and that we may live free. Although your ancestors won freedom on the fields of danger and glory, our ancestors owned it as their birthright, and we have had to purchase it from you as the vilest slaves buy their freedom.

Yet it is said that our present movements are our own voluntary acts—such is not the case. We found ourselves like a benighted stranger, following false guides, until he was surrounded on every side, with fire or water. The fire was certain destruction, and feeble hope was left him of escaping by water. A distant view of the opposite shore encourages the hope; to remain would be utter annihilation. Who would hesitate, or would say that his plunging into the water was his own voluntary act? Painful in the extreme is the mandate of our expulsion. We regret that it should proceed from the mouth of our professed friend, and for whom our blood was commingled with that of his bravest warriors, on the field of danger and death.

But such is the instability of professions. The man who said that he would plant a stake and draw a line around us, that never should be passed, was the first to say he could not guard the lines, and drew up the stake and wiped out all traces of the line. I will not conceal from you my fears, that the present grounds may be removed—I have my foreboding—who of us can tell after witnessing what has already been done, what the next force may be.

I ask you in the name of justice, for repose for myself and my injured people. Let us alone—we will not harm you, we want rest. We hope, in the name of justice, that another outrage may never be committed against us, and that we may for the future be cared for as children, and not driven about as beasts, which are benefitted by a change of pasture.

Taking an example from the American government, and knowing the happiness which its citizens enjoy, under the influence of mild republican institutions, it is the intention of our countrymen to form a government assimilated to that of our white breathern in the United States, as nearly as their condition will permit.

We know that in order to protect the rights and secure the liberties of the people, no government approximates so nearly to perfection as the one to which we have alluded. As east of the Mississippi we have been friends, so west we will cherish the same feelings with additional fervor; and although we may be removed to the desert, still we shall look with fine regard, upon those who have promised us their protection. Let that feeling be reciprocated.

Friends, my attachment to my native land is strong—that cord is now broken; and we must go forth as wanderers in a strange land! I must go—let me entreat you to regard us with feelings of kindness, and when the hand of oppression is stretched against us, let me hope that every part of the United States, filling the mountains and valleys, will echo and say stop, you have no power, we are the sovereign people, and our friends shall no more be disturbed. We ask you for nothing that is incompatible with your other duties.

We go forth sorrowful, knowing that wrong has been done. Will you extend to us your sympathizing regards until all traces of disagreeable oppositions are obliterated, and we again shall have confidence in the professions of our white brethern.

Here is the land of our progenitors, and here are their bones; they left them as a sacred deposit, and we have been compelled to venerate its trust; it is dear to us yet we cannot stay, my people are dear to me, with them I must go. Could I stay and forget them and leave them to struggle alone, unaided, unfriended, and forgotten by our great father? I should then be unworthy the name of a Choctaw, and be a disgrace to my blood. I must go with them; my destiny is cast among the Choctaw people. If they suffer, so will I; if they prosper, then I will rejoice. Let me again ask you to regard us with feelings of kindness.

The American Indian, December 1926, 7, 12.

A White Samaritan
on the Choctaw Trek, 1832

Choctaw removal was a logistical disaster, and some whites living along the path of the trek were horrified by the human misery they witnessed. One Louisiana planter was so moved by the suffering of the starving Indians that he not only allowed them to eat his pumpkins—he noted that they waited for his permission— he also wrote the War Department a stinging criticism about the supplies being provided to them.

LAKE PROVIDENCE, LA., *June* 14, 1832.

DEAR SIR: I see, by some late paper, that a treaty has been made lately with the Creek Indians, and see that one provision of it, which may have been considered important, is, that "each *family shall be furnished with a blanket.*"

It was with yourself the treaty was formed. You have long resided in a cold climate, and from that circumstance may consider *a blanket* enough for a family so far south. This would he an improper esti- mate. But the whole treaty is one that I would not have expected from the head or heart of Governor Cass, acting under General Jackson, as President. It is indeed a narrow thing in every part of it. This treaty, and the report of Houston's case, has induced me to write to you on the subject of the Indians. This, however, I would have done, had neither come to my view.

I live now on the side of, and within forty feet of, the road, and the only one by which the Choctaw Indians have passed, and must pass, that go by land. Their extreme poverty and consequent suf- fering in passing last fall, attracted my particular notice, and the Houston case explained to me in some measure the cause of their extreme suffering from hunger, while passing. I do not yet know who is the contractor for furnishing them rations. But be him or them, who they may, their object is to make money without the least feeling for the suffering of this unfortunate people. From Vicksburg to this place is sixty-eight miles. On this route they received a *scanty* supply, and only then a part of the parties once. Here they received worse than a scanty supply, to do them eighty miles through an uninhabited country, fifty miles of which is an overflowed swamp, and in which distance are two large deep streams that must be crossed in a boat or on a raft, and one other nearly impassable in any way. This, they had to perform or perish, there being no provision made for them on the way. This, too, was to be done during the worst time of weather, I have ever seen in any country—a heavy sleet having broken and bowed down all the small and much of the large timber. And this was to be performed under the pressure of hunger by *old* women and young children, without any covering for their feet, legs, or body, except a cotton under-dress generally. In passing, before they reached the place of getting rations here I gave a party leave to enter a small field in which pumpkins were. They would not enter without leave, though starving. Those they ate *raw* with the greatest avidity.

I furnished part of the beef they got, and was invited to take out the kidney fat, by the man who was to furnish them.

These people have with them a great number of horses, and some cattle, chiefly oxen. The time required to get the horses and cattle together in a morning when travelling through a country thickly covered with strong cane as this is, must be very considerable in good weather, and in bad weather, days are often spent at the same camp. Provision ought to be made to feed them all the way, whatever may be the delay.

I presume it is much in the power of the President to provide, in a cheap way, for the safety, if not the comfort, of these people. If I am correct, I would suggest the propriety of having salt provisions, bacon, furnished for these long marches. Corn they could carry if they got it, but this has not been furnished. I think, too, that instead of a blanket to each family, a blanket to each individual, and a skin to make moccasins and leggings to each, would not be too much. This people have not skins, but they could be had low on contract. I would go still further, I would give each at least a pair of shoes or moccasins, and two pair of short stockings.

I have seen poverty amongst the northern Indians, but theirs is nothing compared to that of those of the south. Friendship for the whites never can exist in the bosom of any of those that passed here last fall. The least sensible of them has been touched too deeply in the tender part ever to become reconciled.

Report says, and I have no doubt of the truth of it, that the Choctaws have been greatly defrauded in the sale of their stock cattle. Indeed, it appears to us, who are near enough to almost see the whole, that few, if any, are sent amongst them, or intrusted to act for or with them, that are not the most unprincipled of the human family. How this should so invariably happen, is difficult to suppose. Blame is due somewhere, and to a great extent.

I am living quite secluded, and write but little, as this letter may be proof of, but the tenor of it will show that I am not an inattentive looker-on, and the hints and opinions here given may perhaps answer some purpose. If it does but remove one cause of complaint, I shall think my time well spent. Be that as it may, be assured that the administration generally, and yourself particularly, have no warmer friend, as to things in general, than I am.

JOSEPH KERR.

Hon. LEWIS CASS, *Secretary of War.*

U.S. Congress, *Correspondence on the Subject of the Emigration of Indians, 1831–1833,* 23rd Cong., 1st sess., 1833, S. Doc. 512, 1: 719–20.

Squatters Take Over Creek Farms, 1832

White squatters encroaching on Indian lands had always been a problem, but the announcement of removal treaties made it impossible to restrain these trespassers, and federal pledges to protect Indians and their property became virtually meaningless. That local officials abetted such offenses especially annoyed federal authorities. In the wake of the Creek removal treaty, Creek federal agent John Crowell reported a case in which whites were simply commandeering Creek farms (called "improvements" by Crowell). These trespassers had secured writs and procured a local sheriff to serve their legal mandates on a U.S. marshal and an army officer trying to stop these depredations. The circumstances Crowell described were common and eventually pushed some Creeks too far.

CREEK AGENCY, *August* 3, 1832.

SIR: The marshal of Alabama has commenced removing intruders from Indian improvements. The first he removed, have

returned with a reinforcement armed, and threaten to defend themselves. I understand they have brought the sheriff of the county,
with writs to serve on the marshal and the officer commanding the
troops, and such Indians as should be found in possession of the
places from which they had been removed; but the marshal and
officer having left the neighborhood, they run the Indians off and
are again in peaceable possession of the improvements from which
they had been removed.

The principal chief of that town was with me yesterday, and
gives a distressing account of the situation of the Indians; the most
of them in the woods, without the means of subsistence, hiding
from the intruders, who treat them cruelly when they meet them.
This chief expressed much regret that the late treaty stipulation, in
relation to the removal of intruders, could not have been executed
by the Government.

I have the honor to be,
Your obedient servant,
JNO. CROWELL,
Agent for Indian Affairs.

The Hon. LEWIS CASS,
Secretary of War, Washington.

U.S. Congress, *Correspondence on the Subject of the Emigration of Indians, 1831–1833,*
23rd Cong., 1st sess., 1833, S. Doc. 512, 3: 413.

Stealing Land from Creeks, 1835

*In addition to simply taking land from Creeks, whites also perpetrated blatant
frauds to steal Indian lands. Federal officials investigating these practices were
appalled and noted how swindlers were so brazen that they bantered about their
misdeeds even as they threatened those trying to stop them. Such crimes were
committed against every tribe after it had consented to removal.*

Near the town of Cusseta, in which Dr. McHenry certified, Indians
were collected in large bodies, amounting to 400 or 500; and from

that to 1,000 were encamped in the woods, which, in the language of one witness, "appeared to be full of them", and were fed by and under the direction avowedly of the agents of those to whom the largest number of contracts was certified; that all regard for appearances even was abandoned, and no attempts at secrecy in their movements was made; and that threats and menace were used by some of those engaged in this business against the persons who exposed their unprincipled proceedings.

That early in March, 1835, "the land stealers were crowding into the office by droves, and certifying contracts very fast, and it appeared as though they would steal all the Indians' land; they seemed to carry on the business in sport"; that a toast was given in a crowd by one of those concerned in these nefarious practices, "Here's to the man that can steal the most land to-morrow without being caught at it;" and that such a flood of fraud inundated the agency that Dr. McHenry closed his books.

Grant Foreman, *Indian Removal: The Emigration of the Five Civilized Tribes of Indians* (Norman: University of Oklahoma Press, 1956), 131–32.

Black Hawk's Farewell, 1835

The so-called Black Hawk War of 1835 was a discreditable incident of removal that ended tragically when the fleeing Sauk-Fox Indians were caught at the Bad Axe River, in modern-day Wisconsin. Almost three-quarters of them died in the ensuing battle. Afterward, Black Hawk had little left but pride in himself and his people—a pride that he resolutely displayed to his white captors.

You have taken me prisoner with all my warriors. I am much grieved, for I expected, if I did not defeat you, to hold out much longer, and give you more trouble before I surrendered. I tried hard to bring you into ambush, but your last general understands Indian fighting. The first one was not so wise. When I saw that I could not beat you by Indian fighting, I determined to rush on you, and fight you face to face. I fought hard. But your guns were well aimed. The

FIGURE 9

Black Hawk—Chief of the Sauk-Fox Indians, Black Hawk opposed removal
but consented to avoid trouble. But his people's move west of the Mississippi
put them at the mercy of hostile Indians, and he led them back into Illinois,
sparking the Black Hawk War. It concluded with his people devastated, he a
captive, and the end of Indian resistance to removal in the Old Northwest.

(Library of Congress)

bullets flew like birds in the air, and whizzed by our ears like the
wind through the trees in the winter. My warriors fell around me;
it began to look dismal. I saw my evil day at hand. The sun rose dim
on us in the morning, and at night it sunk in a dark cloud, and
looked like a ball of fire. That was the last sun that shone on *Black-
hawk*. His heart is dead, and no longer beats quick in his bosom.—
He is now a prisoner to the white men; they will do with him as they
wish. But he can stand torture, and is not afraid of death. He is no
coward. *Black-hawk* is an Indian.

He has done nothing for which an Indian ought to be ashamed.
He has fought for his countrymen, the squaws and papooses,
against white men, who came, year after year, to cheat them and
take away their lands. You know the cause of our making war. It is
known to all white men. They ought to be ashamed of it. The white
men despise the Indians, and drive them from their homes. But the

Indians are not deceitful. The white men speak bad of the Indian, and look at him spitefully. But the Indian does not tell lies; Indians do not steal.

An Indian, who is as bad as the white men, could not live in our nation; he would be put to death, and eat up by the wolves. The white men are bad schoolmasters; they carry false looks, and deal in false actions; they smile in the face of the poor Indian to cheat him; they shake them by the hand to gain their confidence, to make them drunk, to deceive them, and ruin our wives. We told them to let us alone, and keep away from us; but they followed on, and beset our paths, and they coiled themselves among us, like the snake. They poisoned us by their touch. We were not safe. We lived in danger. We were becoming like them, hypocrites and liars, adulterers, lazy drones, all talkers, and no workers.

We looked up to the Great Spirit. We went to our great father. We were encouraged. His great council gave us fair words and big promises; but we got no satisfaction. Things were growing worse. There were no deer in the forest. The opossum and beaver were fled; the springs were drying up, and our squaws and papooses without victuals to keep them from starving; we called a great council, and built a large fire. The spirit of our fathers arose and spoke to us to avenge our wrongs or die. We all spoke before the council fire. It was warm and pleasant. We set up the war-whoop, and dug up the tomahawk; our knives were ready, and the heart of *Black-hawk* swelled high in his bosom, when he led his warriors to battle. He is satisfied. He will go to the world of spirits contented. He has done his duty. His father will meet him there, and commend him.

Black-hawk is a true Indian, and disdains to cry like a woman. He feels for his wife, his children and friends. But he does not care for himself. He cares for his nation and the Indians. They will suffer. He laments their fate. The white men do not scalp the head; but they do worse—they poison the heart; it is not pure with them.— His countrymen will not be scalped, but they will, in a few years, become like the white men, so that you can't trust them, and there must be, as in the white settlements, nearly as many officers as men, to take care of them and keep them in order.

Farewell, my nation! *Black-hawk* tried to save you, and avenge your wrongs. He drank the blood of some of the whites. He has been taken prisoner, and his plans are stopped. He can do no more. He is near his end. His sun is setting, and he will rise no more. Farewell to *Black-hawk*.

Samuel G. Drake, *The Aboriginal Races of North America*, 15th ed. (New York: Hurst & Company, 1880), 657.

Removed Creeks Travel West, 1836

Set upon by white criminals, cheated out of property, and harassed as they wretchedly waited to start their journey, Creeks bound for removal faced a grueling march of almost a thousand miles in bad weather and with inadequate provisions. Like the other southeastern tribes, such as the Cherokees on the infamous Trail of Tears, the Creeks suffered terribly. Lieutenant J. T. Sprague of the United States Marine Corps, who guided a band of Creeks to the Indian Territory in 1836, provided the following summary of such a journey. His measured account does not temper the hardships his charges endured, but he does absolve contractors and government agents of any responsibility for those hardships. Sprague was a good man doing his duty under trying circumstances, but his prejudice shows through with his remark about Indian enmity toward whites being "known to everyone." And his conclusion that the fault for the Creek misery lay with the whites who preyed upon them before removal demonstrates how this ugly policy could blind even a good man.

The excessive bad state of the roads, the high waters, and the extreme cold and wet weather, was enough to embarrass the strongest minds. The distance traveled by the party from Chambers County, Alabama, to their last encampment, was eight hundred miles by land, and four hundred and twenty five by water; occupying ninety-six days. The health of the Indians upon the entire route was much better than might have been anticipated.

Twenty nine deaths were all that occurred; fourteen of these were children and the others were the aged, feeble and intemperate. The unfriendly disposition of the Indians towards the whites from the earliest history of our country, is known to everyone. To what an extent this feeling existed in the party under my charge, I cannot with confidence say, for it was seldom expressed but when in a state of intoxication. But if this be a fair criterion, I have no hesitation in saying it was the most vindictive and malignant kind. To say they were not in a distressed and wretched condition, would be in contradiction to the well known history of the Creeks for the last two years. They were poor, wretchedly, and depravedly poor, many of them without a garment to cover their nakedness. To this there was some exceptions, but this was the condition of a large portion of them. They left their country, at a warm season of the year, thinly clad and characteristically indifferent to their rapid approach to the regions of a climate to which they were unaccustomed, they expended what little they had for intoxicating drinks or for some gaudy article of jewelry.

So long a journey under the most favorable auspices must necessarily be attended with suffering and fatigue. They were in a deplorable condition when they left their homes, and a journey of upwards of a thousand miles could not certainly have improved it. There was nothing within the provisions of the contract by which the Alabama Emigrating Company could contribute to their wants, other than the furnishing of rations and transportation, and a strict compliance with the demands of the officer of the Government; these demands, unquestionably, must come within the letter and spirit of the contract. All these they complied with. The situation of the officers of the Government, at the head of these parties, was peculiarly responsible and embarrassing. They were there to protect the rights of the Indians and to secure to them all the Government designed for them. These Indians, looking up to the officers as a part of the Government, not only appealed for their rights, but their wants. They could sympathize with them, as every one must who saw their condition, but could not relieve them. They had nothing, within their power, for in a pecuniary point they were scarcely better off than those they were willing to assist. All that the contract granted was secured to them. But all this could not shield them from the severity of the weather, cold sleeting storms, and hard frozen ground.

Had a few thousand dollars been placed at the disposal of the officer which he could have expended at his discretion, the great sufferings which all ages, particularly the young, were subjected to, might have been in a measure avoided. But as it was, the officer was obliged to listen to their complaints without any means of redress.* * * Many exaggerated reports are in circulation, respecting the miserable condition of these emigrating Indians. Let these be traced to the proper source and it will be found that the white-men with whom they have been associated for years past have been the principal cause. There is enough in support of this opinion. It is only necessary to advert to the allegations in many instances, well established, of the lands of the Indians having been purchased by some of these citizens at prices much below their real value, or of the purchase money having been in whole or in part, withheld, the prosecution for valid or fictitious debts, commenced at the moment of their departure for the west, and thereby extorting from them what little money they had.

Had they been permitted to retain the fair proceeds of their lands they would have had the means of procuring any additional supplies for their comfort. The stipulations of the treaty were fairly executed; all that was to be furnished the Indians was provided, and if these were inadequate to their comfortable removal and subsistence, no blame can be attached to the agents of the Alabama Emigrating Company or to the officers of the government.

Grant Foreman, *Indian Removal: The Emigration of the Five Civilized Tribes of Indians* (Norman: University of Oklahoma Press, 1956), 174–76.

Cherokees Are Urged to Comply, 1837

Brigadier General John E. Wool was dispatched to north Georgia in 1836 to facilitate voluntary Cherokee removal. Although he had two thousand soldiers under his command, he preferred to use persuasion to disarm the angry and friendly gestures to win over the reluctant Cherokee. Despite Wool's best efforts, many Indians remained unwilling emigrants. In 1837, with time running out, he delivered an impassioned appeal for compliance, and though his warnings must have sounded much like the menacing words Cherokees had endured from adversaries, Wool spoke to them in friendship and out of deep concern for their welfare.

Head Quarters, Army
Cherokee Nation, New Echota, Ga. March 22nd, 1837
CHEROKEES:

It is nearly a year since I first arrived in this country. I then informed you of the objects of my coming among you. I told you that a treaty had been made with your people, and that your country was to be given up to the United States by the 25th May, 1838 a (little more than a year from this time,) when you would all be compelled to remove to the West. I also told you, if you would submit to the terms of the treaty I would protect you in your persons and property, at the same time I would furnish provisions and clothing to the poor and destitute of the Nation. You would not listen, but turned a deaf ear to my advice. You preferred the counsel of

FIGURE 10

John E. Wool—Ordered to round up and enroll Cherokees for removal, Brig. Gen. Wool tempered his instructions with compassion and sincere concern for the Cherokees' welfare. His superiors in Washington censured his actions, and local authorities in the Southeast grew to loath him. His departure from the assignment left the Cherokees all but friendless and set the stage for their grueling journey over what would be dubbed the Trail of Tears. *(Library of Congress)*

those who were opposed to the treaty. They told you, what was not true, that your people had made no treaty with the United States, and that you would be able to retain your lands, and would not be obliged to remove to the West, the place designated for your new homes. Be no longer deceived by such advice! It is not only untrue, but if listened to, may lead to your utter ruin. The President, as well as Congress, have decreed that you should remove from this country. The people of Georgia, of North Carolina, of Tennessee and of Alabama, have decreed it. Your fate is decided; and if you do not voluntarily get ready and go by the time fixed in the treaty, you will then be forced from this country by the soldiers of the United States.

Under such circumstances what will be your condition? Deplorable in the extreme! Instead of the benefits now presented to you by the treaty, of receiving pay for the improvements of your lands, your houses, your cornfields and your ferries, and for all the property unjustly taken from you by the white people, and at the same time, blankets, clothing and provisions for the poor, you will be driven from the country, and without a cent to support you on your arrival at your new homes. You will in vain flee to your mountains for protection. Like the Creeks, you will be hunted up and dragged from your lurking places and hurried to the West. I would ask, are you prepared for such scenes? I trust not. Yet such will be your fate if you persist in your present determination.

Cherokees: I have not come among you to oppress you, but to protect you and to see that justice is done you, as guaranteed by the treaty. Be advised, and turn a deaf ear to those who would induce you to believe that no treaty has been made with you, and that you will not be obliged to leave your country. They cannot be friends, but the worst of enemies. Their advice, if followed, will lead to your certain destruction. The President has said that a treaty has been made with you, and must be executed agreeably to its terms. The President never changes.

Therefore, take my advice: It is the advice of a friend, who would tell you the truth, and who feels deeply interested in your welfare, and who will do every thing in his power to relieve, protect and secure to you the benefits of the treaty. And why not abandon a country no longer yours? Do you not see the white people daily coming into it, driving you from your homes and possessing your houses, your cornfields and your ferries? Hitherto I have been able in some degree, to protect you from their intrusions; in a short time it will no longer be in my power. If, however, I could protect you, you could not live with them. Your habits, your manners and your customs are unlike, and unsuited to theirs. They have no feelings, no sympathies in common with yourselves. Leave then this country, which after the 25th May 1838, can afford you no protection! and remove to the country designated for your new homes, which is secured to you and your children forever; and where you may live under your own laws, and the customs of your fathers, without intrusion or molestation from the white man. It is a country much better than the one you now occupy; where you can grow more corn, and where game is more abundant. Think seriously of what I say to you! Remember that you have but one summer more to plant corn in this country. Make the best use of this time, and dispose of your property to the best advantage. Go and settle with the Commissioners, and with the emigrating Agent, Gen. Smith, receive the money due for your improvements, your houses, your cornfields and ferries, and for the property which has been unjustly taken from you by the whitemen, and at the appointed time be prepared to remove. In the mean time, if you will apply to me or my Agents, I will cause rations, blankets and clothing to be furnished to the poor and destitute of your people.

John E. Wool
Brig. Gen'l
Comdg.

Vicki Rozema, *Voices from the Trail of Tears* (Winston-Salem, NC: John F. Blair, 2003), 67–69.

The Dictates of Conscience, 1837

Wool eventually ran afoul of both state and national authorities for his treatment of the Cherokees. In the fall of 1836, he allowed a large meeting of almost three thousand Cherokees to discuss freely the prospect of removal. When leaders such

as John Ross were able to strengthen anti-removal sentiment, Wool was repri-
manded by the War Department. His practice of sending to Washington rather
than squelching Cherokee protests infuriated President Andrew Jackson, and the
governors of Alabama and Georgia complained that Wool was too soft on Indi-
ans. Finally, he was replaced. Wool, however, saw no contradiction in being both
a compassionate and an obedient officer, and he mounted a firm defense of his
behavior as dictated by conscience, duty, and a code of honorable conduct.

Under the repeated and solemn guarantees of the United States to
the Cherokees for the occupation of their lands not ceded, would
the government have permitted the State of Alabama to have
called upon the military force of her State and expelled these people from her borders by the use of the bayonet? The question need
not be answered. It cannot be doubted by any one familiar with the
condition of the country that they can be as effectually expelled,
though quite so promptly, by means of legislation as by the point of
the bayonet. They have not the privilege of an oath before the
judicial tribunals, no voice in the legislative hall. Is it not equally a
breach of faith to permit that to be accomplished by indirect means
which would be prohibited if attempted directly and forcibly.

The testimony on your records establishes the fact that, if all
controversies of which they have assumed cognizance were submitted to the adjudication of the civil tribunals of that country, it
would be impossible to execute the Cherokee treaty justly and faithfully. There must be some other less interested power to interpose
between them and the white people residing among them, who,
from their superior cunning and knowledge of the laws, and the
fact that the Indian is not allowed his oath, must of necessity be
always successful in defrauding and oppressing them.

With these views of my duty, Mr. President, with my instructions
before me, holding in my hand the late Cherokee treaty, which
solemnly guarantees to the Cherokees the possession of their property, and the free use and occupation of the same until the time
fixed for their removal to the west, what should have been my
course? If I had acted otherwise than I did, I should have considered myself recreant to the sacred trust reposed in me. An Indian

presents himself before me, and in the language of nature details his complaint. He says: I have been dispossessed by the white man of the house which I built, and the fields which I have cultivated for years; my property has been taken from me, and my family turned out to the shelter of the forest; your government is pledged to protect me, you have the treaty before you, and you were sent to enforce it; I ask justice at you hands. I say to him, go to the civil tribunals of the States, they will redress your wrongs. What would be his answer, what would be your answer, or that of any other man in the community? It would be the voice of nature, universal as the human family. He would say, you insult me with such protection; it is a miserable mockery. Is this your justice, this your faith, so often, so solemnly pledge to us? In the language of Scripture he might exclaim, I have asked you for bread, and you have given me a stone.

My crime has been not in using the language here supposed, but in listening to his complaints and redressing his wrongs. I have endeavored to do him justice without inquiry into the particular provisions of this or that State law. I have not perplexed myself with the subtle arguments of politicians about the indivisibility of sovereignty, or such like cobwebs of the brain; but in the path of justice being clear, I but obeyed the still small voice of conscience which frequently, in the advance of reasoning, overleaps those barriers with which subtlety and ingenuity sometimes successfully opposes its progress.

The course of justice and humanity are but the dictates of an enlarged and liberal policy. By such a course the Indians were taught that some remains of justice, some touches of feeling yet existed in the bosoms of white men for their unfortunate and peculiar situation. I trust that it softened in some degree the asperities of their feelings, and caused them to look with come confidence to the future. Suppose a different course had been pursued—that every species of oppression and cruelty was practiced toward them, and they could find no redress. Might they just say: We can but die, let us first be revenged? Do we seek in vain in the pages of history for such resolutions prompted by despair?

American State Papers, 5, *Military Affairs*, 7: 570–71.

Osceola Unbowed, 1834

The Seminoles of Florida were adamantly opposed to leaving their homes, although toward them as with other tribes, the government resorted to the cunning tactic of having a small group of amenable Seminoles purport to speak for all Seminoles. The resulting Treaty of Payne's Landing that relinquished all Indian land in Florida and pledged all Seminoles to removal was an outrage to most of the tribe, and they disputed its legitimacy and renounced its terms. In October 1834, when Seminoles met with Wiley Thompson at the Seminole agency to express these reactions, one of them, Osceola, minced no words. A year

FIGURE 11

Osceola—This Seminole leader was among an influential group that staunchly opposed Seminole removal and ultimately resisted it by force of arms. Army officials captured Osceola by violating a flag of truce, and he died in a fort at Charleston, South Carolina, within a year. *(Library of Congress)*

later, Seminoles under Osceola assailed the agency and killed Thompson while others, in a coordinated attack, massacred a column of U.S. soldiers, deeds that sparked the Second Seminole War.

My Brothers! The white people got some of our chiefs to sign a paper to give our lands to them, but our chiefs did not do as we told them to do; they done wrong; we must do right. The agent tells us we must go away from the lands we live on—our homes, and the graves of our Fathers, and go over the big river [the Mississippi] among the bad Indians. When the agent tells me to go from my home, I hate him, because I love my home, and will not go from it.

My Brothers! When the Great Spirit tells me to go with the white man, I go: but he tells me not to go. The white man says I shall go, and he will send people to make me go; but I have a rifle, and I have some powder and some lead. I say, we must not leave our homes and lands. If any of our people want to go west, we won't let them; and I tell them they are our enemies, and we will treat them so, for the Great Spirit will protect us.

Peter Nabokov, ed. *Native American Testimony: A Chronicle Of Indian-White Relations from Prophecy to The Present, 1492–1992* (New York: Viking, 1991), 125.

Slavery and the Seminole War, 1841

The Second Seminole War was the final chapter in the tragic story of Indian removal. The war became an interminable conflict that ultimately gave rise to protests from a variety of sources, including the soldiers fighting it and, as the following selection shows, abolitionists in Congress. Congressman Joshua Giddings of Ohio believed the real reason behind the war was to reclaim fugitive slaves, and Seminole resistance to removal was stiffened by the belief that their departure would doom blacks left behind to re-enslavement. Despite vehement objections and occasional interruptions, he was able to say as much in February 1841 for the official record. Thus did Indian removal and slavery, the two moral blights of the early Republic, meld in this instance into a single cause for lament.

FIGURE 12

Seminoles at War—The Second Seminole War broke out as a direct result
of U.S. efforts to remove those people from their homes in Florida. It
became the longest Indian war in American history and raised controversies
involving not only removal but also military subordination and slavery.
Many Seminoles would finally be removed, but others continued to resist
and remained in Florida. *(Library of Congress)*

I will take occasion to say that the lands occupied by these Indians
formed no inducement for us to enter upon this war. General Jesup
says, "those lands would not pay for the medicines used by our
troops while employed against the Indiana." The Seminole Indians,
by the treaty entered into at Payne's Landing, on the 9th May, A.D.
1832, agreed to emigrate west of the Mississippi upon certain conditions. I shall not inquire whether those conditions were performed
on our part, or whether the Indians were or were not morally bound
to the observance of this stipulation. It is well known that they
refused to emigrate, and that such refusal induced General Jackson
to order the military force of the United States to Florida to compel them to emigrate. This attempted compulsion brought on the
hostilities which still continue. The important question now proposed, and which I intend to answer, is, Why did they refuse to
emigrate? The answer, however, may be found in Executive documents of the 24th Congress, at its first session, (House Document
No. 271, p. 8,) in an official letter of Wiley Thompson, Indian

agent, to Wm. P. Duval, Governor of Florida, dated January 1, 1834, nearly a year previous to the commencement of hostilities. Speaking of the unwillingness of the Indians to emigrate, General Thompson says: "The principal causes which operate to cherish this feeling hostile to emigration are, first, the fear that their reunion with the Creeks, which will subject them to the government and control of the Creek national council, will be a surrender of a large negro property, now held by those people, to the Creeks, as an antagonistic claimant."

Thus, sir, we have official intelligence that the principal cause of the war was the fear of losing this "negro property."

* * *

On the 6th day of March, 1837, General Jesup entered into a conventional arrangement with the Seminole Indians, by which it was agreed that hostilities should immediately cease; that the Indians should emigrate West of the Mississippi; that they should be secure in their lives and property; and "that negroes, their bona fide property," should accompany them. By the terms of this compact no negroes were included, except those who were called the "bona fide property" of the Indians, and though Governor Duval, General Jesup, and the Indian agent, all unite in saying that the Indians were controlled by the blacks. These blacks comprised both fugitive slaves and free people of color, who were connected with the Indians by marriage and consanguinity. The attempt to separate them appears to have been hopeless.

The Indian who had married a fugitive slave and reared a family of children would not, in my opinion, quietly fold his arms and view his offspring and their mother marched off into interminable slavery, while he himself should go West. Nor do I believe that will ever be done. They are all the enemies of our country, fighting in arms against us. They have already cost us much treasure, and the blood of many freemen. If they will not surrender themselves "prisoners of war," I would send them all West together. No person can doubt our perfect right to do so; and think justice to the nation and to the Indians requires it, and my amendment will be to that effect. General Jesup's attempt to separate them failed, and I believe all further attempts of that kind will fail.

* * *

Of course the war was renewed, and continues, like a mighty maelstrom, draws within its vortex and swallows up the immense resources of the nation. For a period almost equal to that of our Revolutionary war, the people of the Northern States have been taxed for purpose of carrying on this contest, directed principally against the fugitive slaves in Florida. To this war the feelings, the principles, the interests, the honor of the free States are opposed; yet, sir, they have been, arid still are, compelled to furnish means for its prosecution. Revolting as the trading in slaves is to the feelings of our Northern people, they have been constrained to supply the means of purchasing their fellow-beings. Holding, as the people of the North do, "these truths to be self-evident, that man is born free, and is endowed by his Creator with the inalienable right of liberty," they have been obliged to furnish money to pay for the recapture and re-enslaving of those who, fleeing from the power that oppressed them, had sought in the wilds of Florida those rights to which, by the laws of Nature and of Nature's God, they were entitled.

Congressional Globe, Appendix, 26th Cong., 2nd sess., 346, 348, 351.

INTERPRETATIONS

*T*hroughout the early nineteenth century Americans debated the prac-
ticality, morality, legality, necessity, and inevitability of Indian removal.
They reached no consensus. Historians of the twentieth and twenty-first
centuries have continued the argument. Most scholars have concluded that
the United States showed bad faith in its treatment of Indians who were
removed to the West. Even when treaties were not negotiated with a
minority, unrepresentative faction, promises in the treaties for supplies,
transportation, and allotments were rarely kept. As a whole, modern stu-
dents of removal have harshly judged these tragic events, but they have
also disagreed about the inevitability of removal and the motives of the
policy's principal architects, particularly Andrew Jackson.

The value of Indian land for growing cotton and grains, the discovery of gold in north Georgia, and the expansionist attitudes that perme-
ated the age of Manifest Destiny have led some historians to conclude that
removal was inevitable and that even a sympathetic federal government
could not have prevented state governments from victimizing the Indians.
Other historians have defended removal proponents as sincerely wanting to
protect Indians from white influences or wanting a more secure frontier for
the United States.

In his controversial article published in the Journal of American
History in 1969, renowned historian Father Francis Paul Prucha
offered a revisionist view regarding Andrew Jackson's role in removal. He
argued that Jackson's foremost concern was national security. In Prucha's
view, Jackson was alarmed by large numbers of Indians in close proxim-
ity to possible foreign enemies of the United States. Father Prucha was
not alone in his analysis. Other historians, such as Robert V. Remini,
have mounted defenses of Jackson by insisting that he always tried to deal

fairly with Indians and genuinely believed that removal was in everyone's best interest.

Professor Alfred A. Cave of the University of Toledo does not agree. In his seminal article published in The Historian *in 1999, Cave contended that Jackson and his supporters' promises of fair negotiations with Indians and their depiction of removal as a voluntary exercise were merely political ploys to subdue opposition to the policy. Congress did indeed pass the Removal Act, and Cave argues convincingly that Jackson willfully violated its terms by first refusing to protect Indians and then resorting to compulsory removal.*

Andrew Jackson's Indian Policy:
A Reassessment

F. P. PRUCHA

A great many persons—not excluding some notable historians—
have adopted a "devil theory" of American Indian policy. And in
their demonic hierarchy Andrew Jackson has first place. He is
depicted primarily, if not exclusively, as a western frontiersman and
famous Indian fighter, who was a zealous advocate of dispossessing
the Indians and at heart an "Indian-hater." When he became President, the story goes, he made use of his new power, ruthlessly and
at the point of a bayonet, to force the Indians from their ancestral
homes in the East into desert lands west of the Mississippi, which
were considered forever useless to the white man.[1]

This simplistic view of Jackson's Indian policy is unacceptable. It
was not Jackson's aim to crush the Indians because, as an old
Indian fighter, he hated Indians. Although his years in the West had
brought him into frequent contact with the Indians, he by no
means developed a doctrinaire anti-Indian attitude. Rather, as a
military man, his dominant goal in the decades before he became
President was to preserve the security and well-being of the United
States and its Indian and white inhabitants. His military experience, indeed, gave him an overriding concern for the safety of the
nation from foreign rather than internal enemies, and to some
extent the anti-Indian sentiment that has been charged against
Jackson in his early career was instead basically anti-British. Jackson, as his first biographer pointed out, had "many private reasons
for disliking" Great Britain. "In her, he could trace the efficient
cause, why, in early life, he had been left forlorn and wretched,

---

[1] Typical examples of this view are Oscar Handlin, *The History of the United States* (2 vols., New
York, 1967–1968), I, 445; T. Harry Williams, Richard N. Current, and Frank Freidel, *A His-
tory of the United States* (2 vols., New York, 1964), I, 392; Thomas A. Bailey, *The American Pageant:
A History of the Republic* (3rd. ed., New York, 1966), 269; Dale Van Every, *Disinherited: The Lost
Birthright of the American Indian* (New York, 1966), 103; R. S. Cotterill, "Federal Indian Man-
agement in the South, 1789–1825," *Mississippi Valley Historical Review*, XX (Dec. 1933), 347.

without a single relation in the world."[2] His frontier experience, too, had convinced him that foreign agents were behind the raised tomahawks of the red men. In 1808, after a group of settlers had been killed by the Creeks, Jackson told his militia troops: "[T]his brings to our recollection the horrid barbarity committed on our frontier in 1777 under the influence of and by the orders of Great Britain, and it is presumeable that the same influence has excited those barbarians to the late and recent acts of butchery and murder. . . ."[3] From that date on there is hardly a statement by Jackson about Indian dangers that does not aim sharp barbs at England. His reaction to the Battle of Tippecanoe was that the Indians had been "excited to war by the secrete agents of Great Britain."[4]

Jackson's war with the Creeks in 1813–1814, which brought him his first national military fame, and his subsequent demands for a large cession of Creek lands were part of his concern for security in the West.[5] In 1815, when the Cherokees and Chickasaws gave up their overlapping claims to lands within the Creek cession, Jackson wrote with some exultation to Secretary of War James Monroe: "This Territory added to the creek cession, opens an avenue to the defence of the lower country, in a political point of view incalculable."[6] A few months later he added: "The sooner these lands are brought into markett, [the sooner] a permanent security will be given to what, I deem, the most important, as well as the most vulnarable part of the union. This country once settled, our fortifications of defence in the lower country compleated, all [E]urope will cease to look at it with an eye to conquest. There is no other point

[2] John H. Eaton, *The Life of Andrew Jackson, Major General in the Service of the United States: Comprising a History of the War in the South, from the Commencement of the Creek Campaign, to the Termination of Hostilities Before New Orleans* (Philadelphia, 1817), 18.

[3] John Spencer Bassett, ed., *Correspondence of Andrew Jackson* (7 vols., Washington, 1926–1935), I, 188.

[4] Andrew Jackson to William Henry Harrison, Nov. 30, 1811, *ibid.*, 210. See also Jackson to James Winchester, Nov. 28, 1811; Jackson to Willie Blount, June 4, July 10, and Dec. 21, 1812; Jackson to Thomas Pinckney, May 18, 1814, *ibid.*, I, 209, 226, 231–32, 250, II, 3–4.

[5] For the part played by desire for defense and security in the Treaty of Fort Jackson, see Jackson to Pinckney, May 18, 1814, *ibid.*, II, 2–3, and Eaton, *Life of Jackson*, 183–87. Eaton's biography can be taken as representing Jackson's views.

[6] Jackson to James Monroe, Oct. 23, 1816, Bassett, *Correspondence*, II, 261.

of the union (america united) that combined [E]urope can expect to invade with success."[7]

Jackson's plans with regard to the Indians in Florida were governed by similar principles of security. He wanted "to concentrate and locate the F[lorida] Indians at such a point as will promote their happiness and prosperity and at the same time, afford to that Territory a dense population between them and the ocean which will afford protection and peace to all."[8] On later occasions the same views were evident. When negotiations were under way with the southern Indians for removal, Jackson wrote: "[T]he chickasaw and choctaw country are of great importance to us in the defence of the lower country[;] a white population instead of the Indian, would strengthen our own defence much." And again: "This section of country is of great importance to the prosperity and strength of the lower Mississippi[;] a dense white population would add much to its safety in a state of war, and it ought to be obtained, if it can, on any thing like reasonable terms."[9]

In his direct dealings with the Indians, Jackson insisted on justice toward both hostile and peaceful Indians. Those who committed outrages against the whites were to be summarily punished, but the rights of friendly Indians were to be protected. Too much of Jackson's reputation in Indian matters has been based on the first of these positions. Forthright and hard-hitting, he adopted a no-nonsense policy toward hostile Indians that endeared him to the frontiersmen. For example, when a white woman was taken captive by the Creeks, he declared: "With such arms and supplies as I can obtain I shall penetrate the creek Towns, untill the Captive, with her Captors are delivered up, and think myself Justifiable, in laying waste their villiages, burning their houses, killing their warriors and leading into Captivity their wives and children, untill I do obtain a

---

[7] Jackson to Monroe, Jan. 6, 1817, *ibid.*, 272. See also Jackson to Monroe, March 4, 1817, *ibid.*, 277–78.

[8] Jackson to John C. Calhoun, Aug. 1823, *ibid.*, III, 202. See also Jackson's talk with Indian chieftains, Sept. 20, 1821, *ibid.*, 118.

[9] Jackson to John Coffee, Aug. 20, 1826; Jackson to Coffee, Sept. 2, 1826, *ibid.*, 310, 312. See also Fred L. Israel, ed., *The State of the Union Messages of the Presidents, 1790–1966* (3 vols., New York, 1966), 1, 334.

surrender of the Captive, and the Captors."[10] In his general orders to the Tennessee militia after he received news of the Fort Mims massacre, he called for "retaliatory vengeance" against the "inhuman blood thirsty barbarians."[11] He could speak of the "lex taliones,"[12] and his aggressive campaign against the Creeks and his escapade in Florida in the First Seminole War are further indications of his mood.

But he matched this attitude with one of justice and fairness, and he was firm in upholding the rights of the Indians who lived peaceably in friendship with the Americans. One of his first official acts as major general of the Tennessee militia was to insist on the punishment of a militia officer who instigated or at least permitted the murder of an Indian.[13] On another occasion, when a group of Tennessee volunteers robbed a friendly Cherokee, Jackson's wrath burst forth: "that a sett of men should without any authority rob a man who is claimed as a member of the Cherokee nation, who is now friendly and engaged with us in a war against the hostile creeks, is such an outrage, to the rules of war, the laws of nations and of civil society, and well calculated to sower the minds of the whole nation against the united States, and is such as ought to meet with the frowns of every good citizen, and the agents be promptly prosecuted and punished as robers." It was, he said, as much theft as though the property had been stolen from a white citizen. He demanded an inquiry in order to determine whether any commissioned officers had been present or had had any knowledge of this "atrocious act," and he wanted the officers immediately arrested, tried by court-martial, and then turned over to the civil authority.[14]

Again, during the Seminole War, when Georgia troops attacked a village of friendly Indians, Jackson excoriated the governor for "the base, cowardly and inhuman attack, on the old woman [women] and men of the chehaw village, whilst the Warriors of

---

[10] Jackson to Blount, July 3, 1812, Bassett, *Correspondence*, I, 230.

[11] General Orders, Sept. 19, 1813, *ibid.*, 319–20.

[12] Jackson to David Holmes, April 18, 1814, *ibid.*, 505.

[13] Jackson to Colonel McKinney, May 10, 1802, *ibid.*, 62.

[14] Jackson to John Cocke, Dec. 28, 1813, *ibid.*, 415.

that *village* was with me, fighting the battles of our *country* against the common enemy." It was strange, he said, "that there could exist within the U. States, a cowardly monster in human shape, that could violate the sanctity of a flag, when borne by any person, but more particularly when in the hands of a superanuated Indian chief worn down with age. Such base cowardice and murderous conduct as this transaction affords, has not its paralel in history and should meet with its merited punishment." Jackson ordered the arrest of the officer who was responsible and declared: "This act will to the last ages fix a stain upon the character of Georgia."[15]

Jackson's action as commander of the Division of the South in removing white squatters from Indian lands is another proof that he was not oblivious to Indian rights. When the Indian Agent Return J. Meigs in 1820 requested military assistance in removing intruders on Cherokee lands, Jackson ordered a detachment of twenty men under a lieutenant to aid in the removal. After learning that the officer detailed for the duty was "young and inexperienced," he sent his own aide-de-camp, Captain Richard K. Call, to assume command of the troops and execute the order of removal.[16] "Captain Call informs me," he wrote in one report to Secretary of War John C. Calhoun, "that much noise of opposition was threatened, and men collected for the purpose who seperated on the approach of the regulars, but who threaten to destroy the cherokees in the Valley as soon as these Troops are gone. Capt. Call has addressed a letter to those infatuated people, with assurance of speedy and exemplary punishment if they should attempt to carry their threats into execution." Later he wrote that Call had performed his duties "with both judgement, and prudence and much to the interest of the Cherokee-Nation" and that the action would "have the effect in future of preventing the infraction of our Treaties with that Nation."[17]

To call Jackson an Indian-hater or to declare that he believed that "the only good Indian is a dead Indian" is to speak in terms that had

[15] Jackson to Governor of Georgia, May 7, 1818, *ibid.*, II, 369–70.

[16] Jackson to Calhoun, July 9, 1820, *ibid.*, III, 29. See also Jackson's notice to the intruders, *ibid.*, 26n.

[17] Jackson to Calhoun, July 26, Sept. 15, 1820, *ibid.*, 30–31, 31n.

little meaning to Jackson.[18] It is true, of course, that he did not consider the Indians to be noble savages. He had, for example, a generally uncomplimentary view of their motivation, and he argued that
it was necessary to operate upon their fears, rather than on some
higher motive. Thus, in 1812 he wrote: "I believe self interest and
self preservation the most predominant passion. [F]ear is better
than love with an indian."[19] Twenty-five years later, just after he left
the presidency, the same theme recurred; and he wrote: "long experience satisfies me that they are only to be well governed by their
fears. If we feed their avarice we accelerate the causes of their
destruction. By a prudent exertion of our military power we may yet
do something to alleviate their condition at the same time that we
certainly take from them the means of injury to our frontier."[20]

Yet Jackson did not hold that Indians were inherently evil or
inferior. He eagerly used Indian allies, personally liked and respected
individual Indian chiefs, and, when (in the Creek campaign) an
orphaned Indian boy was about to be killed by Indians upon whom his
care would fall, generously took care of the child and sent him home
to Mrs. Jackson to be raised with his son Andrew.[21] Jackson was convinced that the barbaric state in which he encountered most Indians
had to change, but he was also convinced that the change was possible and to an extent inevitable if the Indians were to survive.

Much of Jackson's opinion about the status of the Indians was
governed by his firm conviction that they did not constitute sovereign nations, who could be dealt with in formal treaties as though
they were foreign powers. That the United States in fact did so,
Jackson argued, was a historical fact which resulted from the feeble
position of the new American government when it first faced the
Indians during and immediately after the Revolution. To continue
to deal with the Indians in this fashion, when the power of the
United States no longer made it necessary, was to Jackson's mind
absurd. It was high time, he said in 1820, to do away with the "farce

[18] Note this recent statement: "President Jackson, himself a veteran Indian fighter, wasted little sympathy on the paint-bedaubed 'varmints.' He accepted fully the brutal creed of his fellow Westerners that 'the only good Indian is a dead Indian.'" Bailey, *American Pageant*, 269.
[19] Jackson to Blount, June 17, 1812, Bassett, *Correspondence*, I, 227–28.
[20] Jackson to Joel R. Poinsett, Aug. 27, 1837, *ibid.*, V, 507.
[21] See Jackson to Mrs. Jackson, Dec. 19, 1813, *ibid.*, I, 400–01; Eaton, *Life of Jackson*, 395–96.

of treating with Indian tribes."[22] Jackson wanted Congress to legislate for the Indians as it did for white Americans.

From this view of the limited political status of the Indians within the territorial United States, Jackson derived two important corollaries. One denied that the Indians had absolute title to all the lands that they claimed. The United States, in justice, should allow the Indians ample lands for their support, but Jackson did not believe that they were entitled to more. He denied any right of domain and ridiculed the Indian claims to "tracts of country on which they have neither dwelt nor made improvements, merely because they have seen them from the mountain or passed them in the chase."[23]

A second corollary of equal import was Jackson's opinion that the Indians could not establish independent enclaves (exercising full political sovereignty) within the United States or within any of the individual states. If their proper status was as subjects of the United States, then they should be obliged to submit to American laws. Jackson had reached this conclusion early in his career, but his classic statement appeared in his first annual message to Congress, at a time when the conflict between the Cherokees and the State of Georgia had reached crisis proportions. "If the General Government is not permitted to tolerate the erection of a confederate State within the territory of one of the members of this Union against her consent," he said, "much less could it allow a foreign and independent government to establish itself there." He announced that he had told the Indians that "their attempt to establish an independent government would not be countenanced by the Executive of the United States, and advised them to emigrate beyond the Mississippi or submit to the laws of those States."[24] "I have been unable to perceive any sufficient reason," Jackson affirmed, "why

[22] Jackson to Calhoun, Sept. 2, 1820, Bassett, *Correspondence*, III, 31–32. See also Jackson to John Quincy Adams, Oct. 6, 1821; Jackson to Calhoun, Sept. 17, 1821, Walter Lowrie and Walter S. Franklin, eds., *American State Papers: Miscellaneous* (2 vols., Washington, 1834), II, 909, 911–12.

[23] Israel, *State of the Union Messages*, I, 310. See also Jackson to Isaac Shelby, Aug. 11, 1818, Bassett, *Correspondence*, II, 388.

[24] Israel, *State of the Union Messages*, I, 308–09. Jackson dealt at length with this question in his message to the Senate, Feb. 22, 1831. James D. Richardson, ed., *A Compilation of the Messages and Papers of the Presidents* (11 vols., Washington, 1897–1914), II, 536–41. See also Jackson to Secretary of War [1831?], Bassett, *Correspondence*, IV, 219–20.

the Red man more than the white, may claim exemption from the municipal laws of the state within which they reside; and governed by that belief, I have so declared and so acted."[25]

Jackson's own draft of this first annual message presents a more personal view than the final public version and gives some insight into his reasoning. He wrote:

> The policy of the government has been gradually to open to them the ways of civilisation; and from their wandering habits, to entice them to a course of life calculated to present fairer prospects of comfort and happiness. To effect this a system should be devised for their benefit, kind and liberal, and gradually to be enlarged as they may evince a capability to enjoy it. It will not answer to encourage them to the idea of exclusive self government. It is impracticable. No people were ever free, or capable of forming and carrying into execution a social compact for themselves until education and intelligence was first introduced. There are with those tribes, a few educated and well informed men, possessing mind and Judgment, and capable of conducting public affairs to advantage; but observation proves that the great body of the southern tribes of Indians, are erratic in their habits, and wanting in those endowments, which are suited to a people who would direct themselves, and under it be happy and prosperous.[26]

Jackson was convinced from his observation of the political incompetence of the general run of Indians that the treaty system played into the hands of the chiefs and their white and half-breed advisers to the detriment of the common Indians. He said on one occasion that such leaders "are like some of our bawling politicians, who loudly exclaim we are the friends of the people, but who, when the[y] obtain their views care no more for the happiness or wellfare of the people than the Devil does—but each procure[s] influence through the same channell and for the same base purpose, *self-agrandisement.*"[27]

Jackson was genuinely concerned for the well-being of the Indians and for their civilization. Although his critics would scoff at the idea of placing him on the roll of the humanitarians, his

[25] Draft of Second Annual Message, Series 8, vol. 174, nos. 1409–1410, Andrew Jackson Papers (Manuscript Division, Library of Congress). This statement does not appear in the final version.

[26] Draft of First Annual Message, Dec. 8, 1829, Bassett, *Correspondence,* IV, 103–04.

[27] Jackson to Robert Butler, June 21, 1817, *ibid.,* II, 299. See also Jackson to Coffee, June 21, 1817; U. S. Commissioners to Secretary Graham, July 8, 1817, *ibid.,* 198, 300.

assertions—both public and private—add up to a consistent belief that the Indians were capable of accepting white civilization, the hope that they would eventually do so, and repeated efforts to take measures that would make the change possible and even speed it along.

His vision appears in the proclamation delivered to his victorious troops in April 1814, after the Battle of Horseshoe Bend on the Tallapoosa River. "The fiends of the Tallapoosa will no longer murder our Women and Children, or disturb the quiet of our borders," he declared. "Their midnight flambeaux will no more illumine their Council house, or shine upon the victim of their infernal orgies. They have disappeared from the face of the Earth. In their places a new generation will arise who will know their duties better. The weapons of warefare will be exchanged for the utensils of husbandry; and the wilderness which now withers in sterility and seems to mourn the disolation which overspreads it, will blossom as the rose, and become the nursery of the arts."[28]

The removal policy, begun long before Jackson's presidency but whole-heartedly adopted by him, was the culmination of these views. Jackson looked upon removal as a means of protecting the process of civilization, as well as of providing land for white settlers, security from foreign invasion, and a quieting of the clamors of Georgia against the federal government. This view is too pervasive in Jackson's thought to be dismissed as polite rationalization for avaricious white aggrandizement. His outlook was essentially Jeffersonian. Jackson envisaged the transition from a hunting society to a settled agricultural society, a process that would make it possible for the Indians to exist with a higher scale of living on less land, and which would make it possible for those who adopted white ways to be quietly absorbed into the white society. Those who wished to preserve their identity in Indian nations could do it only by withdrawing from the economic and political pressures exerted upon their enclaves by the dominant white settlers. West of the Mississippi they might move at their own pace toward civilization.[29]

Evaluation of Jackson's policy must be made in the light of the feasible alternatives available to men of his time. The removal program cannot be judged simply as a land grab to satisfy the President's western and southern constituents. The Indian problem that

---

[28] Proclamation, April 2, 1814, *ibid.*, I, 494.

[29] Israel, *State of the Union Messages,* I, 310, 335, 354, 386–87.

Jackson faced was complex, and various solutions were proposed. There were, in fact, four possibilities.

First, the Indians could simply have been destroyed. They could have been killed in war, mercilessly hounded out of their settlements, or pushed west off the land by brute force, until they were destroyed by disease or starvation. It is not too harsh a judgment to say that this was implicitly, if not explicitly, the policy of many of the aggressive frontiersmen. But it was not the policy, implicit or explicit, of Jackson and the responsible government officials in his administration or of those preceding or following his. It would be easy to compile an anthology of statements of horror on the part of government officials toward any such approach to the solution of the Indian problem.

Second, the Indians could have been rapidly assimilated into white society. It is now clear that this was not a feasible solution. Indian culture has a viability that continually impresses anthropologists, and to become white men was not the goal of the Indians. But many important and learned men of the day thought that this was a possibility. Some were so sanguine as to hope that within one generation the Indians could be taught the white man's ways and that, once they learned them, they would automatically desire to turn to that sort of life. Thomas Jefferson never tired of telling the Indians of the advantages of farming over hunting, and the chief purpose of schools was to train the Indian children in white ways, thereby making them immediately absorbable into the dominant culture. This solution was at first the hope of humanitarians who had the interest of the Indians at heart, but little by little many came to agree with Jackson that this dream was not going to be fulfilled.

Third, if the Indians were not to be destroyed and if they could not be immediately assimilated, they might be protected in their own culture on their ancestral lands in the East—or, at least, on reasonably large remnants of those lands. They would then be enclaves within the white society and would be protected by their treaty agreements and by military force. This was the alternative demanded by the opponents of Jackson's removal bill—for example, the missionaries of the American Board of Commissioners for Foreign Missions. But this, too, was infeasible, given the political and military conditions of the United States at the time. The fed-

eral government could not have provided a standing army of sufficient strength to protect the enclaves of Indian territory from the
encroachments of the whites. Jackson could not withstand Georgia's demands for the end of the *imperium in imperio* represented by
the Cherokee Nation and its new constitution, not because of some
inherent immorality on his part but because the political situation
of America would not permit it.

The jurisdictional dispute cannot be easily dismissed. Were the
Indian tribes independent nations? The question received its legal
answer in John Marshall's decision in *Cherokee Nation v. Georgia,* in
which the chief justice defined the Indian tribes as "dependent
domestic nations." But aside from the juridical decision, were the
Indians, in fact, independent, and could they have maintained their
independence without the support—political and military—of the
federal government? The answer, clearly, is no, as writers at the
time pointed out. The federal government could have stood firm in
defense of the Indian nations against Georgia, but this would have
brought it into head-on collision with a state, which insisted that its
sovereignty was being impinged upon by the Cherokees.

This was not a conflict that anyone in the federal government
wanted. President Monroe had been slow to give in to the demands
of the Georgians. He had refused to be panicked into hasty action
before he had considered all the possibilities. But eventually he
became convinced that a stubborn resistance to the southern states
would solve nothing, and from that point on he and his successors,
John Quincy Adams and Jackson, sought to solve the problem by
removing the cause. They wanted the Indians to be placed in some
area where the problem of federal versus state jurisdiction would
not arise, where the Indians could be granted land in fee simple by
the federal government and not have to worry about what some
state thought were its rights and prerogatives.[30]

The fourth and final possibility, then, was removal. To Jackson this
seemed the only answer. Since neither adequate protection nor quick

[30] For the development of the removal idea see Annie Heloise Abel, "The History of Events
Resulting in Indian Consolidation West of the Mississippi," *Annual Report of the American Historical Association for the Year 1906* (2 vols., Washington, 1908), I, 233–450; Francis Paul Prucha,
American Indian Policy in the Formative Years: The Indian Trade and Intercourse Acts, 1790–1834 (Cambridge, 1962), 224–49.

assimilation of the Indians was possible, it seemed reasonable and necessary to move the Indians to some area where they would not be disturbed by federal-state jurisdictional disputes or by encroachments of white settlers, where they could develop on the road to civilization at their own pace, or, if they so desired, preserve their own culture.

To ease the removal process Jackson proposed what he repeatedly described as—and believed to be—*liberal* terms. He again and again urged the commissioners who made treaties to pay the Indians well for their lands, to make sure that the Indians understood that the government would pay the costs of removal and help them get established in their new homes, to make provision for the Indians to examine the lands in the West and to agree to accept them before they were allotted.[31] When he read the treaty negotiated with the Chickasaws in 1832, he wrote to his old friend General John Coffee, one of the commissioners: "I think it is a good one, and surely the religious enthusiasts, or those who have been weeping over the oppression of the Indians will not find fault with it for want of liberality or justice to the Indians."[32] Typical of his views was his letter to Captain James Gadsden in 1829:

> You may rest assured that I shall adhere to the just and humane policy towards the Indians which I have commenced. In this spirit I have recommended them to quit their possessions on this side of the Mississippi, and go to a country to the west where there is every probability that they will always be free from the mercenary influence of White men, and undisturbed by the local authority of the states: Under such circumstances the General Government can exercise a parental control over their interests and possibly perpetuate their race.[33]

The idea of parental or paternal care was pervasive. Jackson told Congress in a special message in February 1832: "Being more and more convinced that the destiny of the Indians within the settled portion of the United States depends upon their entire and speedy migration to the country west of the Mississippi set apart for their permanent residence, I am anxious that all the arrangements necessary to the complete execution of the plan of removal and to the

---

[31] See, for example, Jackson to Coffee [Sept. 1826?], Bassett, *Correspondence,* III, 315–16.

[32] Jackson to Coffee, Nov. 6, 1832, *ibid.,* IV, 483.

[33] Jackson to James Gadsden, Oct. 12, 1829, *ibid.,* 81.

ultimate security and improvement of the Indians should be made without further delay." Once removal was accomplished, "there would then be no question of jurisdiction to prevent the Government from exercising such a general control over their affairs as may be essential to their interest and safety."[34]

Jackson, in fact, thought in terms of a confederacy of the southern Indians in the West, developing their own territorial government which should be on a par with the territories of the whites and eventually take its place in the Union.[35] This aspect of the removal policy, because it was not fully implemented, has been largely forgotten.

In the bills reported in 1834 for the reorganization of Indian affairs there was, in addition to a new trade and intercourse act and an act for the reorganization of the Indian Office, a bill "for the establishment of the Western Territory, and for the security and protection of the emigrant and other Indian tribes therein." This was quashed, not by western interests who might be considered hostile to the Indians, but by men like John Quincy Adams, who did not like the technical details of the bill and who feared loss of eastern power and prestige by the admission of territories in the West.[36]

Jackson continued to urge Congress to fulfill its obligations to the Indians who had removed. In his eighth annual message, in December 1836, he called attention "to the importance of providing a well-digested and comprehensive system for the protection, supervision, and improvement of the various tribes now planted in the Indian country." He strongly backed the suggestions of the commissioner of Indian affairs and the secretary of war for developing a confederated Indian government in the West and for establishing military posts in the Indian country to protect the tribes. "The best hopes of humanity in regard to the aboriginal race, the welfare of our rapidly extending settlements, and the honor of the United States," he said, "are all deeply involved in the relations existing between this Government and the emigrating tribes."[37]

[34] Richardson, *Messages and Papers of the Presidents*, II, 565–66.

[35] Jackson to Coffee, Feb. 19, 1832; Jackson to John D. Terrill, July 29, 1826, Bassett, *Correspondence*, IV, 406, III, 308–09.

[36] Prucha, *American Indian Policy in the Formative Years*, 269–73.

[37] Israel, *State of the Union Messages*, I, 465–66.

Jackson's Indian policy occasioned great debate and great opposition during his administration. This is not to be wondered at. The
"Indian problem" was a complicated and emotion-filled subject,
and it called forth tremendous efforts on behalf of the Indians by
some missionary groups and other humanitarians, who spoke loudly
about Indian rights. The issue also became a party one.

The hue and cry raised against removal in Jackson's administration should not be misinterpreted. At the urging of the American
Board of Commissioners for Foreign Missions, hundreds of church
groups deluged Congress with memorials condemning the removal
policy as a violation of Indian rights; and Jeremiah Evarts, the secretary of the Board, wrote a notable series of essays under the
name "William Penn," which asserted that the original treaties
must be maintained.[38] It is not without interest that such opposition
was centered in areas that were politically hostile to Jackson. There
were equally sincere and humanitarian voices speaking out in support of removal, and they were supported by men such as Thomas
L. McKenney, head of the Indian Office; William Clark, superintendent of Indian affairs at St. Louis; Lewis Cass, who had served
on the frontier for eighteen years as governor of Michigan Territory; and the Baptist missionary Isaac McCoy—all men with long
experience in Indian relations and deep sympathy for the Indians.

Jackson himself had no doubt that his policy was in the best
interests of the Indians. "Toward this race of people I entertain the
kindest feelings," he told the Senate in 1831, "and am not sensible
that the views which I have taken of their true interests are less
favorable to them than those which oppose their emigration to the
West."[39] The policy of rescuing the Indians from the evil effects of
too-close contact with white civilization, so that in the end they too
might become civilized, received a final benediction in Jackson's
last message to the American people—his "Farewell Address" of
March 4, 1837. "The States which had so long been retarded in

[38] See the indexes to the *House Journal,* 21 Cong., 1 Sess. (Serial 194), 897–98, and the *Senate
Journal,* 21 Cong., 1 Sess. (Serial 191), 534, for the presentation of the memorials. Some of
the memorials were ordered printed and appear in the serial set of congressional documents.
Jeremiah Evarts' essays were published in book form as [Jeremiah Evarts,] *Essays on the
Present Crisis in the Condition of the American Indians; First Published in the National Intelligencer, Under
the Signature of William Penn* (Boston, 1829).

[39] Richardson, *Messages and Papers of the Presidents,* II, 541.

their improvement by the Indian tribes residing in the midst of them are at length relieved from the evil," he said, "and this unhappy race—the original dwellers in our land—are now placed in a situation where we may well hope that they will share in the blessings of civilization and be saved from that degradation and destruction to which they were rapidly hastening while they remained in the States; and while the safety and comfort of our own citizens have been greatly promoted by their removal, the philanthropist will rejoice that the remnant of that ill-fated race has been at length placed beyond the reach of injury or oppression, and that the paternal care of the General Government will hereafter watch over them and protect them."[40]

In assessing Jackson's Indian policy, historians must not listen too eagerly to Jackson's political opponents or to less-than-disinterested missionaries. Jackson's contemporary critics and the historians who have accepted their arguments have certainly been too harsh, if not, indeed, quite wrong.

F. P. Prucha, "Andrew Jackson's Indian Policy: A Reassessment," *Journal of American History* 566 (December 1969): 527–39.

Abuse of Power: Andrew Jackson and the Indian Removal Act of 1830

ALFRED A. CAVE

While virtually all historical accounts of the Jackson era, both scholarly and popular, devote some space to the relocation of Indian inhabitants of the eastern United States to an Indian territory west of the Mississippi, very few acknowledge that the process as it was carried out by the Jackson administration violated guarantees contained in the congressional legislation which authorized

---

[40] *Ibid.*, III, 294. See the discussion in John William Ward, *Andrew Jackson: Symbol for an Age* (New York, 1955), 40–41.

removal. Indeed, historians frequently misunderstand and often misrepresent the provisions of this law. One recent writer, for example, claims erroneously "in 1830 the United States Congress passed . . . a statute authorizing use of military force to compel the relocation of all indigenous peoples east of the Mississippi River to points west."[1] A widely read survey of American history maintains that the law empowered "the President to send any eastern tribe beyond the Mississippi if he wished, using force if needed." Other textbooks contain the same claim.[2] While specialists familiar with the primary sources are certainly aware of the limits of the legislation passed in 1830, they have generally focused on the removal process itself and, for the most part, have devoted little if any attention to the discrepancy between the law's provisions and the administration's actions.[3] Neither of the two major studies of Jacksonian Indian removal devote any space to that issue.[4] Others note in passing that the law did not authorize the measures Jackson used, but

---

[1] Ward Churchill, *A Little Matter of Genocide* (San Francisco, 1997), 144.

[2] Quotation from Irvin Unger, *The United States: The Questions of Our Past* (Upper Saddle River, N.J., 1999), 235. For other examples of textbook accounts that imply, or state explicitly, that the act authorized forced removal, see George Brown Tindall and David E. Shi, *America: A Narrative History* (New York, 1992), 1: 411; Joseph R. Conlin, *The American Past* (Fort Worth, 1993), 242–43; John Mack Faragher, Mari Jo Buhle, Daniel Czitrom, and Susan H. Armitage, *Out of Many: A History of the American People* (Upper Saddle River, N.J., 1999), 178; Gary B. Nash, et al., *The American People: Creating a Nation and a Society* (New York, 2000), 310; Carol Berkin, Christopher L. Miller, Robert W. Cherny, and James L. Gormly, *Making America: A History of the United States* (Boston, Mass., 1995), 322–23.

[3] Jackson's misuse of the Indian Removal Act is recognized in Anthony F. C. Wallace, *The Long Bitter Trail: Andrew Jackson and the Indians* (New York, 1993). Wallace's very perceptive book, a popular supplemental text, is brief and lacks footnotes. But other accounts of the Indian Removal Act in the specialized literature are less satisfactory. Quite often, Jacksonian scholars have simply ignored the connection between legislation and removal. To cite two recent examples, Charles Sellers in *The Market Revolution* (New York, 1991) condemns Jacksonian Indian policy (308–12), but does not discuss the Indian Removal Act. Andrew Burstein, in *The Passions of Andrew Jackson* (New York, 2003), writes of the "devastating effect that Andrew Jackson's Indian policy had on his country" (236), but makes no mention of the law.

[4] Michael Paul Rogin, *Fathers and Children: Andrew Jackson and the Subjugation of the American Indian* (New York, 1975), offers a detailed, highly critical account of Jackson's tactics in dealing with Indians, but ignores the opposition to Indian removal and does not deal specifically with the Indian Removal Act. Rogin consequently fails to place the removal program within its political context. Ronald N. Satz, *American Indian Policy in the Jacksonian Era* (Lincoln, Neb., 1975), provides a fairly good account of the coercive measures employed by the Jackson administration in carrying out its removal policy (97–115), but fails to note the discrepancy between

provide few details.[5] As a result, the impression that Jackson had received congressional authorization to remove Indians from their homelands at the point of a bayonet remains widespread.

The Indian Removal Act passed by Congress in 1830 neither authorized the unilateral abrogation of treaties guaranteeing Native American land rights within the states, nor the forced relocation of the eastern Indians. Yet both occurred, on a massive scale, during Andrew Jackson's administration and were the result, not of an explicit congressional mandate, but of an abuse of presidential power. In engineering removal, Jackson not only disregarded a key section of the Indian Removal Act, but also misused the powers granted to him under the Trade and Intercourse Act of 1802. Furthermore, he failed to honor promises made in his name in order to win congressional support of the removal, and he broke a number of federal treaty commitments to Indians, including some that he had personally negotiated. While Jackson was not the only president who abused powers granted to him by the legislative branch, disregard of the extralegal character of much of his Indian policy has contributed to the over-simplistic view of Indian removal found in much of the historical literature.

---

those measures, Jackson's earlier promises, and the terms of the law. Satz states simply that "the Removal Act of 1983 provided the Jackson administration with congressional sanction and the necessary funds to begin relocating eastern tribes in the trans-Mississippi west" (64).

[5] Francis Paul Prucha, in *Indian Policy in the Formative Years: The Indian Trade and Intercourse Acts, 1780–1834* (Cambridge, 1962), declared that while the law "made no mention of coercion to remove the Indians, and on the surface it seemed harmless and humane enough . . . those who knew the policy and practice of Jackson and the Georgians understood that force would be inevitable" (238–39). In a similar vein, Robert Remini in *Andrew Jackson and His Indian Wars* (New York, 2001) observes that under the Removal Act, "Indians had to sign treaties by which they formally gave their consent to migrate. And that could prove exceedingly difficult" (233). However, neither writer fully explored the conflict between the law and the actions of the administration. Prucha and Remini are both apologists for Jackson, stressing not only the political constraints he faced, but his presumed benevolent desire to protect and preserve Indians through removal. Both, in this writer's estimation, downplay and in some instances ignore the illegality of much of Jackson's Indian policy. There is also a tendency among some writers to interpret the law in the light of the outcome of the removal controversy. Thus Jill Norgren, in *The Cherokee Cases: The Confrontation of Law and Politics* (1996), recognizes that the law ostensibly continued the voluntary, treaty-based removal program in place prior to Jackson's election. Norgren claims, however, that "the tenor of the pro-removal debate and the very nature of the bill questioned tribal sovereignty and aboriginal land titles" (85–86). The result is a discounting of the very real opposition to coerced removal and an oversimplification of this tragic episode in American history.

In a message to the Congress of the United States dated 8 December 1829 Jackson declared of removal: "This emigration should be voluntary, for it would be as cruel as unjust to compel the aborigines to abandon the graves of their fathers, and seek a home in a distant land." The president added that "our conduct toward these people" would reflect on "our national character."[6] This perspective on Indian affairs is particularly interesting in light of Jackson's treatment of Indians during his first year of office, which reflected his long-standing belief that Indian treaties were not really binding on the nation. The Jackson administration had refused to bintervene to protect the Cherokee from the state of Georgia, which by legislative act had denied the Cherokees' right to tribal self-government and challenged their ultimate ownership of their land. Repudiating all past constitutional precedents, Andrew Jackson had declared that the federal government could not interfere with the states' management of Indian affairs within their own borders. In his 1829 message to Congress, Jackson noted that "years ago I stated to them my belief that if the states chose to extend their laws over them it would not be in the power of the federal government to prevent it."[7] Secretary of War Eaton, speaking for the President, several months earlier had informed Cherokee leaders that the guarantees in treaties with the United States that they claimed protected their rights against encroachment by Georgia in fact were nothing more than temporary grants of privilege awarded by a conquering power—the United States—to a vanquished people, the Cherokee. There were, Eaton declared, no guarantees in any treaty that could be considered permanent, nor could any clause be construed as "adverse to the sovereignty of Georgia."[8] Indeed, in the early stages of Congress's deliberations on Indian removal, the report of the House Committee on Indian Affairs, written by close associates of the president, dismissed Indian treaty-making as nothing more than an "empty gesture" to placate Indian "vanity." Such treaties were not really

[6] James D. Richardson, *A Compilation of the Messages and Papers of the Presidents*, 10 vols. (Washington, D.C., 1896–99), 2: 457–59.

[7] First Annual Message, 18 December 1829, in Richardson, *Messages and Papers of the Presidents*, 2: 458.

[8] John Eaton to the Cherokee Delegation, 18 April 1829, OIALS.

treaties, the committee declared, but were only a "stately form of intercourse" useful in gaining Indian acquiescence in peacemaking and land cession. Although that view was rejected in the bill finally presented to Congress, it was reflected still in the words of some pro-removal congressmen and thereby served to arouse suspicion of the administration's real intent with regard to Indian removal.[9]

Although privately in favor of coerced removal (and as a former treaty commissioner, skilled and experienced in the coercing of Indians), President Jackson recognized that he could not obtain from Congress the aggressive removal law that many writers imagine was actually passed. Hence, Jackson did not ask that Congress author-ize forced deportation, but instead sought authorization and fund-ing to continue his predecessors' policy of granting land west of the Mississippi to tribes willing to relinquish their eastern holdings. The Indian Removal Act of 1830 made provision for the president to negotiate for land exchanges and make payments for "improve-ments" (i.e., houses, barns, orchards, etc.) that Indians had made on their lands. The president was also authorized to pay transportation costs to the West. An appropriation of $500,000 was provided for those purposes.[10] Significantly, there was no provision in the bill authorizing the seizure of land that Indians declined to cede by treaty.

Members of Jackson's administration underscored the presumed voluntary nature of the president's removal program. Secretary of War John Henry Eaton assured skeptical congressmen that "noth-ing of a compulsory nature to effect the removal of this unfortunate race of people has ever been thought of by the President, despite assertions to the contrary."[11] Worried by the extensive anti-removal campaign recently mounted by the Boston-based American Board of Commissioners of Foreign Missions and by some of Jackson's political opponents, Eaton in confidential correspondence twice warned the Governor of Georgia that the state must be careful to avoid "the appearance of harshness towards the Indians." Should Georgia be suspected of "injustice," it might well prove impossible

[9] House Committee on Indian Affairs, H.R. 227(1830), 11.

[10] The text of the Indian Removal Act is reprinted in many places, including Wallace, *Long Bitter Trail*, 125–26.

.[11] Quoted in Rogin, *Fathers and Children*, 241.

to secure broad based support for Jackson's removal program.[12] To reassure the general public, Michigan Governor and Jackson loyalist Lewis Cass, in an unsigned article in the influential *North American Review* in January 1830, declared that the administration not only understood that "no force should be used," but was determined that Indians "shall be liberally remunerated for all they may cede."[13]

Jackson's supporters in Congress also assured doubters that the administration did not intend to force a single Indian to move against his or her will. To cite three typical examples, Senator Robert Adams of Mississippi denied that the legislation Jackson requested would give the president any power "to drive those unfortunate people from their present abode." Indian relocation, the senator insisted, would remain "free and voluntary."[14] Congressman James Buchanan of Pennsylvania assured the House that there was no cause for concern, as Jackson had never considered "using the power of the government to drive that unfortunate race of men across the Mississippi."[15] Congressman Wilson Lumpkin of Georgia assured his colleagues that "no man entertains kinder feelings towards Indians than Andrew Jackson."[16] Jackson's supporters in Congress reminded skeptics of the president's assurances that Indians belonging to tribes that had signed removal treaties, but who did not themselves wish to accompany their kinsmen on the trek westward, would receive individual land grants after tribal claims had been extinguished and would then be welcome to

---

[12] Eaton to John Forsyth, 15 September, 14 October 1829, Office of Indian Affairs, Letters Sent, Microfilm, National Archives, Washington, D.C. Hereafter cited as OIALS. Writing under the assumed name "William Penn," the Society's secretary, Jeremiah Evarts, published a series of essays in the *National Intelligencer* between 5 August and 19 December 1829 that mobilized evangelicals and others in opposition to Jackson's proposed Indian removal legislation. Widely circulated in a pamphlet edition during the 1830's, the Penn essays have been more recently reprinted in Francis Paul Prucha, ed., *Cherokee Removal: The William Penn Essays and Other Writings* (Knoxville, Tenn., 1981). On Evarts's career, see John A. Andrews, III, *From Revivals to Removal: Jeremiah Evarts: The Cherokee Nation, and the Search for the Soul of America* (Athens, Ga., 1992).

[13] Lewis Cass, "Removal of the Indians," *North American Review* 30 (January 1830): 62–121.

[14] *Register of Debates*, 21 Cong., I Sess., 20 April 1830, 357–69.

[15] Quoted in Rogin, *Fathers and Children*, 214.

[16] *Register of Debates*, 21 Cong., I Sess., 17 May 1830, 1021–24.

remain behind as citizens of the states, where they would, in Jackson's words, be "protected in their persons and property."[17]

The Indian Removal Act passed by Congress included a clause guaranteeing that "nothing in this act contained shall be construed as authorizing or directing the violation of any existing treaty between the United States and any of the Indian tribes." Without that guarantee, and without Jackson's promise of legal protection for Indians who chose not to relocate, it is unlikely that the removal act would have passed the House of Representatives.

The Jacksonians' insistence on the voluntary nature of their removal program was a political ploy aimed at winning badly needed votes in the House of Representatives. In both houses of Congress, a substantial block of legislators stated bluntly that they did not believe that Andrew Jackson could be trusted to deal fairly with Indians, a suspicion confirmed when War Department correspondence discussing possible means of bribing and intimidating Indians reluctant to sign removal treaties fell into the hands of the opposition.[18] As a result, Jackson's congressional critics demanded yet more explicit procedural protection of existing Indian treaty rights. In the Senate, Theodore Frelinghuysen of New Jersey offered two amendments that, by affirming explicitly that treaty rights transcended state authority, would have guaranteed continuing federal protection of "tribes and nations" that rejected removal. One amendment stipulated that in the absence of a removal treaty, the "tribes or nations . . . shall be protected in their present possessions, and in the enjoyment of all their rights of territory and government, as heretofore exercised and enjoyed, from all interruptions and encroachments." The second declared that changes in Indian status could be made only through the traditional treaty-making process, thus denying that Indian nations were subordinate to the states.[19] In spite of significant support, however, determined opposition from southern senators meant that both amendments failed. A similar

[17] Richardson, *Messages and Papers of the Presidents*, 2: 457–59.

[18] *Register of Debates*, 21 Cong., I Sess., 9 April 1830, 310.

[19] Ibid., 309–20. Frelinghuysen's speech may also be found in (Jeremiah Evarts), *Speeches on the Passage of the Bill for the Removal of the Indians, Delivered in the Congress of the United States April and May 1830* (Boston, 1830), 1–30.

fate befell a variety of other proposed amendments, both in the Senate and the House, that would have provided more explicit federal protection of the property both of Indians who remained behind, and of those who relocated, and that would have mandated congressional inspection of the proposed Indian Territory.

The amendment that came closest to passing was introduced by Pennsylvania congressman Joseph Hemphill, a Jacksonian Democrat. Hemphill's amendment would have delayed action for a year, pending the report of "three disinterested commissioners" who would be charged with responsibility for ascertaining the real wishes of each of the eastern tribes and for certifying the suitability of the western lands earmarked for their use.[20] That measure almost passed, with Speaker of the House Andrew Stevenson, a Jacksonian loyalist, breaking a ninety-eight to ninety-eight tie vote.

When efforts to amend the Indian Removal Act failed, Old Hickory's congressional critics then sought to vote down the act, arguing that the administration's refusal to agree to more specific protections of Indian rights exposed Jackson's true intentions. While in the Senate the removal bill passed easily, with twenty-eight votes in favor and nineteen opposed, it came close to failing in the House of Representatives and passed only when Jackson, scared by the near success of the Hemphill amendment, "pressured and bullied" the recalcitrant.[21] In the end, the House voted for the Indian Removal Act by the narrow margin of 102 to 97. An analysis of the roll call reveals that the vote was sectional: a substantial majority of congressmen who represented districts north of the Mason-Dixon line opposed this legislation. Northeastern representatives were overwhelmingly opposed, with seventy-nine voting against the bill and only forty-two in favor. In the delegations from the northwest, opinion was divided. Twenty-seven western congressmen supported the bill; seventeen voted against it. There was little division in the South: sixty out of seventy-five southern representatives voted with the administration. Although the vote on the Removal Bill is usually represented as a partisan vote, a number of northern

[20] *Register of Debates*, 21 Cong. I Sess., 18 May 1830, 1132–33.

[21] Robert Remini, *The Legacy of Andrew Jackson: Essays on Democracy, Indian Removal and Slavery* (Baton Rouge, La., 1988), 66. The nickname "Old Hickory" was given to Jackson by militiamen during the Creek War. The men boasted that their general was tough as hickory wood.

Jacksonians, despite pressure from the White House, broke with Old Hickory on this issue. Some others, fearful of both their anti-removal constituents and of the president, as Martin Van Buren recalled, "felt themselves constrained to shoot the pit," and absented themselves on the day of the vote.[22]

Opposition to the act was particularly strong in Quaker Pennsylvania. Of that state's twenty-five Democratic congressmen, seventeen voted against the removal bill. Other Jacksonian Democrats also broke party ranks, with six from New York, six from New England, four from Ohio, one from Indiana, and six from the South opposing removal. In the Senate, five pro-Jackson senators from New England, joined by a Senator from Pennsylvania, one from Ohio, and one from Missouri, had refused to support the president on this issue. By contrast, seven anti-Jackson congressmen from the South and one from Indiana supported the Indian Removal Act.[23] While the measure's support was primarily southern, Jackson's efforts to impose party discipline had secured a narrow victory empowering him to grant land west of the Mississippi to eastern Indians willing to relocate.

Indian removal as carried out by Jackson and his successor Martin Van Buren was anything but a voluntary relocation program. Numerous contemporary witnesses provide damning testimony regarding fraud, coercion, corruption, and malfeasance both in the negotiation of removal treaties and in their execution. In their zeal to secure removal treaties, agents of the Jackson administration resorted to extensive bribery of compliant and corrupt tribal officials and frequently threatened independent Indian leaders opposed to relocation. In a series of blatant violations of the specific guarantees that Andrew Jackson and his supporters had offered to Congress in 1830, federal officials, by a variety of ruses, in effect denied antiremoval majorities within Indian tribes the right to vote on the ratification of removal treaties. Furthermore, the administration systematically removed Indian agents who either opposed the removal policy or were less than zealous in coercing compliance. Moreover, Indians endeavoring to make good on Jackson's

[22] Martin Van Buren, *Autobiography*, ed. John E. Fitzpatrick (Washington, D.C., 1920), 289.

[23] Fred S. Rolater, "The American Indian and the Origin of the Second American Party System," *Wisconsin Magazine of History* 76 (1993): 193.

promise that they could remain within the states as individuals were subjected to all manner of harassment from state officials, speculators, and Indian-hating mobs as the federal government looked the other way.[24]

Andrew Jackson's defenders over the years have suggested that Old Hickory ought not to be held responsible for the abuses associated with removal. Those abuses, in their view, were the work of lesser officials over whom he had little control. Jackson biographer Robert Remini, for example, has written that Old Hickory "struggled to prevent fraud and corruption" in the removal process, and sought through their relocation to protect "Indian life and culture."[25] Furthermore, according to Remini, "as far as Jackson was concerned, the Indians could refuse to remove and stay where they were." He only asked that they acknowledge the authority of the state in which they resided. Remini recognizes that few of those who wished to remain were actually able to do so, but assures us that Andrew Jackson was not personally to blame. "Unfortunately the President's noble desire to give the Indians a free choice between staying and recovery, one devoid of coercion, was disregarded by land greedy state and federal officials, who practiced fraud and deception to enrich themselves and their friends at the expense of the native tribes."[26]

In these assertions, Remini and other Jackson apologists are mistaken. Close examination of administrative correspondence and personal memoranda suggests that Jackson's guarantees in 1829 and early 1830 that removal would be voluntary and that those Indians who did not wish to relocate would be protected in their personal and property rights were politically expedient but fundamentally dishonest. Some rough notes in his personal papers offers some insights into the president's private thoughts about Indians as citizens of the states. In a set of points he intended to raise with his

---

[24] The literature on the execution of Indian removal is extensive. A useful guide is Regan A. Lutz, *West of Eden: The Historiography of the Trail of Tears* (Ph.D. diss., University of Toledo, 1995).

[25] Robert Remini, *Andrew Jackson and the Course of American Freedom 1822–1832* (New York, 1981), 264. For a more detailed statement of his views on this issue, see Remini's *Legacy of Andrew Jackson*, 45–82 and his more recent *Andrew Jackson and His Indian Wars*, 226–53. The most uncritical modern defense of Jackson is to be found in Francis Paul Prucha, "Andrew Jackson's Indian Policy: A Reassessment," *Journal of American History* 56 (1969): 527–39.

[26] Remini, *Andrew Jackson and His Indian Wars*, 237.

envoy to Mexico, scribbled in the summer of 1829, Jackson lists
among the advantages of the possible acquisition of Texas the
prospect that the "additional territory" could be used for "concentrating the Indians," thereby "relieving the states of the inconveniences which the residue within their limits at present afford."[27]
Jackson's own draft of his 1829 message to Congress contains no
reference to voluntary removal. The eloquent acknowledgement
that forced removal would be an act of cruelty that would reflect
adversely on our national honor was added later, perhaps at the
insistence of advisers hoping to reassure some northern congressmen.[28] Jackson himself was more concerned about other political
considerations. In a draft of a position paper probably written in
1831, he argued that if the states indeed had no jurisdiction over
Indian lands within their boundaries and thus lacked the right to
take that land when needed by white settlers, then numerous land
grants, and with them countless white land titles, in the frontier
states of the upper South were "void." "Such a doctrine," he wrote,
"would not be well received in the west."[29]

Jackson understood from the outset that the states would not in
fact extend the full protection of the law to those Indians who
remained behind. When the governor of Georgia informed Jackson
that no Indian would be given a land allotment in his state, Jackson
offered no objection. Instead, he warned Indians that the federal
government could not protect them if they chose not to emigrate.
When the Cherokee leadership indicated that they would accept a
removal treaty that included the sort of allotment option earlier
made available to the Choctaw, Creek, and Chickasaw, Jackson told
them that they could have no land in Georgia. It is telling that in
his 1830 annual message to Congress, Jackson in effect repudiated
his 1829 observations about the cruelty of compelling "aborigines
to abandon the graves of their fathers and seek a home in a distant
land." "Doubtless," the president now declared, "it will be painful

[27] "Notes on Poinsett's Instructions," 3 August 1829, Jackson Papers, Library of Congress
Microfilm.

[28] Draft of the First Annual Message, 8 December 1829, Jackson Papers, Library of Congress Microfilm.

[29] Andrew Jackson to the secretary of war [1831?], Jackson Papers, Library of Congress
Microfilm.

for them to leave the graves of their forefathers, but what do they do more than our ancestors did or our children are now doing?"[30]

Jackson regarded state harassment of Indians as a useful means of encouraging removal. Georgia officials claimed that Jackson himself in 1829 told a congressman disturbed by the delays in the Cherokee removal, "Build a fire under them. When it gets hot enough, they'll move."[31] While Jackson himself made no record of that conversation, Georgia's governor later sent a confidential letter to Jackson expressing satisfaction with "your general plans and policy in relieving the states from their remnant Indian population." The Governor was gratified that Jackson understood that "Indians cannot live in the midst of a White Population and be governed by the same laws." As for the Cherokee, who still refused to sign a removal treaty, "starvation and destruction await them if they remain much longer in their present abodes."[32] There is no doubt that Jackson shared those sentiments. Several months after the passage of the Removal Act, he assured a correspondent concerned about delays in the forthcoming Choctaw negotiations: "Indians could not possibly live under the laws of the states." He added: "If now they refuse to accept the liberal terms offered, they only must be responsible for whatever evils and difficulties may arise."[33] Shortly thereafter, Jackson, frustrated by the refusal of several

[30] Prior to his election to the presidency, Jackson had entertained the possibility that some Indians might well choose to abandon their "ancient customs and habits" and accept "agricultural pursuits, civil life, and a government of laws." Those Indians, he advised John Coffee in 1817, should be allowed to remain on individual land allotments within the states. He anticipated that they would be protected by state laws, and become a part of "civilized society" Andrew Jackson to John Coffee, 13 July 1817, quoted in Remini, *Legacy of Andrew Jackson*, 56. As we have seen, his early comments on the removal bill held out the same prospect. Yet Jackson was soon declaring the necessity for total removal even of those who had adopted "agricultural pursuits, civil life, and a government of laws." He justified his repudiation of [his] earlier position by claiming that whites and Indians could not coexist in the same territory. It may be that the intransigent position of Georgia, combined with pressure from other southern states, explains Jackson's apparent change of position. However, some of his earlier statements, cited elsewhere in this paper, suggest that he was never willing [to] tolerate any substantial Indian presence east of the Mississippi.

[31] Quoted in Samuel Carter III, *Cherokee Sunset: A Nation Betrayed* (Garden City, N.J., 1976), 83.

[32] Governor Wilson Lumpkin to Jackson, 9 February 1835, Bassett, *Correspondence*, V: 327.

[33] Andrew Jackson to John Pitchlynn, 5 August 1830, Bassett, *Correspondence*, IV: 169.

southeastern Indian nations to heed his summons to meet with him at Franklin, Tennessee, to discuss removal, wrote his close associate William B. Lewis to predict that the activities of former Attorney General William Wirt and other antiremoval activists "will lead to the destruction of the poor ignorant Indians." "I have used all the persuasive means in my power," the president declared, "I have exonerated the national character from all imputations, and now leave the poor deluded Creeks and Cherokees to their fate, and their annihilation, which their wicked advisers has [sic] induced."[34]

Jackson repeatedly warned that those Indians who did not agree to removal would lose their right of self-government and be subject to the laws of the states in which they resided. In so doing, he far exceeded his legal mandate under the Indian Removal Act of 1830. That law, as we have seen, explicitly upheld existing treaty rights and obligations. Rather than enforcing the laws that forbade white settlement on treaty lands, Jackson informed Indian leaders that he lacked the power to protect them from even the most extreme and oppressive actions of the state governments and of lawless whites. One chief, self-described as "old and feeble," wrote to his "Great Father" Andrew Jackson to complain that treaty provisions were no longer honored and that whites invaded Indian country to "steal our property." Making matters worse, the federal soldiers in the area refused to help the Indians, but when Indians tried to resist the squatters, they were hunted down and shot "as if . . . they had been so many wild dogs." Only the Great Father, the chief pleaded, could protect his Indian children and restore peace.[35] We have no record of Jackson's reply. But a typical example of Jackson's response to Indian petitioners is found in his message to the Cherokee, dated 16 March 1835, wherein he declared, "you cannot remain where you now are. Circumstances that cannot be controlled, and which are beyond the reach of human laws, render it impossible that you can flourish in the midst of a civilized community. . . . Deceive yourselves no longer. . . . Shut your ears to bad counsels."[36] While it is true that Jackson on occasion sought to curb the excesses

[34] Jackson to Major William B. Lewis, 25 August 1830, Ibid., IV: 177.

[35] Tiskinhah-haw to Andrew Jackson, 21 May 1831, OIALR.

[36] Jackson Talk to the Cherokee, March 1831, Jackson Papers, Library of Congress.

of some of the more corrupt Indian removal contractors, and ordered some reforms in the process, a close examination of the record suggests that he was primarily concerned with dealing with those who defrauded the government, or who cheated other whites, and was relatively indulgent with those who defrauded Indians.

While some writers have explained Jackson's refusal to protect the sovereignty of Indian nations against the claims of the states as an act consistent with his deep respect for states' rights, one must remember that Andrew Jackson not only refused to honor the obligations contained in treaties negotiated by his predecessors, but also ignored treaty promises made by his own administration.[37] His newly negotiated removal treaties generally guaranteed Indians federal protection from the depredations of white squatters prior to the completion of land surveys. While the federal government clearly possessed both the right and the obligation to enforce those guarantees, Secretary of War Cass, although required by the removal treaties to direct his agents to eject intruders on Indian land, made it clear that Andrew Jackson did not want federal officers to be particularly diligent in doing so. In a letter to United States Marshal Robert L. Crawford, he wrote: "it is the President's desire" that the order "be executed with as much regard for the feelings and situations of the persons (white squatter), whose cases are embraced by it, as possible." Force, the marshal was told, should be used "only when absolutely necessary," and then only after explaining the situation at length to those who were asked to move.[38] Soon thereafter, Jackson's administration abandoned even the pretext of removing illegal occupants of Indian land. Southern politicians had made it clear that their constituents would not tolerate any real enforcement of the protective clauses in the removal treaties. In Mississippi, Congressman Franklin Plummer declared that the settlers who had occupied Choctaw lands came from "numerous families of the first respectability" and had been encouraged by the federal agent to plant their crops on Indian land. He further warned that Mississippi would resent their eviction.[39] Similarly, in

[37] Ronald Satz, Robert Remini, and Francis Paul Prucha, in the works cited earlier, all stress the constraints imposed by Jackson's states rights philosophy.

[38] House Document No. 452, 21 Cong., 2 Session, II, 806.

[39] Plummer to Cass, 28 May 1832, Senate Document 512, 23 Cong., 1 Sess., 3: 361–63.

Alabama, federal efforts to deal with an unusually violent group of squatters provoked an armed confrontation, and a period of tension between the state and the administration that ended with an agreement that the treaty provision calling for the removal of all intruders on Creek land would not be enforced.[40]

Plummer's claim of federal collusion was well founded. Jackson's agents from the outset understood that the president expected them to be considerate of white squatters, not of the Indians the squatters had so often dispossessed. Thus they not only did not challenge state officials who encouraged whites to occupy Indian lands prior to removal, but also on occasion actively encouraged the violation of removal treaty guarantees. The removal treaties envisioned an orderly process whereby whites purchasing Indian land would take possession only after the original owners had departed. But when Congressman Plummer in the spring of 1832 expressed concern that a provision in the recent Choctaw treaty which forbade white occupation of land in Choctaw territory occupied before September 1833 might be used to disallow the rights of some Mississippians who had already bought Indian titles, Secretary of War Cass replied: "The President is happy . . . that he is not called upon to execute [those] . . . provisions of the treaty."[41] As to the political reasons for Jackson's happiness, General Winfield Scott, in correspondence with Secretary of War Cass, noted that use of federal troops to eject white occupants of Indian land "would inflame the passions of Virginia, North Carolina, South Carolina, Georgia, and Mississippi, and thus give wider spread to the heresies of nullification and secession."[42]

Jackson was well aware of the misdeeds of his Indian agents. After leaving office, he told Francis P. Blair that dealing with the Indian office was "the most arduous part of my duty, and I watched over it with great vigilance, and could hardly keep it under proper restraint, and free from abuse and injury to the administration."[43]

[40] William Irvin to Lewis Cass, 30 July 1832 Senate Document No. 512, 23 Cong., 1 Sess., 3: 410; Young, *Redskins, Ruffleshirts, and Rednecks,* 76–82

[41] Cass to Plummer, 23 May 1832, *American State Papers: Public Lands,* 38 vols. (Washington, D.C., 1832–1861), VII: 611.

[42] Quoted in Young, *Redskins, Ruffleshirts, and Rednecks,* 80.

[43] Jackson to Francis P. Blair, 4 July 1838, Bassett, *Correspondence,* V: 553.

His claim that he had displayed "great vigilance" must be placed in proper context. Jackson was speaking of those who cheated the government or other whites, not those who abused Indians. One combs the record in vain for evidence that Jackson took any particular pains to protect Indians from speculators and swindlers. Consider, for example, Jackson's intervention in the Choctaw removal. In Mississippi, Indian agent William Ward refused to provide the land allotments within the state promised by treaty to those Choctaws who chose not to relocate. Often drunk, Ward was seldom available at the registration office, frequently destroyed records, and—refusing to meet with concerned Choctaw leaders, or with those who had not been able to obtain their promised allotments— reported to his superiors in Washington, D.C. that only sixty-nine Choctaw had qualified for land in the state. He admitted that many others had tried to register, but reported that he had denied them a place on the register because he suspected that opponents of the removal program had influenced them. Despite Ward's acknowledgement that he had violated the treaty, the administration initially took no action. When Choctaws victimized by Ward appealed to Jackson, his first reaction was to brush aside their complaints. As president, he declared, he could do nothing. The Choctaw should look to Congress for relief. But when certain prominent Democrats who had hoped to profit from the purchase and re-sale of lands in Mississippi allocated to those Choctaw who stayed behind complained about Ward, Jackson suddenly discovered that he did have power to do something about it and promptly issued orders to investigate and resolve Choctaw claims.[44]

In the event, over one thousand Choctaw allotments were subsequently registered. But much of the best allotment land soon fell into the hands of speculators. Remarking upon this, Secretary of War Cass noted that, "our citizens were disposed to buy, and the Indians to sell," but when fraud occurred as it often did, Cass disavowed any responsibility for protecting the Choctaws from their

---

[44] William Ward to Samuel Hamilton, 21 June 1831; Anthony Campbell to Lewis Cass, 5 August 1832; William Armstrong to George Gibson, 13 October 1832, Senate Document 512, 23 Cong., I Sess., I: 386; 2: 493; 3: 416–18; William Ward to Samuel Hamilton, 29 October 1831, OIALS; "Application for Indemnity, for Being Deprived of Reservations, of the Choctaw Indians," 1 February 1832, *American State Papers: Public Lands*, 8: 432.

own "improvident habits." If Indians made bad contracts that rendered them destitute, they had only themselves to blame.[45] The allotment fraud investigations in Mississippi, which extended over a decade, pitted white settlers against speculators. Jackson denounced speculators, but regarded Indian removal as the sole means of protecting Indians from the unprincipled and the corrupt. In those cases where claims commissioners found evidence that Choctaws had been illegally dispossessed, they did not restore them to their allotments, but rather ordered that they be issued paper script in the value of $1.25 per acre. Even this compensation was limited in practice, however, since half the script was never actually issued while much of the rest fell into the hands of speculators. As for Ward, he remained in office until the progress of Choctaw removal made his office superfluous.[46] By contrast, Jackson did not hesitate to replace Indian agents whose commitment to removal was less than total; indeed, within two years of the passage of the Indian Removal Act, Jackson had fired over half of the Indian agents and subagents in the field.[47]

Jackson's flexible understanding of presidential power was also manifest in his selective enforcement of the Indian Trade and Intercourse Act of 1802. That law mandated federal action to remove whites that intruded on Indian land. Reluctant to use the law against traders, speculators, and squatters who cheated or abused Indians, Jackson was quite willing to invoke its provisions in order to silence his critics. Thus, even before the passage of the Indian Removal Act, the administration invoked the authority of the 1802 Act to detain and eject from Indian Territory missionaries and other white philanthropists who opposed the Indian removal program.[48]

[45] Cass to R. J. Meigs, 11 October 1834; OIALS.

[46] On the activities of speculators, and of Agent Ward, see the depositions in *American State Papers: Public Lands*, 7: 641–53, 8: 337, 629–32, 691–93; and the correspondence in Senate Document 512, 23 Cong. Ist Sess. 1: 386; 2: 473; 3: 416–418. The history of the Choctaw allotments controversy is carefully analyzed in Mary E. Young, *Redskins, Ruffleshirts, and Rednecks*, 47–62. See also Arthur DeRosier, *The Removal of the Choctaw Indians* (Knoxville, Tenn., 1970): 136–37; Satz, *American Indian Policy in the Jacksonian Era*, 89; Rogin, *Fathers and Children*, 221.

[47] Remini, *Andrew Jackson and His Indian Wars*, 229.

[48] McKinney to Indian Agents, 17 February 1829; Eaton to Ward, 11 July 1829; Randolph to Ward, 20 October 1830, OIALS; Rogin, *Fathers and Children*, 222–23.

Jackson was also willing to send federal troops into the states to deal with Indians who sought to obstruct removal. Worried about resistance in Tennessee, the president offered to dispatch federal troops to protect cooperative Indians from coercion by tribal governments. Likewise, disturbed by reports of violence against whites in the Cherokee Nation, the president directed his agents in Georgia to warn Cherokee principal chief John Ross and his council that the full power of the federal government would be used to punish Indian malefactors who harassed or harmed emigrants, pro-emigration chiefs, or government agents. Moreover, Ross himself would be held personally accountable "for every murder committed by his people."[49]

As we have noted, Jackson's presidential activism in dealing with crime in the Indian country did not extend to the protection of Indians from corrupt Indian agents or land speculators. His intervention in the controversies over Creek land allotments offers further evidence of his failure to enforce the law in an even-handed manner. The Creek Indians, who had earlier relinquished their Georgia lands but still lived in Alabama, refused to sign a treaty providing for their relocation west of the Mississippi. However, in March 1832 they agreed to give up most of their Alabama territory in exchange for the promise that they could remain on individual allotments within the state. The 1832 treaty contained guarantees both of the Creek right to land ownership and of their immunity from forced removal.[50] But as soon as they sought to claim the land titles promised to them, the Creeks were victimized by hordes of unprincipled whites who, when other means failed, often gained title for themselves by hiring people to impersonate the real owners and lay claim to their land. The Creek governing council begged the secretary of war to enforce the treaty and remove the intruders. "We are surrounded . . . our lives are in jeopardy, we are daily threatened."[51] The local federal marshal confirmed the Creeks' description of the crisis, reporting one instance in which white squatters "had not

[49] Andrew Jackson to B. F. Curry and H. Montgomery, 3 September 1834, Bassett, *Correspondence,* V: 288.

[50] *7 Statutes at Large,* 366–68.

[51] Neah Micco et al. to Lewis Cass, 26 September 1832, Senate Document 512, 23 Cong., I Sess., III: 464, 470.

only taken the Indians' land from them and burnt and destroyed their houses and corn, but used violence to their persons."[52] The administration's response was to advise the Creeks to emigrate. Those who found themselves thrown off their lands by unscrupulous speculators or by squatters received little help from federal agents and investigators. Although willing to investigate and provide for federal adjudication of the conflicting claims of whites who defrauded one another in the purchase of Creek land allotments in Alabama, the Jackson administration showed little concern for Creeks victimized by those frauds. An agent in the field, Robert McHenry, noted that "the interest of the Indian is not much at hart [sic]" in antifraud proceedings in Alabama.[53] Another federal official, describing the condition of the Creeks in 1833, wrote: "How the Indians are going to subsist the present year I can't imagine. Some of them are sustaining themselves upon roots. They have, apparently, very little corn, and scarcely any flock. The game is gone, and what they are to do, God only knows."[54] Jackson was not unaware of their situation. The administration's own special investigator had advised that nowhere in the world could one find "a greater mass of corruption . . . than has been engendered by the Creek treaty." But when a few angry and starving Creeks raided some white farms in their former homeland in 1836, Jackson ordered the army to deport the entire nation by force.[55]

By contrast, Old Hickory showed great leniency in dealing with Indian Agent Benjamin Smith. A friend and supporter of the president, Smith had attained notoriety by stealing thousands of dollars of Chickasaw funds and by defrauding tribal members by paying

---

[52] Robert Crawford to Lewis Cass, 31 August 1832, Senate Document 512, 23 Cong., I Sess., III, 440, 231. For a very judicious survey of the evidence on allotment frauds, see Mary E. Young, "The Creek Frauds: A Study in Conscience and Corruption," *Mississippi Valley Historical Review* 42 (1955): 411–37, and *Redskins, Ruffleshirts, and Rednecks*, 73–98.

[53] Robert McHenry to Lewis Cass, 25 May 1835, Senate Document No. 425, 24 Cong., I Sess., 280–81.

[54] Enoch Parson to Cass, 13 January 1833, Senate Document 512, 4: 29.

[55] John B. Hogan to Lewis Cass, 30 March 1836, quoted in Rogin, *Fathers and Children*, 231. For the Creek removal, see Michael D. Green, *The Politics of Indian Removal: Creek Government and Society in Crisis* (Lincoln, Neb., 1983), and Foreman, *Indian Removal*, 107–92. For the background of the so-called "Second Creek War," see the documents in "Causes of the Hostilities of the Creek and Seminole Indians" *American State Papers: Military Affairs*, VI: 574–783.

their claims in depreciated "rag money." He lost his job, but was not prosecuted and thus kept his ill-gotten gains.[56] It is also worth noting that in Florida, a notoriously corrupt agent named John Phagan was finally cashiered, not for his abuse of the Seminoles or his role in provoking an Indian war, but for embezzling public funds.[57] A memorandum that Jackson prepared for the United States Senate but never sent suggests that the president was not terribly concerned about the means agents employed as long as they achieved the desired end without creating a public scandal. In that memo, Jackson responded to Ohio senator Ewing's complaint that one of his Indian agents had resorted to "deceptions, frauds, and treacheries" by declaring that whether those charges were true or not, they "would in no manner affect the validity of the Treaties" he had negotiated.[58] Andrew Jackson did nothing to honor his own guarantee that those Indians who wished to remain as citizens of the states could do so. Hence, Cherokee efforts to negotiate an accommodation that would grant them citizenship rights and allotments in Georgia in exchange for relinquishment of their claim of sovereignty and a substantial land cession received no encouragement from the White House.[59]

Soon after Jackson signed the Removal Bill, Henry Clay, declaring that it "threatens to bring a foul and lasting stain upon the good faith, humanity, and character of the nation," proposed that Jackson's opponents in the House of Representatives seek to block its enforcement by withholding appropriations, and that the Senate support those efforts by refusing to ratify removal treaties.[60]

[56] Rogin, *Fathers and Children*, 223.

[57] John Mahon, *History of the Second Seminole War 1835–1842* (Gainesville, Fla., 1985), 84–85.

[58] Jackson to the United States Senate, 16 January 1832, Jackson Papers, Library of Congress Microfilm.

[59] John Ross, "Letter in Answer to Inquiries from a Friend, July 2, 1836," *Niles Weekly Register*, 1 October 1836.

[60] Henry Clay to Daniel Webster, 7 June 1830 in *The Papers of Daniel Webster, Correspondence*, Charles M. Wilste, et al., eds., 7 vols. (Hanover, N.H., 1974–88), III: 80–82 and Webster to Edward Everett, 7 May 1836, ibid., IV: 110; Robert Remini, *Daniel Webster: The Man and His Times* (New York, 1997), 447; Robert Remini, *Henry Clay: Statesman for the Union* (New York, 1991), 386. Historians of the Whig party have generally ignored the Indian Removal issue. Most give it only a few sentences. The most thorough history, Michael Holt, *The Rise and Fall of the American Whig Party* (New York, 1999), although over a thousand pages in length, makes no mention of Whig opposition to removal.

Although he had little admiration for Native Americans or their culture, Clay had long opposed what he had described in 1819 as Andrew Jackson's "cruel violence" towards Indians.[61] Whig opposition to removal was driven in part by public pressure from evangelicals and others moved by humane considerations. In the William Penn essays of 1829, Jeremiah Evarts had warned that if the Jacksonian removal proposal were adopted, there would be "much suffering ... much exposure, sickness, hunger, nakedness, either on the journey, or after arrival. . . . The crowding together [in the Indian Territory] of different tribes, speaking languages entirely unintelligible to each other, and accustomed to different habits, will be productive of quarrels." Federal agents, Evarts predicted, would not effectively protect their charges during and after the removal process. "Judging from all past experience, some of them would be profane, licentious, and over bearing, and a majority would be selfish, looking principally at the emoluments of office and caring little for the Indians." Stripped of all claims of sovereignty, the Indians after removal would be entirely defenseless. With these words, Evarts anticipated the horrors of the Trail of Tears—a prophecy that Jackson's opponents would recall throughout the 1830s.[62]

If some Whigs were motivated by a concern for Indians, others were political opportunists seizing on Jackson's possible abuse of Indians as a means of embarrassing and discrediting the president.[63] Even more critical to Jackson's opposition than either humanitarianism or opportunism, however, was the issue of states' rights. To conservatives committed to the premise that the federal government must play a major role in promoting economic growth through positive legislation on the tariff, internal improvements, and banking, Jackson's invocation of states' rights principles in dealing with Indian matters had distressing implications. Ever mindful

[61] Remini, *Andrew Jackson and His Indian Wars*, 163.

[62] Prucha, *Cherokee Removal*, 201–11.

[63] A conversation between John Quincy Adams and Henry Clay during the Adams presidency is particularly revealing. As Adams noted in his diary on 22 December, 185, "Mr. Clay said he thought it was impossible to civilize Indians. . . . He believed they were destined to extinction, and although he would never use or countenance inhumanity towards them, he did not think them, as a race, worth preserving." Adams added that he feared Clay's assessment was well founded. John Quincy Adams, *Memoirs of John Quincy Adams*, ed. Charles Francis Adams, 12 vols. (Philadelphia, Pa., 1874–77), 7: 89–90.

that the Constitution declares treaties as well as acts of Congress the supreme law of the land, Whigs regarded Andrew Jackson's refusal to use federal power to secure their enforcement as nothing short of a dereliction of duty that opened the door to the dismantling of federal authority through state nullification.[64]

Many conservatives were equally disturbed by the confiscation of Cherokee property. Whigs were well aware of the fact that the Cherokee leaders who were dispossessed by the Georgians were not impoverished primitives living close to nature, but were actually often wealthy landowners, slaveholders, or merchants. The president's failure to enforce those provisions of the federal Trade and Intercourse Act mandating forced removal of those who illegally occupied Indian land, combined with his acquiescence in Georgia's confiscation of Cherokee-owned farms and plantations, raised grave questions about the sanctity of private property and the government's role in protecting property rights. Even in Georgia, Whigs challenged the premise that states had the right to seize Indian property by legislative mandate.[65]

Whigs also deplored Jackson's overly vigorous use of presidential prerogatives, as they held a view of the constitutional separation of powers that reflected long-standing conservative fears of the accession to executive power of a popular demagogue not deferential to the rights and interests of the propertied and the prominent. During the debate on the Indian Removal Act, Congressman Henry Stores of New York, after charging Jackson with acting as "a military chieftain" rather than as chief magistrate of a free Republic, intoned what would become the Whig mantra: "the concentration of power in the hands of the executive leads to despotism."[66]

Whig advocacy of ongoing federal protection of the Indian can also be seen as an outgrowth of their continuing if often unacknowledged belief in the politics of deference and in the chain of mutual obligations and benefits which, in their view, bound the social classes together. In the hierarchical, organic society that many Whig leaders envisioned as their ideal, the strong had an obligation to protect,

[64] Henry Clay to Samuel Southard, 14 February 1831, in *The Papers of Henry Clay*, ed. James F. Hopkins, 10 vols. (Lexington, Ky., 1959–1991), VIII: 323.

[65] Paul Murray, *The Whig Party in Georgia* (Chapel Hill, N.C., 1948), 194–95.

[66] *Register of Debates in Congress*, 21 Cong., 1 Sess., 15 May 1830, 1002.

discipline, and improve the weak and vulnerable.[67] Laissez-faire individualism, of the sort upheld by Secretary Cass in his refusal to protect Indians from the consequences of their own bad judgment in land transactions, was a Jacksonian, not a Whig, dogma. Moreover, although it certainly does not fit all cases, historian Alexander Saxton is correct in contrasting the "hard racism" of Jacksonian Democracy, with its undercurrent of Indian hating, with Whig "soft racism," with its paternalistic determination to uplift "savages."[68]

When the first of Jackson's removal treaties came before the Senate, the opposition voted down the preamble, which stated, "the President cannot protect the Choctaw people in their property, rights, and possessions, in the State of Mississippi." But their bid to reject the treaty itself failed by three votes.[69] Later efforts to reform or terminate the removal process also ended in failure. Despite persistent public criticism of removal abuses, Jackson's opponents (known as Whigs after the merger of the National Republican Party with various other anti-Jackson elements) generally were unable to muster the votes required to deny the Jacksonians the two-thirds majority needed for treaty ratification. In 1832, Jackson assured his friend John Coffee that Clay and his associates had won little support for their efforts to block removal and had therefore "abandoned their opposition." Jackson believed that his administration's refusal to accept and enforce the Supreme Court decision in *Worcester* v. *Georgia*, which upheld Cherokee treaty rights and declared Georgia's legislative aggression against the Cherokee Republic unconstitutional, would settle the issue. His alleged quip, "John Marshall has made his decision, now let him enforce it" may be apocryphal, but Jackson did write to John Coffee that "the

[67] Whig ideas about the nature of society are best approached through examination of the files of *The American Whig Review*, published between 1845 and 1852. See in particular the two-part article "Human Rights According to Modern Philosophy" published in October and November of 1845. The secondary literature is not extensive. Daniel Walker Howe, *The Political Culture of the American Whigs* (Chicago, Ill., 1979); Thomas Brown, *Politics and Statesmanship: Essays on the American Whig Party* (New York, 1985); and John Ashworth, *Agrarians and Aristocrats: Party Political Ideology in the United States, 1837–1846* (Cambridge, 1987) contain valuable insights.

[68] Alexander Saxton, *The Rise and Fall of the White Republic* (London, 1990), 53–76.

[69] Senate Journal 22, Cong. I Sess., 21 February 1831, 236. The vote on the preamble was twenty-five in favor, nineteen opposed. The treaty itself was ratified by a vote of thirty-five to twelve.

decision of the Supreme Court has fell still born . . . it cannot coerce Georgia to yield to its mandate."[70] He added that even if he were so inclined, he could not persuade "one regiment of militia" to fight to protect the Cherokees from Georgia. Should they resist removal, Jackson declared "the arm of the government is not sufficiently strong to preserve them from destruction."[71] When John Ridge, speaker of the Cherokee National Council, asked Jackson directly if the federal government would enforce the court's finding that Georgia had no right to impose its laws on the Cherokee, Jackson made it clear that would never happen.[72] There is, however, some evidence that Jackson was worried about further legal controversy, as he wrote to Governor Lumpkin to advise that Georgia "do no act that would give the Federal court a legal jurisdiction over a case that might arise with the Cherokee." He used his influence to persuade Lumpkin to release the missionaries.[73]

In the spring of 1833, Senator Frelinghuysen concluded that the Cherokee would be well-advised to seek the most favorable terms possible and move west as further resistance seemed futile. John Ridge agreed. The missionary Samuel Worcester, whose incarceration under a Georgia law forbidding whites to live in Indian territory without a state license was the basis of the Supreme Court decision against Georgia, concurred.[74] In 1835, presenting a petition to the Senate from the Cherokee "Removal Party" (a minority faction headed by Ridge), Massachusetts senator Edward Everett, hitherto one of the most eloquent opponents of removal, concluded that the Cherokee now had little hope of remaining in their homeland.[75] Paradoxically, Jackson's successful opposition to South

[70] Horace Greeley claimed he learned of Jackson's remark from Massachusetts Congressman George N. Briggs. See *The American Conflict: A History of the Great Rebellion in the United States of America 1860–54*, 2 vols. (Hartford, 1865) I: 106. Robert Remini argues that Jackson probably did not say it. Since there was no federal habeas corpus statute applicable to state prisoners in 1832, there was no way to force Georgia to release the missionaries. *Legacy of Andrew Jackson*, 70.

[71] Andrew Jackson to John Coffee, 7 April 1832, Bassett, *Correspondence*, IV: 429.

[72] Remini, *Legacy of Andrew Jackson*, 73.

[73] Jackson to Lumpkin, 22 June 1832, Bassett, *Correspondence*, IV: 451.

[74] Frelinghuysen to David Greene, 23 April 1832, quoted in Edwin Miles, "After John Marshall's Decision," *Journal of Southern History* 39 (November 1973): 530.

[75] *Register of Debates*, 25 Cong., 2 Sess., 10 January 1835, 1008.

Carolina's nullification of the tariff in 1832–33 weakened Whig resolve to defend Indians from removal abuses. Conservatives feared that, if South Carolina successfully evaded federal tariff legislation, the federal government's capacity to promote economic growth through legislation would be permanently impaired. Southerners, by contrast, feared that denial of a state's right to block tyrannical and unconstitutional assertions of national power could lead to federal interference with slavery. Jackson's support of Indian removal represented a concession to states' rights in dealing with Georgia's treatment of the Cherokee that helped defuse this issue. As one scholar notes, "in other southern states—Alabama, Georgia, Mississippi, and Tennessee—Jackson's support for Indian removal had lessened antipathy toward the tariff and diminished the power of the common cause involving states rights." Hence, conservative politicians were fearful "that agitation over the Cherokee would add to the danger of civil dissension in the United States. In some quarters, there was a political excitement bordering on panic."[76]

Even so, the removal issue would not die, and the passing of the nullification crisis relieved momentary Whig fears of continued identification with the antiremoval cause. Reports of the horrendous hardships endured by those Indians outraged many Americans. The petition campaign against removal continued throughout the 1830s. On one occasion, Congressman John Quincy Adams presented a petition from New York City that was forty-seven yards long. Jacksonian efforts to pass a resolution that all petitions on the Indian removal question be tabled automatically failed in the House by a vote of ninety-one to ninety-two.[77] Jackson was mistaken in his belief that his opponents would drop the Indian removal issue. Whig leaders soon discovered that many of their constituents did not agree that the matter was settled, and so the leaders responded accordingly. A sectional issue from the outset, party leaders sought to transform support or opposition to Indian removal into a litmus test of party loyalty. Historian Fred S. Rolater's analysis of roll call votes in Congress from 1830 to 1842 reveals that on no issue were Whigs more united. Overall, 84.74 percent [of] Whig congressional

[76] Norgren, *Cherokee Cases,* 126.

[77] Leonard L. Richards, *The Life and Times of Congressman John Quincy Adams* (New York, 1986), 149.

votes on the issue were cast in opposition to removal measures. Democrats, by contrast, supported the administration in 80.74 percent of the votes they cast on congressional legislation implementing the policy.[78] Continued popular opposition in the North made it inexpedient for some Democratic congressmen to be identified with removal, although pressure from party leaders and the White House brought many into line. Southern Whigs faced comparable difficulties in opposing the policy.

Substantial Democratic legislative majorities throughout the decade assured that there would be no significant congressional interference with the removal program. Antiremoval forces were, of course, strongest in the House of Representatives, where the South controlled only a minority of the seats. But treaty ratification was the prerogative of the Senate, where southerners and their northern Democratic allies had little difficulty mustering the votes needed to implement the removal program. There was one close call. Jackson's opponents almost defeated the notorious Treaty of New Echota (removing the Cherokees) in 1835. The treaty, approved by a small faction of the Cherokee and opposed by an overwhelming majority, was ratified in the Senate by a one-vote margin. In the acrimonious week-long debate in the Senate, Daniel Webster, a powerful Whig leader who earlier in his career had expressed little interest in Indian policy, charged that the record revealed that Democrats had "no concern for Indian rights" whatsoever. When the treaty was ratified, by a one-vote margin, Webster wrote to Edward Everett to express disgust with the behavior of Senator Robert Goldsborough of Maryland, a Whig whom he had mistakenly considered as "a man of honor and religion." Had Goldsborough not voted with the Jacksonians, the treaty would have been defeated. Stung by the loss, Webster wondered what he could do "to clear myself from the shame and sin of the treaty."[79] His conversion to the cause of Indian rights gives telling evidence of the importance of opposition to Jacksonian Indian policy to the Whig program in the mid-1830s. The ongoing execution of the removal process

[78] Rolater, "The American Indian and the Origin of the Second American Party System," 197.

[79] *Register of Debates,* 24 Cong., I Sess., 1415–16, 1527–28; Webster to Edward Everett, 7 May 1836, in *The Papers of Daniel Webster, Correspondence,* IV: 110; Remini, *Daniel Webster,* 447.

removed the issue from politics, as by the early 1840s there were few Indians left in the states east of the Mississippi.[80] Clearly the process could not easily be reversed, as the former Indian territories east of the Mississippi were now occupied by white landowners. In 1841, former president John Quincy Adams, once a proponent of voluntary removal, described the Jacksonian program as "among the heinous sins of this nation, for which God will one day bring them to judgment." But as a practical political matter, Adams concluded that it was too late to redress the injustices of the past decade. He accordingly declined to chair the House Committee on Indian Affairs, confiding to his diary that "the only result would be to keep a perpetual harrow upon my feelings, with a total impotence to render any useful service."[81]

Antiremoval protestors frequently charged that Andrew Jackson's refusal to execute the Indian treaties and laws of the United States "constituted a gross abuse of presidential power."[82] The charge was well-founded. Nothing in the Indian Removal Act of 1830 authorized his denial of Indian treaty rights in the removal process. While the law's affirmation that prior treaties remained in force was not as strong as Jackson's critics wished, it was nonetheless part of the law. By disregarding the obligations placed upon him by legislation providing for protection of Indian property, by denying the legitimacy of prior federal treaty commitments to Indian nations, by ignoring the promises written into his own removal treaties, and by tacitly encouraging the intimidation and dispossession of Indians, Jackson transformed the voluntary removal program authorized by Congress into a coerced removal sanctioned by the White House. The failure of subsequent Congresses dominated by Jacksonian loyalists to deal with those abuses does not alter the fact that the president was operating outside the law. It is doubtful that Jackson could have achieved his objectives in

[80] An exception is New York, where opponents of removal were able to secure a compromise that protected some Iroquois holdings. See Stephen J. Valone, "William Seward, Whig Politics and the Compromised Indian Removal Program in New York State, 1838–1843," *New York History* 82 (spring 2001): 107–34.

[81] Adams, *Memoirs*, 10: 491–92.

[82] Philip R. Fendall to Henry Clay, 27 August 1832, in *The Papers of Henry Clay* James Hopkins et al. (Lexington, Ky., 1984) 8: 563.

Indian removal had he either accepted the constraints contained in the enabling legislation, or honored the promises made to Congress to secure passage of that law. It is a mark of Jackson's political success that so many historians over the years have conveyed to their readers the impression that neither the constraints nor the promises existed.

Cave, Alfred A., "Abuse of Power: Andrew Jackson and the Indian Removal Act of 1830," *Historian* 65 (Winter 2003), 1330–53.

SUGGESTED READINGS

Biography

Andrew, John A. *From Revivals to Removal: Jeremiah Evarts, the Cherokee Nation, and the Search for the Soul of America.* Athens: University of Georgia Press, 1992.

Bartlett, Irving H. *John C. Calhoun: A Biography.* New York: W. W. Norton, 1993.

Bass, Althea. *Cherokee Messenger.* Norman: University of Oklahoma Press, 1936.

Burstein, Andrew. *The Passions of Andrew Jackson.* New York: Alfred A. Knopf, 2003.

Callahan, North. *Henry Knox, General Washington's General.* New York: Rinehart, 1958.

Chapman, George. *Chief William McIntosh: A Man of Two Worlds.* Atlanta, GA: Cherokee, 1988.

Coit, Margaret L. *John C. Calhoun, American Portrait.* Boston: Houghton Mifflin, 1950.

Cole, Donald B. *The Presidency of Andrew Jackson.* Lawrence: University Press of Kansas, 1993.

Cutter, Donald C. "President Andrew Jackson and the West." *Journal of the West* 31 (1992): 38–43.

Dowd, Gregory Evans. *A Spirited Resistance: The North American Indian Struggle for Unity, 1745–1815.* Baltimore: Johns Hopkins University Press, 1992.

Eckert, Allan W. *A Sorrow in Our Heart: The Life of Tecumseh*. New York: Bantam, 1992.

Edmunds, R. David. *The Shawnee Prophet*. Lincoln: University of Nebraska Press, 1983.

————. *Tecumseh and the Quest for Indian Leadership*. Boston: Little, Brown, 1984.

Gabriel, Ralph H. *Elias Boudinot, Cherokee and His America*. Norman: University of Oklahoma Press, 1941.

Griffith, Benjamin W. *McIntosh and Weatherford, Creek Indian Leaders*. Tuscaloosa: University of Alabama Press, 1988.

Hartley, William B., and Ellen Hartley. *Osceola, the Unconquered Indian*. New York: Hawthorn Books, 1973.

Hendricks, Rickey L. "Henry Clay and Jacksonian Indian Policy: A Political Anachronism." *Filson Club History Quarterly* 60 (1986): 218–38.

James, Marquis. *The Life of Andrew Jackson*. Indianapolis: Bobbs-Merrill, 1938.

McLoughlin, William G. "Thomas Jefferson and the Beginning of Cherokee Nationalism, 1806 to 1809." *William and Mary Quarterly* 32 (1975): 547–80.

Latner, Richard B. *The Presidency of Andrew Jackson: White House Politics, 1829–1837*. Athens: University of Georgia Press, 1979.

Mooney, Chase C. *William H. Crawford, 1772–1834*. Lexington: University Press of Kentucky, 1974.

Moulton, Gary E. *John Ross: Cherokee Chief*. Athens: University of Georgia Press, 1978.

Parsons, Lynn Hudson. " 'A Perpetual Harrow upon My Feelings': John Quincy Adams and the American Indian." *New England Quarterly* 46 (1973): 339–79.

Prucha, Francis Paul. "Andrew Jackson's Indian Policy: A Reassessment." *Journal of American History* 56 (1969): 527–39.

————. "Protest by Petition: Jeremiah Evarts and the Cherokee Indians." *Proceedings of the Massachusetts Historical Society* 97 (1985): 42–58.

————. "Thomas L. McKenny and the New York Indian Board." *Mississippi Valley Historical Review* 48 (1961–1962): 635–55.

Remini, Robert V. *Andrew Jackson and the Course of American Democracy, 1833–1845.* New York: Harper & Row, 1984.

————. *Andrew Jackson and the Course of American Empire, 1767–1821.* New York: Harper & Row, 1977.

————. *Andrew Jackson and the Course of American Freedom, 1822–1832.* New York: Harper & Row, 1981.

Rogin, Michael. *Fathers and Children: Andrew Jackson and the Subjugation of the American Indians.* New York: Knopf, 1975.

Satz, Ronald N. "Remini's Andrew Jackson (1767–1821): Jackson and the Indians." *Tennessee Historical Quarterly* 38 (1979): 158–66.

Schlesinger, Arthur M., Jr. *The Age of Jackson.* Boston: Little, Brown, 1945.

Sugden, John. *Tecumseh: A Life.* New York: Henry Holt, 1998.

Vipperman, Carl J. "The 'Particular Mission' of Wilson Lumpkin." *Georgia Historical Quarterly* 66 (1982): 295–316.

Wells, Mary Ann. *Searching for Red Eagle: A Personal Journey into the Spirit World of Native America.* Jackson: University Press of Mississippi, 1998.

Wilkins, Thurmond. *Cherokee Tragedy: The Story of the Ridge Family and the Decimation of a People.* New York: Macmillan, 1970.

Wiltse, Charles M. *John C. Calhoun.* 3 vols. Indianapolis: Bobbs-Merrill, 1944–1951.

Cherokee

Anderson, William L. *Cherokee Removal: Before and After.* Athens: University of Georgia Press, 1991.

Breyer, Stephen. "The Cherokee Indians and the Supreme Court." *Georgia Historical Quarterly* 87 (2003): 408–26.

Burnett, John G. "The Cherokee Removal through the Eyes of a Private Soldier." *Journal of Cherokee Studies* 3 (1978): 180–85.

Conser, Walter H., Jr. "John Ross and the Cherokee Resistance Campaign, 1833–1838." *Journal of Southern History* 44 (1978): 191–212.

Duffield, Lathel F. "Cherokee Emigration: Reconstructing Reality." *Chronicles of Oklahoma* 80 (2002): 314–47.

Ehle, John. *Trail of Tears: The Rise and Fall of the Cherokee Nation.* New York: Anchor Books, 1989.

Feder, Bernard. "The Ridge Family and the Death of a Nation." *American West* 15 (1978): 61–63.

Filler, Louis, and Allen Guttman, eds. *The Removal of the Cherokee Nation: Manifest Destiny or National Dishonor?* Boston: Heath, 1962.

Finger, John R. "The Abortive Second Cherokee Removal, 1841–1844." *Journal of Southern History* 47 (1981): 207–26.

Flanagan, Sharon P. "The Georgia Cherokees Who Remained: Race, Status, and Property in the Chattahoochee Community." *Georgia Historical Quarterly* 73 (1989): 584–609.

Franks, Kenny A. "Political Intrigue in the Cherokee Nation, 1839." *Journal of the West* 13 (1974): 17–25.

Gibson, Wayne Dell. "Cherokee Treaty Party Moves West: The Bell-Deas Overland Journey, 1838–1839." *Chronicles of Oklahoma* 79 (2001): 314–35.

Gilbert, Joan. *The Trail of Tears across Missouri.* Columbia: University of Missouri Press, 1996.

Grinde, Donald. "Cherokee Removal and American Politics." *New England Social Studies Bulletin* 44 (1987): 28–45.

Halliburton, R., Jr. *Red over Black: Black Slavery among the Cherokee Indians.* Westport, CT: Greenwood, 1977.

Hauptman, Laurence M. "General John E. Wool in Cherokee Country, 1836–1837: A Reinterpretation." *Georgia Historical Quarterly* 85 (2001): 1–26.

Hoig, Stan. *Night of the Cruel Moon: Cherokee Removal and the Trail of Tears.* New York: Facts on File, 1996.

Ishii, Izumi. "Alcohol and Politics in the Cherokee Nation Before Removal." *Ethnohistory* 50 (2003): 671–95.

King, Duane H. *The Cherokee Indian Nation: A Troubled History.* Knoxville: University of Tennessee Press, 1979.

Mails, Thomas E. *The Cherokee People: The Story of the Cherokee from Earliest Origins to Contemporary Times.* Tulsa, OK: Council Oak, 1992.

Malone, Henry Thompson. *Cherokees of the Old South: A People in Transition.* Athens: University of Georgia Press, 1956.

McLoughlin, William Gerald. *After the Trail of Tears: The Cherokees' Struggle for Sovereignty, 1839–1890.* Chapel Hill: University of North Carolina Press, 1993.

————. "Cherokees and Methodists, 1824–1834." *Church History* 50 (1981): 44–63.

————. *Cherokees and Missionaries, 1789–1839.* New Haven: Yale University Press, 1984.

————. *Cherokee Renascence in the New Republic.* Princeton: Princeton University Press, 1986.

————. *The Cherokees and Christianity, 1794–1870: Essays on Acculturation and Cultural Persistence.* Athens: University of Georgia Press, 1994.

————. *The Cherokee Ghost Dance: Essays on the Southeastern Indians, 1789–1861.* Macon, GA: Mercer University Press, 1984.

————. "Georgia's Role in Instigating Compulsory Indian Removal." *Georgia Historical Quarterly* 70 (1986): 605–32.

_____. "The Murder Trial of the Reverend Evan Jones, Baptist Missionary to the Cherokee in North Carolina, 1833." *North Carolina Historical Review* 62 (1985): 157–78.

Miles, Edwin A. "After John Marshall's Decision." *Journal of Southern History* 39 (1973): 519–44.

Miles, Tiya. *Ties That Bind: The Story of an Afro-Cherokee Family in Slavery and Freedom.* Berkeley: University of California Press, 2005.

Moulton, Gary E. "Chief John Ross and Cherokee Removal Finances." *Chronicles of Oklahoma* 52 (1974): 342–59.

Norgren, Jill. *The Cherokee Cases: Two Landmark Federal Decisions in the Fight for Sovereignty.* Norman: University of Oklahoma Press, 2004.

Owen, Christopher H. " 'To Refrain from . . . Political Affairs': Southern Evangelicals, Cherokee Missions, and the Spirituality of the Church." *Tennessee Historical Quarterly* 53 (1994): 20–29.

Peacock, Mary Thomas. "Methodists Mission Work among the Cherokee Indians before Removal." *Methodist History* 3 (1965): 20–39.

Perdue, Theda. "Cherokee Planters, Black Slaves, and African Colonization." *Chronicles of Oklahoma* 60 (1982): 322–31.

_____. "Cherokee Women and the Trail of Tears." *Journal of Women's History* 1 (1989): 14–30.

_____. *Cherokee Women: Gender and Culture Change, 1700–1835.* Lincoln: University of Nebraska Press, 1998.

_____. *Slavery and Evolution of Cherokee Society, 1540–1866.* Knoxville: University of Tennessee Press, 1979.

Remini, Robert V. "Andrew Jackson Versus the Cherokee Nation." *American History* 36 (2001): 48–56.

Satz, Ronald N. "The Cherokee Trail of Tears: A Sesquicentennial Perspective." *Georgia Historical Quarterly* 73 (1989): 431–66.

Scherer, Mark R. " 'Now Let Him Enforce It': Exploring the Myth of Andrew Jackson's Response to Worcester v. Georgia (1832)." *Chronicles of Oklahoma* 74 (1996): 16–29.

Strickland, Rennard. *Fire and the Spirits: Cherokee Law from Clan to Court.* Norman: University of Oklahoma Press, 1975.

Thornton, Russell. "Cherokee Population Losses during the Trail of Tears: A New Perspective and a New Estimate." *Ethnohistory* 31 (1984): 289–300.

Vipperman, Carl J. "The Bungled Treaty of New Echota: The Failure of Cherokee Removal, 1836–1838." *Georgia Historical Quarterly* 73 (1989): 540–58.

————. " 'Forcibly If We Must': The Georgia Case for Cherokee Removal, 1802–1832." *Journal of Cherokee Studies* 3 (1978): 103–10.

Wardell, Morris L. *A Political History of the Cherokee Nation, 1838–1907.* Norman: University of Oklahoma Press, 1938.

Wishart, David M. "Evidence of Surplus Production in the Cherokee Nation Prior to Removal." *Journal of Economic History* 55 (1995): 120–38.

Young, Mary Elizabeth. "The Cherokee Nation: Mirror of the Republic." *American Quarterly* 33 (1981): 502–24.

————. "The Exercise of Sovereignty in Cherokee Georgia." *Journal of the Early Republic* 10 (1990): 43–63.

Chickasaw

Atkinson, James R. *Splendid Land, Splendid People: The Chickasaw Indians to Removal.* Tuscaloosa: University of Alabama Press, 2004.

Clark, Blue. "Chickasaw Colonization in Oklahoma." *Chronicles of Oklahoma* 54 (1976): 44–59.

Gibson, Arrell M. *The Chickasaws.* Norman: University of Oklahoma Press, 1971.

Littlefield, Daniel, Jr. *The Chickasaw Freedmen: A People without a Country.* Westport, CT: Greenwood Press, 1980.

Choctaw

Akers, Donna. *Living in the Land of Death: The Choctaw Nation, 1830–1860.* East Lansing: Michigan State University, 2004.

————. "Removing the Heart of the Choctaw People: Indian Removal from a Native Perspective." *American Indian Culture and Research Journal* 23 (1999): 63–76.

Birzer, Bradley J. "Choctaw Economic Success in Indian Territory, 1831–1861." *Continuity* 24 (2000): 31–51.

Carson, James Taylor. *Searching for the Bright Path: The Mississippi Choctaws from Prehistory to Removal.* Lincoln: University of Nebraska Press, 1999.

Debo, Angie. *The Rise and Fall of the Choctaw Republic.* Norman: University of Oklahoma Press, 1961.

DeRosier, Arthur H. "Andrew Jackson and Negotiations for the Removal of the Choctaw Indians." *Historian* 29 (1967): 343–62.

————. "The Choctaw Removal of 1831: A Civilian Effort." *Journal of the West* 6 (1967): 237–47.

————. *The Removal of the Choctaw Indians.* Knoxville: University of Tennessee Press, 1970.

————. "Thomas Jefferson and the Removal of the Choctaw Indians." *Southern Quarterly* 1 (1962): 52–62.

Haag, Marcia. *Choctaw Language and Culture: Chahta Anumpa.* Norman: University of Oklahoma Press, 2001.

Huggard, Christopher J. "Culture Mixing: Everyday Life on Missions among the Choctaws." *Chronicles of Oklahoma* 70 (1992–1993): 432–49.

Jordan, H. Glenn. "Choctaw Colonization in Oklahoma." *Chronicles of Oklahoma* 54 (1976): 16–33.

Kidwell, Clara Sue. *Choctaws and Missionaries in Mississippi, 1818–1918*. Norman: University of Oklahoma Press, 1995.

Reeves, Carolyn. *The Choctaw before Removal*. Jackson: University Press of Mississippi, 1985.

Syndergaard, Rex. "The Final Move of the Choctaws, 1825–1830." *Chronicles of Oklahoma* 52 (1974): 207–19.

Van Hoak, Stephen P. "The Poor Red Man and the Great Father: Choctaw Rhetoric, 1540–1860." *Chronicles of Oklahoma* 81 (2003): 298–315.

———. "Untangling the Roots of Dependency: Choctaw Economics, 1700–1860." *American Indian Quarterly* 23 (1999): 113–28.

Wells, Samuel J., and Roseanna Tubby. *After Removal: The Choctaw in Mississippi*. Jackson: University Press of Mississippi, 1986.

Creek

Braund, Kathryn E. Holland. *Deerskins & Duffels: The Creek Indian Trade with Anglo-America, 1685–1815*. Lincoln: University of Nebraska Press, 1993.

———. "Guardians of Tradition and Handmaidens to Change: Women's Roles in Creek Economic and Social Life during the Eighteenth Century." *American Indian Quarterly* 14 (1990): 239–53.

Debo, Angie. *The Road to Disappearance*. Norman: University of Oklahoma Press, 1941.

Ellisor, John T. "'Like So Many Wolves': Creek Removal in the Cherokee Country, 1835–1838." *Journal of East Tennessee History* 71 (1999): 1–24.

Ethridge, Robbie. *Creek Country: The Creek Indians and Their World*. Chapel Hill: University of North Carolina Press, 2003.

Frank, Andrew. *Creeks & Southerners: Biculturalism on the Early American Frontier*. Lincoln: University of Nebraska Press, 2005.

Garrison, Tim Alan. "Beyond Worcester: The Alabama Supreme Court and the Sovereignty of the Creek Nation." *Journal of the Early Republic* 19 (1999): 423–50.

Green, Michael D. *The Politics of Indian Removal: Creek Government and Society in Crisis*. Lincoln: University of Nebraska Press, 1982.

Heidler, David S., and Jeanne T. Heidler. "Between a Rock and a Hard Place: United States-Creek Indian Relations, 1814–1818." *Alabama Review* 50 (1997): 267–89.

Hodges, Bert. "Notes on the History of the Creek Nation and Some of Its Leaders." *Chronicles of Oklahoma* 43 (1965): 9–18.

Jones, Warrick Lane. "A Lettered Portrait of William McIntosh: Leader of the Creek Nation." *Chronicles of Oklahoma* 74 (1996): 76–95.

Littlefield, Joel W. *Africans and Creeks: From the Colonial Period to the Civil War*. Westport, CT: Greenwood Press, 1979.

Martin, Joel W. *Sacred Revolt: The Muskogees' Struggle for a New World*. Boston: Beacon, 1991.

Saunt, Claudio. *A New Order of Things: Property, Power, and the Transformation of the Creek Indians, 1733–1816*. New York: Cambridge University Press, 1999.

Savage, William W., Jr. "Creek Colonization in Oklahoma." *Chronicles of Oklahoma* 54 (1976): 34–43.

Southerland, Henry deLeon, and Jerry Elijah Brown. *The Federal Road through Georgia, the Creek Nation, and Alabama, 1806–1836*. Tuscaloosa: University of Alabama Press, 1989.

Stiggins, George. *Creek Indian History: A Historical Narrative of the Genealogy, Traditions, and Downfall of the Ispocoga or Creek Indian Tribe of Indians*. Birmingham: Birmingham Public Library Press, 1989.

Swanton, John Reed. *Early History of the Creek Indians and Their Neighbors*. Gainesville: University Presses of Florida, 1998.

Wright, J. Leitch. *Creeks & Seminoles: The Destruction and Regeneration of the Muscogulge People*. Lincoln: University of Nebraska Press, 1986.

Young, Mary Elizabeth. "The Creek Frauds: A Study in Conscience and Corruption." *Mississippi Valley Historical Review* 42 (1955): 411–37.

General

Abel, Annie Heloise. "The History of Events Resulting in Indian Consolidation West of the Mississippi." *Annual Report of the American Historical Association for the Year 1906*. 2 vols. Washington, DC: American Historical Association, 1908. 2: 233–450.

Berkhofer, Robert F. *The White Man's Indian: Images of the American Indian from Columbus to the Present*. New York: Random House, 1978.

Bolton, S. Charles. "Jeffersonian Indian Removal and the Emergence of Arkansas Territory." *Arkansas Historical Quarterly* 62 (2003): 253–71.

Champagne, Duane. *Social Order and Political Change: Constitutional Government among the Cherokee, the Choctaw, the Chickasaw, and the Creek*. Stanford, CA: Stanford University Press, 1992.

Coward, John M. *The Newspaper Indian: Native American Identity in the Press, 1820–1890*. Urbana: University of Illinois Press, 1999.

Cushman, H. B. *History of the Choctaw, Chickasaw and Natchez Indians*. Greenville, TX: Headlight Printing House, 1899; reprint, Stillwater, OK: Redlands Press, 1962.

Debo, Angie. *And Still the Waters Run: The Betrayal of the Five Civilized Tribes*. Revised edition, Princeton: Princeton University Press, 1972.

Dillon, Merton. *The Abolitionists: The Growth of a Dissenting Minority*. New York: W. W. Norton, 1979.

Ellenberg, George B. "An Uncivil War of Words: Indian Removal in the Press." *Atlanta History* 33 (1989): 48–59.

Feller, Daniel. *The Jacksonian Promise: America, 1815–1840*. Baltimore: Johns Hopkins University Press, 1995.

Foreman, Grant. *The Five Civilized Tribes*. Norman: University of Oklahoma Press, 1934.

_____. *Indian Removal: The Emigration of the Five Civilized Tribes of Indians*. Norman: University of Oklahoma Press, 1972.

Gitlin, Jay. "Private Diplomacy to Private Property: States, Tribes, and Nations in the Early National Period." *Diplomatic History* 22 (1998): 85–99.

Heidler, David S., and Jeanne T. Heidler. *Manifest Destiny*. Westport CT: Greenwood Press, 2003.

Hershberger, Mary. "Mobilizing Women, Anticipating Abolition: The Struggle Against Indian Removal in the 1830s." *Journal of American History* 86 (1999): 15–40.

Horsman, Reginald. *Race and Manifest Destiny: The Origins of American Racial Anglo-Saxonism*. Cambridge: Harvard University Press, 1981.

Hoxie, Frederick E., Ronald Hoffman, and Peter J. Albert, eds. *Native Americans and the Early Republic*. Charlottesville: University Press of Virginia, 1999.

Hudson, Charles H. *Four Centuries of Southern Indians*. Athens: University of Georgia Press, 1975.

Hurt, R. Douglas. *The Indian Frontier, 1763–1846*. Albuquerque: University of New Mexico Press, 2002.

Kelleher, Michael. "The Removal of Southeastern Indians: Historians Respond to the 1960s and the Trail of Tears." *Chronicles of Oklahoma* 78 (2000): 346–53.

Konkle, Maureen. *Writing Indian Nations: Native Intellectuals and the Politics of Historiography, 1827–1863*. Chapel Hill: University of North Carolina Press, 2004.

Lefler, Lisa J., and Frederic W. Gleach. *Southern Indians and Anthropologists: Culture, Politics, and Identities*. Athens: University of Georgia Press, 2002.

Mancall, Peter C., and James H. Merrell, eds. *American Encounters: Natives and Newcomers from European Contact to Indian Removal, 1500–1850.* New York: Routledge, 2000.

May, Katja. *African Americans and Native Americans, the Creek and Cherokee Nations, 1830s to 1920s: Collision and Collusion.* New York: Garland Publishing, 1996.

McEwan, Bonnie G., ed. *Indians of the Greater Southeast: Historical Archaeology and Ethnohisotry.* Gainesville: University Presses of Florida, 2000.

McKivigan, John R., and Stanley Harrold. *Antislavery Violence: Sectional, Racial, and Cultural Conflict in Antebellum America.* Knoxville: University of Tennessee Press, 1999.

Minges, Patrick. "Beneath the Underdog: Race, Religion, and the Trail of Tears." *American Indian Quarterly* 25 (2001): 453–79.

Prucha, Francis Paul. *American Indian Policy in the Formative Years: The Indian Trade and Intercourse Acts, 1790–1834.* Cambridge: Harvard University Press, 1962.

————. *The Great Father: The United States Government and the American Indians.* 2 vols. Lincoln: University of Nebraska Press, 1984.

Remini, Robert Vincent. *Andrew Jackson & His Indian Wars.* New York: Viking, 2001.

————. *The Legacy of Andrew Jackson: Essays on Democracy, Indian Removal, and Slavery.* Baton Rouge: Louisiana State University Press, 1988.

Rolater, Fred S. "The American Indian and the Origin of the Second American Party System." *Wisconsin Magazine of History* 76 (1993): 180–203.

Ronda, James P. " 'We Have A Country': Race, Geography, and the Invention of Indian Territory." *Journal of the Early Republic* 19 (1999): 739–55.

Satz, Ronald N. *American Indian Policy in the Jacksonian Era.* Lincoln: University of Nebraska Press, 1975.

Sellers, Charles. *The Market Economy: Jacksonian America, 1815–1846.* New York: Oxford University Press, 1991.

Sheehan, Bernard W. *Seeds of Extinction: Jeffersonian Philanthropy and the American Indian.* Chapel Hill: University of North Carolina Press, 1973.

Shoemaker, Nancy, ed. *Negotiators of Change: Historical Perspectives on Native American Women.* New York: Routledge, 1995.

Stein, Gary C. "Indian Removal as Seen by European Travelers in America." *Chronicles of Oklahoma* 51 (1973–1974): 399–410.

Theodore, Alisse. "'A Right To Speak on the Subject': The U.S. Women's Antiremoval Petition Campaign, 1829–1831." *Rhetoric & Public Affairs* 5 (2002): 601–23.

Usner, Daniel, Jr. "American Indians on the Cotton Frontier: Changing Economic Relations with Citizens and Slaves in the Mississippi Territory." *Journal of American History* 72 (1985): 297–317.

Van Deusen, Glydon G. *The Jacksonian Era, 1828–1848.* New York: Harper, 1959.

Van Every, Dale. *Disinherited: The Lost Birthright of the American Indian.* New York: Morrow, 1966.

Wallace, Anthony F. C. *Jefferson and the Indians: The Tragic Fate of the First Americans.* Cambridge: Belknap Press of Harvard University Press, 1999.

———. *The Long Bitter Trail: Andrew Jackson and the Indians.* New York: Hill and Wang, 1993.

Watson, Harry L. *Liberty and Power: The Politics of Jacksonian America.* New York: Hill and Wang, 1990.

White, Richard. *The Middle Ground: Indians, Empires, and Republics in the Great Lakes Region, 1650–1815.* New York: Cambridge University Press, 1991.

William, Walter L. *Southeastern Indians since the Removal Era.* Athens: University of Georgia Press, 1979.

Young, Mary Elizabeth. "Conflict Resolution on the Indian Frontier." *Journal of the Early Republic* 16 (1996): 1–19.

————. "Indian Removal and Land Allotment: The Civilized Tribes and Jacksonian Justice." *American Historical Review* 64 (1958): 31–45.

————. "Racism in Red and Black: Indians and Other Free People of Color in Georgia Law, Politics, and Removal Policy." *Georgia Historical Quarterly* 73 (1989): 492–518.

————. *Redskins, Ruffleshirts and Rednecks: Indian Allotments in Alabama and Mississippi, 1830–1860.* Norman: University of Oklahoma Press, 1961.

Primary Sources

American State Papers, Indian Affairs. 2 vols. Washington, DC: Gales & Seaton, 1832.

American State Papers, Military Affairs. 7 vols. Washington, DC: Gales & Seaton, 1832–1861.

Boudinot, Elias. *Cherokee Editor: The Writings of Elias Boudinot.* Edited by Theda Perdue. Knoxville: University of Tennessee Press, 1983.

Calhoun, John C. *The Papers of John C. Calhoun.* Edited by Robert Meriwether, William Edwin Hemphill, and Clyde Norman Wilson. 20 vols. Columbia: University of South Carolina Press, 1959–1988.

Dale, Edward E., and Gaston Little, eds. *Cherokee Cavaliers: Forty Years of Cherokee History as told in the Correspondence of the Ridge-Watie-Boudinot Family.* Norman: University of Oklahoma Press, 1939.

Giddings, Joshua R. *The Exiles of Florida; or the Crimes Committed by Our Government against the Maroons Who Fled from South Carolina and Other States, Seeking Protection under Spanish Laws.* Gainesville: University of Florida Press, 1964.

Hawkins, Benjamin. *The Collected Works of Benjamin Hawkins, 1796–1810.* Edited by Thomas Foster. Tuscaloosa: University of Alabama Press, 2003.

_____. *Letters, Journals, and Writings of Benjamin Hawkins.* 2 vols. Edited by C. L. Grant. Savannah: Beehive Press, 1980.

Homer, Davis A., ed. *Constitution and Laws of the Chickasaw Nation: Together with the Treaties of 1832, 1833, 1834, 1837, 1852, 1855, and 1866.* Wilmington, DE: Scholarly Resources, 1973.

Henegar, H. B. "Recollections of Cherokee Removal." *Journal of Cherokee Studies* 3 (1978): 177–79.

Jackson, Andrew. *The Correspondence of Andrew Jackson.* Edited by John Spencer Bassett. 7 vols. Washington, DC: Carnegie Institution of Washington, 1927–1928.

_____. *The Papers of Andrew Jackson.* Edited by Sam B. Smith, Harriett C. Owsley, Harold Moser, et al. 6 vols. Knoxville: University of Tennessee Press, 1980–2003.

Jefferson, Thomas. *Notes on the State of Virginia.* Edited by William Peden. Chapel Hill: University of North Carolina Press, 1982.

Kilpatrick, Jack R., and Anna G. Kilpatrick. *New Echota Letters: Contributions of Samuel Worcester to the Cherokee Phoenix.* Dallas: Southern Methodist University Press, 1968.

Lumpkin, Wilson. *The Removal of the Cherokee Indians from Georgia.* 2 vols. New York: Arno Press, 1969.

Nabokov, Peter, ed. *Native American Testimony: A Chronicle of Indian White Relations from Prophecy to the Present, 1492–1992.* New York: Viking, 1991.

Perdue, Theda, and Michael D. Green. *The Cherokee Removal: A Brief History with Documents.* Boston: Bedford Books of St. Martin's Press, 1995.

Prucha, Francis Paul, ed. *Cherokee Removal: The "William Penn" Essays and Other Writings.* Knoxville: University of Tennessee Press, 1981.

Prucha, Francis Paul, comp. *The Indian in American History.* New York: Holt, Rinehart, and Winston, 1971.

11 1111 11111111111

Ross, John. *The Papers of Chief John Ross.* 2 vols. Edited by Gary E. Moulton. Norman: University of Oklahoma Press, 1985.

Scott, Winfield. "If Not Rejoicing, At Least in Comfort: General Scott's Version of Removal." *Journal of Cherokee Studies* 3 (1978): 138–42.

Whalen, Brett E., comp. "A Vermonter on the Trail of Tears, 1830–1837." *Vermont History* 66 (1998): 31–38.

Seminole

Coe, Charles H. *Red Patriots: The Story of the Seminoles.* Edited by Charlton W. Tebeau. Gainesville: University Presses of Florida, 1974.

Covington, James W. *The Seminoles of Florida.* Gainesville: University Presses of Florida, 1993.

Fairbanks, Charles Herron. *The Florida Seminole People.* Phoenix: Indian Tribal Series, 1973.

Heidler, David S., and Jeanne T. Heidler. *Old Hickory's War: Andrew Jackson and the Quest for Empire.* Mechanicsburg, PA: Stackpole Books, 1996; reprint, Baton Rouge: Louisiana State University Press, 2003.

Klos, George. "Blacks and the Seminole Removal Debate, 1821–1835." *Florida Historical Quarterly* 68 (1989): 55–78.

Littlefield, Daniel F. *Africans and Seminoles: From Removal to Emancipation.* Oxford: University Press of Mississippi, 2001.

Mahon, John K. "The Treaty of Moultrie Creek, 1823." *Florida Historical Quarterly* 40 (1962): 350–72.

McReynolds, Edwin C. *The Seminoles.* Norman: University of Oklahoma Press, 1957.

Welsh, Louise. "Seminole Colonization in Oklahoma." *Chronicles of Oklahoma* 54 (1976): 77–103.

States

Carson, James Taylor. "State Rights and Indian Removal in Mississippi, 1817–1835." *Journal of Mississippi History* 57 (1995): 25–41.

Finger, John R. *Tennessee Frontiers: Three Regions in Transition.* Bloomington: Indiana University Press, 2001.

Garrison, Tim Alan. *The Legal Ideology of Removal: The Southern Judiciary and the Sovereignty of Native American Nations.* Athens: University of Georgia Press, 2002.

Nichols, David A. "Land, Republicanism, and Indians: Power and Policy in Early National Georgia, 1780–1825." *Georgia Historical Quarterly* 85 (2001): 199–226.

Rensi, Raymond Charles. *Gold Fever: America's First Gold Rush.* Atlanta: Georgia Humanities Council, 1988.

Satz, Ronald N. *Tennessee's Indian Peoples: From White Contact to Removal, 1540–1840.* Knoxville: University of Tennessee Press, 1979.

Valone, Stephen J. "William Seward, Whig Politics, and the Compromised Indian Removal Policy in New York State, 1838–1843." *New York History* 82 (2001): 106–34.

Williams, David. *The Georgia Gold Rush: Twenty-niners, Cherokees, and Gold Fever.* Columbia: University of South Carolina Press, 1993.

Young, Mary Elizabeth. "The Exercise of Sovereignty in Cherokee Georgia." *Journal of the Early Republic* 10 (1990): 43–63.

_____. "Racism in Red and Black: Indians and Other Free People of Color in Georgia Law, Politics, and Removal Policy." *Georgia Historical Quarterly* 73 (1989): 492–518.

U.S. Government

Cave, Alfred A. "Abuse of Power: Andrew Jackson and the Indian Removal Act of 1830." *Historian* 65 (2003): 1330–53.

Christianson, James R. "Removal: A Foundation for the Formation of Federal Indian Policy." *Journal of Cherokee Studies* 10 (1985): 215–29.

Fritz, Henry E. "Humanitarian Rhetoric and Andrew Jackson's Indian Removal Policy." *Chronicles of Oklahoma* 79 (2001): 62–91.

Keller, Christian B. "Philanthropy Betrayed: Thomas Jefferson, the Louisiana Purchase, and the Origins of Federal Indian Removal Policy." *Proceedings of the American Philosophical Society* 144 (2000): 39–66.

Meyers, Jason. "No Idle Past: Uses of History in the 1830 Indian Removal Debates." *Historian* 63 (2001): 53–65.

Scherer, Mark R. " 'Now Let Him Enforce It': Exploring the Myth of Andrew Jackson's Response to Worcester v. Georgia (1832)." *Chronicles of Oklahoma* 74 (1996): 16–29.

Wars

Adams, George R. "The Caloosahatchee Massacre: Its Significance in the Second Seminole War." *Florida Historical Quarterly* 48 (1970): 368–80.

Buker, George E. *Swam Sailors: Riverine Warfare in the Everglades, 1835–1842.* Gainesville: University Presses of Florida, 1975.

Eby, Cecil D. *"That Disgraceful Affair": The Black Hawk War.* New York: W. W. Norton, 1973.

Fiorato, Jacqueline. "The Cherokee Mediation in Florida." *Journal of Cherokee Studies* 3 (1978): 111–19.

Francke, Arthur E. *Fort Mellon, 1837–1842: A Microcosm of the Second Seminole War.* Miami: Banyan, 1977.

Laumer, Frank. *Dade's Last Command.* Gainesville: University Press of Florida, 1995.

_____. *Massacre!* Gainesville: University of Florida Press, 1968.

Mahon, John K. *History of the Second Seminole War, 1835–1842.* Gainesville: University Presses of Florida, 1991.

Owsley, Frank Lawrence. *Struggle for the Gulf Borderlands: The Creek War and the Battle of New Orleans, 1812–1815.* Gainesville: University Presses of Florida, 1981.

Porter, Kenneth W. "Negroes and the Seminole War, 1835–1842." *Journal of Southern History 30* (1964): 427–50.

Tucker, Phillip Thomas. "John Horse: Forgotten African-American Leader of the Second Seminole War." *Journal of Negro History* 77 (1992): 74–83.

Valliere, Kenneth L. "The Creek War of 1836, A Military History." *Chronicles of Oklahoma* 57 (1979–1980): 463–85.

Walton, George H. *Fearless and Free: The Seminole Indian War, 1835–1842.* Indianapolis: Bobbs-Merrill, 1977.

INDEX